The Druze

D1104129

VILLA JULIE COLLEGE LIBRARY
STEVENSON, MD 21153

The Druze

Robert Brenton Betts

Yale University Press
New Haven and London

Published with assistance from the Kingsley Trust Association Publication Fund established by the Scroll and Key Society of Yale College

Copyright © 1988 by Yale University.
All rights reserved.
This book may not be reproduced, in whole or in part, including illustrations, in any form (beyond that copying permitted by Sections 107 and 108 of the U.S. Copyright Law and except by reviewers for the public press), without written permission from the publishers.

Designed by Sujata Guha and James J. Johnson and set in Bembo Roman type by Brevis Press, Bethany, Connecticut.
Printed in the United States of America by Braun-Brumfield, Inc., Ann Arbor, Michigan.

Library of Congress Cataloging-in-Publication Data

Betts, Robert Brenton.
The Druze / Robert Brenton Betts.
p. cm.
Bibliography: p.
Includes index.
1. Druzes. I. Title.
DS59.D78B47 1988
305.6'97—dc19 87-22696
CIP

ISBN 0-300-04100-4 (cloth)
0-300-04810-6 (pbk)

The paper in this book meets the guidelines for permanence and durability of the Committee on Production Guidelines for Book Longevity of the Council on Library Resources.

10 9 8 7 6 5 4 3 2

9.50

68442

To the memory of my mother,
Wanda Ellen Betts (née Carl), 1904–1986,
whose journey into the Druze country
in April of 1975 is still remembered and
remarked upon.

Contents

List of Maps and Illustrations

PLATE 9. The village of al-Mukhtara in the central Shuf Mountains, July 1975. Plates 9–22 photographed by the author

PLATE 10. The shrine of the Druze saint al-Nabi Ayyub in the southern Shuf Mountains near the village of Niha, July 1975

PLATE 11. Entrance to the shrine of al-Nabi Ayyub, showing the Druze star, July 1975

PLATE 12. The tomb of al-Nabi Ayyub, July 1975

PLATE 13. Druze *shaykhs* on the steps of the *khalwa* of Qanawat in the Jabal al-Druze, Syria, July 1975

PLATE 14. Druze farmer threshing grain near Qanawat, July 1975

PLATE 15. The ruins of the Byzantine church at Qalb Lawzah, Jabal al-Aʿla, July 1985

PLATE 16. Entrance to the former palace of the Junbalat family (now a school) in Aleppo, Syria, July 1985

PLATE 17. Entrance to the new *majlis* of ʿAyn al-Zaman in Suwayda, Jabal al-Druze, July 1985

PLATE 18. ʿAnz, a mixed Druze, Christian, and Muslim village in the southern Jabal al-Druze, July 1985

PLATE 19. A new *mawqaf* at ʿAnz, July 1985

PLATE 20. A *mudafa* in the remote village of Mushannaf in the eastern Jabal al-Druze, July 1985

PLATE 21. The Druze shrine of al-Nabi Shuʿayb, near Tiberias in Galilee, Israel, September 1985

PLATE 22. Entrance to the shrine of al-Nabi Shuʿayb, with a version of the Druze flag, September 1985

Preface

The Druze of Lebanon, Syria, and Israel hold a unique and influential position in the Arab world. Theirs is a fascinating and complex story, and a book of this sort invites an explanation. During one of the more horrendous and seemingly incomprehensible periods of intercommunal slaughter in Lebanon several years ago, friends in the American diplomatic service who were veteran Middle East hands made the inevitable suggestion. Knowing of my long-term interest in the Druze, which had grown out of my doctoral thesis on Christian Arab minorities in the area,[1] they proposed a book that would make what knowledge did exist on the Druze more readily available to Western readers—and possibly help prevent casual observers in the media from pontificating irresponsibly, often with serious inaccuracy, on a subject of considerable human and political interest.

I was fortunate to have gained a personal perspective that few others could claim through a close friendship with a large Druze family in the Shuf mountains of Lebanon, which had led to dozens of visits to their village between 1969 and 1975 and reciprocal visits by them to my home in Athens, until the father's death in 1981. Having been a student of Arabic, Islam, and the Middle East for more than twenty years, most of it spent in or near the

1. Robert Brenton Betts, "The Indigenous Arabic-Speaking Communities of Greater Syria and Mesopotamia" (unpublished Ph.D. diss., Johns Hopkins University, 1968). This research provided the basis for a book on the subject, *Christians in the Arab East: A Political Study* (London and Atlanta: The SPCK and John Knox Press, 1978).

region, and having organized and taught a whole range of courses on the history and politics of the area for an overseas American university program, I felt encouraged to attempt such a book despite the difficulties involved. Like any complex subject, the Druze appear increasingly intimidating the more one learns about them. One runs the risk, moreover, of falling into the trap of pursuing various tangential intricacies to the detriment of a comprehensive overall picture. One is also threatened with being repetitive, given the existence of other studies, no matter how narrowly specialized.

Conscious of these and other potential pitfalls, I nonetheless hope that this essay will help those interested in Islamic and Middle Eastern studies better to understand the Druze in the present Middle Eastern political context. I have tried to use as many sources as possible and to cite those that are most readily available. Where an English and an Arabic source exist side by side I have used the former, with apologies to Arabists, in order to make quick reference that much easier for most readers. To those with little or no background in the history, religion, and culture of the area, I would recommend prior reading of at least one general survey[2] for an overall view into which they might better fit the complex historical sidelights contained in this study. A quick look at the maps following page 161 below will help familiarize the reader with the place names that constantly reappear throughout the study, and the Glossary at the back provides a brief guide to various terms, persons, and places. I follow the most commonly accepted scheme of transliteration from Arabic into English, but in the case of frequently used terms such as *Druze* I cite a more correct transliteration (*al-Duruz*) where it first appears in the text and then continue with the more familiar Western usage. I omit all diacritical marks other than the *hamza* and the *ʿayn,* except in the Glossary.

In discussing the Druze since the independence of the three countries in which they are found in substantial numbers—Lebanon, Syria, and Israel—I treat each state separately, given that in each they play a different role in national political life. In Lebanon they were until 1975 the pivotal group that held the balance between the ruling Christian majority, declining in relative numerical strength since 1932, and the growing Muslim minority. For many years grudgingly supportive of the Christian (predominantly Maronite) establishment, the Druze broke away at the outbreak of civil war in 1975, and they have continued to play a major role far in excess of their numerical strength in political developments that may one day lead to a restructured Lebanese political system in which they are certain to play an even greater part.

In Syria the Druze were looked upon by the ruling Sunnis as a troublesome, separatist minority to be dealt with as little as was necessary. The present ruling *Baʿth* (Renaissance) party elite, drawn overwhelmingly from

2. For example, Sydney Nettleton Fisher, *The Middle East,* 3d ed. (New York: Alfred A. Knopf, 1979).

the Alawite minority of Latakia (*al-Ladhiqiya*), sees the Druze in much the same light, though the Druze in no way pose the threat to Colonel Asad's hegemony that the frustrated, politically emasculated Sunni majority does. The Syrian Druze, only peripherally involved in the government in Damascus, have but one card to play if their existence in this country is threatened: secession from Syria of their principal area of concentration, the Jebel Druze (*Jabal al-Duruz*), to join with either Israel or Jordan—a remote but not entirely fanciful possibility that Syrian governments must always be prepared to contend with.

In Israel, although they are the smallest of the country's three Arab communities, the Druze are the most favored by an Israeli government that considers them to be the only Arabs who can be trusted. Indeed the government has tried, unsuccessfully, to create in the minds of the Druze the myth that they are in fact a race apart from their Christian and Muslim Palestinian neighbors. Their communal interests are carefully looked after, and any complaints or problems receive prompt attention. In response, Druze men serve in the Israeli Defense Force (IDF), and their community leaders are loudly supportive of the state. Nevertheless, their position in Israel is not without its problems, particularly with regard to the recalcitrant Syrian Druze of the Golan Heights (*al-Julan*), unhappily annexed to Israel in December 1981.[3]

In each of these countries the Druze have their own group structure and religious, tribal, and political leadership. Yet a strong communal sense binds them together into a unity whose cohesiveness transcends geopolitical boundaries in all matters except political issues. I try to consider not only these overall community traits but also the tripartite national political development in which they are involved. In discussing the religious and historical background of the Druze I refer to the various theories and hypotheses advanced over the centuries since the faith was established, granting deference to the three contemporary *apologiae* by Druze writers, Abdallah Najjar's *The Druze* (1965), Sami Makarem's *The Druze Faith* (1975), and Nejla M. Abu-Izzeddin's *The Druzes* (1984). Although not in complete agreement on all points, the three authors do tend to discuss their common belief from a member's perspective and to discount or ignore the contributions and theories of outsiders, many of which contain information (or, to be fair, speculation) that is of considerable interest and relevance. In each case I attempt not to pass judgment, opting rather to acquaint the reader with existing material, both factual and theoretical.

There are many aspects of Druze society that I only touch upon and that are in need of further detailed scholarly investigation. Aharon Layish's excellently documented study of marriage, divorce, and inheritance among

3. The formal annexation took place on Dec. 14, 1981, but the event had been a foregone conclusion since July of the previous year when the Israeli Parliament (Knesset) passed a law offering Israeli citizenship to all Golan Druze. See Elfi Pallis, "We Are Not Israelis," *Middle East International,* Dec. 21, 1981, p. 5.

the Druze of Israel and Nura Alamuddin's monograph on Lebanese Druze marriage[4] are examples of the kind of much-needed research that can successfully be undertaken. I hope that my own general survey will encourage further specialized studies and that in the meantime it will serve to shed some light on the Druze in their contemporary Middle Eastern setting by providing a useful overview of their history, tradition, and relations with other peoples of this troubled region.

4. Aharon Layish, *Marriage, Divorce and Succession in the Druze Family* (Leiden: E. J. Brill, 1982), and Nura S. Alamuddin and Paul D. Starr, *Crucial Bonds: Marriage among the Lebanese Druze* (Delmar, N.Y.: Caravan Books, 1980).

Part I

Origins and Beliefs

1

The Rise of Druzism as a Political and Religious Movement

The distance between the urban decay surrounding the mosque of the Fatimid Imam-caliph al-Hakim biʿAmr Allah, which abuts the northeastern walls of medieval Cairo, and the pine-scented Mediterranean slope of Mount Hermon (*Jabal al-Shaykh* in Arabic) is not far in terms of miles. But in between lies one of the world's most politically turbulent landscapes, Palestine. Ironically, the continuing instability that has marked the region politically since the death of the main builder of that celebrated mosque in Cairo, whose life and ambition gave birth to the Druze faith, has contributed in large measure to the survival of the religion and community of the Druze (*al-Duruz*), who today number some nine hundred thousand Arabic-speaking citizens of Lebanon, Syria, Israel, and Jordan, scattered in towns and villages all within a few hours' travel of the mountain of Old Testament fame.

Al-Hakim's mosque, begun in A.D. 990

during the reign of his father, the caliph al-ʿAziz, was completed in 1013, eight years before al-Hakim's disappearance.[1] Like its more famous contemporary structure, the mosque and university of al-Azhar, completed in 972, it is a reflection of the political power and cultural achievement of the Fatimid caliphate. By the time of al-Hakim, the caliphate's boundaries stretched from modern-day Tunisia eastward through Egypt, where the capital lay (a new city called Cairo, *al-Qahira* in Arabic, founded in 969 and built on the edge of earlier capitals of earlier empires), north into Palestine and Lebanon, and south to the holy cities of Medina (*al-Madina*) and Mecca (*al-Makka*). The caliph and most of his Muslim subjects (at that time only half the population of Egypt and less than that in Palestine and Lebanon)[2] were, at least nominally, of the *Ismaʿili* branch of the *Shiʿa* sect of Islam.

Originally the outgrowth of a political dispute within Islam over the issue of the succession to the prophet Muhammad's mantle of power (the Shia having opted for a hereditary caliphate through the sons of the prophet's only surviving child, his daughter Fatima), Shi'ism had been ruthlessly suppressed by the dominant Sunni (or "orthodox," for want of a better word) branch of Islam in the years following the assassination of Fatima's husband (and cousin), ʿAli, the fourth and last of the so-called orthodox (*al-rashidun*) caliphs, who ruled from al-Kufa in Iraq (656–661). Ali's murder set a bloody precedent that was visited upon all his Shia successors, called imams (*aʾima*), until the twelfth and last, al-Muntazar, died, disappeared, or went into hiding sometime after 872.[3] The faithful held to the belief that he had gone into a state of suspended animation or "occultation" (*qhayba*),[4] from which he would return as the mahdi (redeemer) to usher in the final years of Islamic

1. K. A. C. Creswell, *The Muslim Architecture of Egypt* (Oxford: Clarendon Press, 1959), vol. 1, pp. 65ff.

2. It was not until the persecution and enforced conversion of Egyptian Christians by al-Hakim that the native Copts ceased to be a majority of the population of Egypt and shrank to their present share of 10–15 percent of the total population. The noted authority on the Copts, Otto F. A. Meinardus, states in his *Christian Egypt Ancient and Modern* (Cairo: American University of Cairo Press, 1965), p. 8, that "by the fourteenth century, the number of Copts in Egypt had decreased to one-tenth or even one-twelfth of the population, a percentage which more or less has been maintained to this day." In Palestine, Christians were a majority until the collapse of the Crusading states in 1291, and in Lebanon they maintained their majority well into the present century. Jews were an inconsequential minority everywhere in the Fatimid domains outside the major cities.

3. According to ʾAllamah S. M. H. Tabatabaʾi in his *Shi'ite Islam* (London: George Allen and Unwin, 1975), p. 211, "the occultation of the twelfth Imam is, therefore, divided into two parts: the first, the minor occultation (*ghaybat-i sughrā*) which began in 260/872 and ended in 329/939, lasting about seventy years; the second, the major occultation (*ghaybat-i-Kubrā*) which commenced in 329/939 and will continue as long as God wills it." Philip Hitti in *The History of the Arabs* (New York: St. Martin's Press, 1967), p. 441, cites the year 264/878 as the beginning of al-Muntazar's disappearance. Bernard Lewis in *The Origins of Ismaʿilism* (Cambridge: W. Heffer and Sons, Ltd., 1940) gives the same Muslim year as Tabatabaʾi (260) but places it later in the Christian calendar, 873–74.

4. Hitti, *History of the Arabs*, p. 441.

greatness before the end of the world and the dreadful Day of Judgment (*yawm al-din,* or day of faith). In the interim they were guided by religious leaders, the *mujtahids* (higher theologians). As God's spokesmen and His intermediaries with men,[5] they were by necessity secretive and given to protecting themselves from persecution by the mainstream Sunni[6] Muslims whose caliph ruled over the Islamic world first from Damascus under the Umayyad dynasty (661–750) and then from Baghdad (750–1254) under the Iranianized Abbasids.

During the early centuries when Sunni political power was dominant, the Shia's secrecy and isolation from traditional religious thought led to a gradual departure from orthodox Islamic beliefs and practices and to the infusion of many outside influences, including Christian mysticism with its emphasis on martyrdom (as among the Christians of Cordoba in Muslim Spain who in the ninth century deliberately courted death for their faith).[7] A further development was the virtual deification of the caliph Ali and his martyred son Husayn. Also included in the Shia hagiology was Husayn's elder brother Hasan, who, if we can believe Sunni accounts, was not martyred at all but pensioned off to a luxurious retirement in Medina, where he died of what Victorian writers used to term "the excesses of the Harem." The Shia, whose popular tenets almost demanded the martyrdom of their religious leaders, insist that he was poisoned.

Whereas Sunni religious practices are austere, dispassionate, and devoid of any attempt at direct contact with the deity (such as through the eucharist in Christianity),[8] the Shia came to hold that their imams, as direct descendants of the prophet, were born with an innate knowledge that came directly from God.[9] As the cult of the martyrdom of Husayn grew, a kind of passion play developed around it that is celebrated with elaborate pageantry and ferocious self-flagellation by impassioned devotees throughout the Shia world on the tenth day (the *ʿashuraʾ*) of the Muslim month of *al-Muharram,* the day in the Christian year 661 that Husayn and his band of followers were massacred near Karbalaʾ in Iraq by the forces of the second Umayyad caliph, Yazid I (680–683). Their imams, moreover, were often reputed, like Christ, to work miracles.

At the same time as the political power of the Sunni caliphate in

5. *Ibid.*

6. Literally, the followers of the *sunna,* or path of the prophet Muhammad.

7. Reinhart Dozy, *Spanish Islam* (London: Chatto and Windus, 1913), pp. 292–94.

8. A Sunni Muslim would not pray to God for a specific request, since he would not find it necessary (or worthy) to remind God of something He must by His nature already be aware of. If it is in God's plan to remedy the situation He will do so without further petition. The exception to this dispassionate approach to the deity within Sunni Islam is that of the Sufi mystics. For most Sunnis, however, dervishes of the Sufi or any other Muslim semimonastic order are regarded as beyond or at least at the very outer limits of orthodox acceptability.

9. According to Hitti they possessed *ʿisma,* or infallibility, as well as the divine gift of impeccability. Hitti, *History of the Arabs,* p. 440.

Baghdad began to deteriorate during the last half of the ninth Christian century, the Shia, who from the beginning had periodically been rent by dissension and factional splintering, saw the emergence of a major force within their own community. This was the faction known today alternatively as the Isma'ili or Sevener sect, after Ismaʿil ibn Jaʿfar, who died circa 760, the elder brother of the seventh Shia imam. His father had denied him the title of imam because he was a known drunkard, but the Isma'ilis refused to accept this as a sufficient reason for his being passed over ("as an infallible being [he] could not prejudice his case by such a thing as drinking wine");[10] for these radical Shia he became the "hidden" mahdi.[11] Most other Shia continued to follow Isma'il's younger brother Musa and his successors through the twelfth and, for them, final imam, Muhammad al-Muntazar, the true mahdi and "master of time" (*qaʾim al-zaman*), a young child who disappeared at the time of his father's death.[12]

The Isma'ilis, however, followed the discredited Isma'il and his son Muhammad ibn Ismaʿil (both regarded by the faithful as hidden imams), on through Muhammad's adopted son ʿAbd Allah ibn Maymun al-Qaddah and a series of imams and hidden imams directly to the Fatimid imam-caliphs themselves.[13] Although a minority within a minority, they came to constitute a vital force within the Islamic world[14] and in the early part of the tenth Christian century established their own political power base in North Africa. After their conquest of Egypt in 969 they founded a heretical caliphate to rival that of the Sunni Abbasids in Baghdad, whose real power had fallen to a succession of foreign palace guards and advisers.

Between the frontier of the Fatimid caliphate and the Abbasids lay a patchwork of small principalities, some Sunni and some Shia. Their rulers included some of the more interesting and culturally active figures of Islamic history, such as Sayf al-Dawlah al-Hamdani of Aleppo (944–967), but most were prey both to their own petty rivalries and to the incursions of the Byzantine emperors, notably Nikiforos Fokas (963–969), John I Tzimiskis (969–976), and Basil II (976–1025). And after the Byzantine collapse at Man-

10. *Ibid.*, p. 442.

11. *Ibid.*

12. *Ibid.*, p. 441. Also Moojan Momen, *An Introduction to Shiʿi Islam* (New Haven and London: Yale University Press, 1985), p. 45.

13. Thus the Fatimids were "Alids" (i.e., direct descendants of Ali and Fatima) only in "a spiritual sense" (Lewis, *Origins of Ismaʿilism,* p. 21). But since in Isma'ili tradition and practice regarding spiritual adoption "the pupil, not the physical son is the true heir," the lack of a physical descent was not important (*ibid.*). In fact, for the Isma'ilis "the material relationship between father and son, affecting only the insignificant and transitory body, was regarded as less important and less real than the spiritual relationship between teacher and pupil, which springs from the immortal soul" (*ibid.*, p. 44). In an apparent attempt to discredit the heretical Fatimids, several Sunni historians published the so-called Jewish Legend, which asserts that ʿAbd Allah ibn Maymun was a Jew and that "he was the true ancestor of the Fāṭimid caliphs, who were thus of Jewish descent" (*ibid.*, p. 67).

14. Hitti, *History of the Arabs,* p. 443.

zikert in 1071 the principalities were subjected to the growing power of the Saljuq Turks. Finally the rivalries between all four of these groups (Fatimids, Byzantines, Turks, and Abbasids) allowed the leaders of the First Crusade to achieve their amazing success with the capture of Jerusalem in 1099, thus introducing a fifth factor to an already complicated equation. It was into this period of extreme political volatility, exceptional even for this region, that the Druze religion was born—and flourished.

It is difficult to imagine a Druze-Cairo connection today. The outgrowth of a deity cult encouraged (at least in its early stages) by the caliph al-Hakim, the Druze movement in Egypt hardly survived the end of his rule. But in the last hectic years of al-Hakim's reign the movement spread to the northern frontier of his empire, the mountainous region of present-day southern Lebanon (then a stronghold of Isma'ili Shi'ism),[15] where it was difficult for the Fatimids to stamp it out once they began to lose control of the area. During the eleventh and twelfth centuries A.D. the area passed back and forth from one ruler to another in such relatively rapid succession that none was able or concerned enough to prevent the new religion's spread and survival.

It is also difficult to imagine Cairo as a center of Isma'ili Shi'ism. Today Egypt's Muslim population is exclusively Sunni, and has been so since the end of the Fatimid caliphate in 1174. According to most authorities Egyptian Muslims were never enthusiastic Shia but simply accepted the will of their rulers, until the overthrow of the Fatimids by Saladin allowed them to take up their former Sunni practices again. Al-Azhar mosque and university, which had been founded as Shia Fatimid establishments, are now the center, insofar as there has been one since the abolition of the caliphate by Atatürk in 1924, of Sunni Islamic political and intellectual consciousness. Yet extremist Shia thought was taken very seriously indeed by the Fatimid ruling class in the Cairo of al-Hakim biʾAmr Allah, and it was here that the concept of the Shia leadership imbued with divine knowledge was taken to its utmost extension of equating that divinely inspired leadership to the divinity itself.

The mosque that al-Hakim completed in his own honor must have been splendid in its time. The ensuing years have not been altogether kind, and the bulky, square-shaped bases added to the bottom halves of the otherwise graceful minarets during the Bahri Mamluk period (as a possible protection against earthquakes) have given them a curious, chunky appearance. The mosque itself was turned into a stable by the conquering Sunni, Saladin, and in recent years it has served as the Islamic Museum and a boys' school. It is now a functioning mosque once again, thanks to the restoration work of the Bohoras, an Indian Isma'ili sect who uphold the claims of al-Mustaʿli—1094–1101—to succeed his father, al-Mustansir, rather than his brother Nizar, whose adherents became the famous Assassins. Despite its

15. Kamal Salibi, *A Modern History of Lebanon* (London: Weidenfeld and Nicolson, 1965), p. xv.

strikingly Indian interior furnishings donated by devout Shia, it nonetheless caters to a Sunni congregation. The surrounding area, once a magnificent medieval city, is now a crumbling, desperately overcrowded adjunct to the late twentieth-century metropolis of Cairo, home to between ten and fifteen million Egyptians. The splendid Fatimid city gates of Bab al-Futuh and Bab al-Nasr that flank the mosque on either side now lead from a decaying medieval urban blight into a slightly more modern and equally unsettling one.

Yet it is not too difficult to conjure up the grandeur that must have clothed those few remnants of the imperial city in the time of al-Hakim. And it must be remembered that before the discovery of a sea route around Africa to India in 1498, a substantial amount of the trade with the Orient passed through Egypt. With this lucrative commerce as its financial base, Fatimid Cairo had become the power center of the Islamic world, eclipsing its rivals, caliphal Baghdad to the east and Cordoba in Spain, which had declared itself the capital of a third (and second Sunni) caliphate in 929. So the historical events out of which the Druze faith was born took their course not in the capital of the struggling, "third-world" country that is Egypt today but in a wealthy world power center rivaled in its time by Constantinople alone. The consequences for Islam and the world had it succeeded cannot even be guessed. But that a living remnant of such a brief episode in Islamic history is still with us as an important force in the power structure and political balance of the region is testimony to the seriousness of its impact at the time.

The Isma'ili theology that dominated the Fatimid empire and its government, credited by Hitti as having "organized one of the most subtle and effective means of politico-religious propaganda that the world of Islam had ever experienced,"[16] promised a radical political change that, somewhat like the promises of theoretical Marxism in Russia, failed to materialize. The failure of the Isma'ilis once in power to achieve their universalist aims led to a disillusionment that spawned Druzism. The "messianic kingdom" of the Isma'ilis became an ordinary state little different in structure from that of the Abbasid (or Byzantine) enemy. The people still looked for messianic rule, and other would-be messiahs began to appear. "Such desperation," writes Sadik Assaad, "clearly accounts for the appearance of the Drūz movement."[17]

Out of this vortex of messianic expectation grew the belief that the caliph al-Hakim was indeed the expected deliverer. Druzism as a religious movement can be said to have begun in the thirteenth year of the caliph's reign (A.H. 400, or A.D. 1009–1010),[18] when a number of Isma'ili religious

16. Hitti, *History of the Arabs,* p. 443.

17. Sadik A. Assaad, *The Reign of Al-Hakim bi Amr Allah* (Beirut: The Arab Institute for Research and Publishing, 1974), p. 39.

18. The Muslim calendar, which begins with the flight (*al-hijra,* often mistransliterated in Western texts as *hegira*) of Muhammad and his followers from Mecca to Medina to avoid persecution in A.D. 622 is based on twelve lunar months, two weeks shorter than the Christian year, and therefore the two never correspond.

leaders in Cairo began publicly to discuss al-Hakim in these terms, quoting "passages from revealed scriptures which they interpreted as pointing to Hākim as the fulfillment of the promise."[19] Whether the caliph himself actively encouraged this speculation at the outset or simply allowed it to grow of its own accord cannot be ascertained. Certainly there is sufficient mystery and myth surrounding the historical personage of al-Hakim to make dissemination of a belief in his own divinity at his own instigation not unlikely.

The year in which Druzism began was ushered in by extraordinary political moves by the caliph, including the destruction of the Church of the Holy Sepulcher in Jerusalem, restrictions on traditional Muslim religious practices such as the *hajj* (the annual pilgrimage to Mecca required of all faithful at least once in their lifetime if at all possible), and the persecution of local Jews and Christians. The remaining eleven years of his reign were marked by unusual, even irrational, actions both public and personal that created an image in the Christian world of the caliph as a madman.[20] For many of his subjects, however, his behavior gave increasing evidence of the divinity that was claimed by and for him. As Abu-Izzeddin notes, "his astonishing independence of all established ways marked him as superhuman."[21]

Certainly some of the seemingly more bizarre examples of his behavior usually cited by Christian authors as evidence of mental imbalance (see Hitti, *History of the Arabs,* p. 620) do take on an aura of rationality and cunning when seen in the proper context of the political and religious instability of the age.

The general picture that emerges is of a brilliant megalomaniac who dreamed of uniting the Islamic world under his own aegis at whatever cost—a goal toward which all his political moves, internal reforms, and even the creation of a new religious movement with himself as the divine center were aimed. Either he disappeared after despairing of ever achieving his goals or he was murdered by his enemies. Druze apologists emphasize his role as a social reformer. Abu-Izzeddin, quoting the Christian contemporary chronicler, Yahya ibn Saʿid al Antaki, writes: "Of his justice no one has heard the

19. Nejla M. Abu-Izzeddin, *The Druzes: A New Study of Their History, Faith and Society* (Leiden: E. J. Brill, 1984), p. 101.

20. Druze historians, such as Makarem, Najjar, and Abu-Izzeddin, tend to discount the extremes of al-Hakim's personality, yet even they are forced to come to terms with his extraordinary behavior. Abdullah Najjar, *The Druze: Millennium Scrolls Revealed,* translated by Fred I. Massey under the auspices of the American Druze Society (n.p., 1973), p. 147, admits that he was "capricious." Abu-Izzeddin describes him as "whimsical and enigmatic," noting that "his zeal was excessive and when thwarted turned to violence" (*Druzes,* p. 75); but, she concludes, "by sifting the likely and probable from the malicious accounts, and keeping in mind Hakim's vehement desire for reform and pressing need, in the circumstances, for the establishment of order and tranquility, a picture nearer the truth can be constructed" (*ibid.*).

21. Abu-Izzeddin, *Druzes,* p. 101, quoting Marshall G. S. Hodgson, "Al-Darazi and Hamza in the Origin of the Druze Religion," *Journal of the American Oriental Society* 82 (first quarter 1962): 14–17.

like" (*Druzes,* p. 76). One of the more "capricious" and "whimsical" of his many reputed idiosyncratic activities is found in the tale related by the somewhat maliciously witty, but academically reliable, Desmond Stewart in his *Great Cairo* (p. 73). Though it is a story from which the sexually conservative Druze must indeed recoil, it at once attests to al-Hakim as the impartial administrator of immediate justice and to the enigmatic nature of his image in the West as a madman. The traditional Western view of the Druze religious founder is perhaps best summed up in the words of John P. Durbin, a nineteenth-century American Protestant academic, who noted in his *Observations in the East* (vol. 2, p. 88*n.*) that "Hakim was not only eccentric, but impious, superstitious, and cruel. Twenty thousand persons, mostly Christians, perished by his hands or orders. When he appeared or his name was pronounced, everybody was required to prostrate themselves on the ground. At length he became intolerable even to his friends, and was assassinated by order of his sister, as he walked alone at night in a retired part of Mount Mokattam, and his body was concealed. This gave rise to the report that he had fled the earth for its wickedness, but will return again. Yet this creature is the object of Druze worship."

The catalyst that was to bring these widely held views to the status of an officially proclaimed belief appeared in the personage of Hamza ibn ʿAli ibn Ahmad al-Zuzani, a Persian Isma'ili theologian from an area of present-day western Afghanistan. Arriving in Cairo in the year A.H. 407 / A.D. 1016, Hamza soon became the leading figure among the devotees of al-Hakim as the Mahdi, a group which since the beginning of the Druze movement had "renounced the world and led a life of the spirit."[22] On the first day of the following year (408 / 1017) the caliph issued a proclamation (*sijill*) in which he revealed himself to be the manifestation of the deity and encouraged his followers publicly to practice this belief in their regular worship.

The mortal duties of the imamate now fell to Hamza, who for the next three years actively pursued the *daʿwa* (or "Divine Call," as Makarem terms it) of the new faith throughout the Fatimid empire. As Marshall Hodgson notes in his definitive study of the early years of the Druze movement,[23] "Hamza's crucial innovation seems to have been to make al-Hakim not merely an *imām* on however exalted a level, but the indefinable One itself (Hamza himself succeeding to the vacant *imam*ate)." He was aided in his missionary endeavors by two disciples in particular, Bahaʾ al-Din al-Samuqi and Muhammad al-Darazi, called "Nashtakin" (from the word *nestegin,* meaning the son of a Turk by a non-Turkish woman); it is al-Darazi whom some sources (chiefly Sibt ibn al-Jawzi) credit with having planted the new religion in the region of southern Lebanon that is regarded as its cradle today, and with having given these converts the name by which they became commonly known (singular *durzi,* plural *duruz*).[24]

22. Abu-Izzeddin, *Druzes,* p. 102.
23. Hodgson, "Al-Darazi and Hamza," p. 13.

The zeal of Hamza and his followers bore fruit quickly as Druzism spread throughout the empire and even beyond to Aleppo (where it took particularly firm root) and Damascus. It must be recognized that even in its earliest stages Druzism was not merely a sect of Islam but a new religion, which aimed at establishing a new world order. As Hodgson states, "Hamza evidently looked to al-Ḥākim to introduce, by his caliphal power, the messianic culmination of history, forcing all men to discard the various symbolisms of the old revealed religions, including Ismāʿīlism, and to worship the One alone, revealed clearly in al-Ḥākim."[25] Within a year, however, an irreconcilable split between Hamza and al-Darazi arose over who was to exercise the imamate and how converts were to be brought to the faith (Darazi advocating force, Hamza insisting on the strength of reasoned argument). Hamza publicly rebuked Darazi, calling his activities "destructive and calamitous."[26]

On the last day of 410 / 1019, Darazi was assassinated (probably with the blessing of al-Hakim, who saw him as a divisive force in the movement) and then anathematized by the Druze faith as a heretic. The spread of Druzism continued unabated until the sudden disappearance of al-Hakim in the tenth month of 411 / February 1021. In a proclamation that was found affixed to mosques immediately afterward, the caliph stated his disillusion with the results of his efforts to correct the religious divisions, social disparities, and moral ills of his time.

There are many theories surrounding the disappearance and presumed death of the imam al-Hakim in A.D. 1021. The generally accepted one is that he was murdered with the collusion of his sister, Sitt al-Mulk, whom he had accused of immoral behavior. Assaad suggests that it was the handiwork of the Druze themselves to create yet another disappeared and hidden imam who could reinforce their *daʿwa,* or religious call. The Christian historians Bar Hebraeus and Al-Antaki maintain that al-Hakim, whose mother was a Christian from a patriarchal Orthodox family, disappeared in order to be-

24. Sami Makarem, *The Druze Faith* (Delmar, New York: Caravan Books, 1975), p. 11. According to Abu-Izzeddin, "the statement that Ḥākim sent Darazi to Syria to spread the new doctrine among mountain people, especially in Wādī al-Taym, is not correct. Darazi did not leave Egypt and he disappeared at an early stage in the *daʿwa*" (*Druzes,* p. 104), a theory that Hodgson proposed ("Al-Darazi and Hamza," p. 5). Abu-Izzeddin does accept the derivation of the term *Druze* from Darazi, however, "probably because of the stir he created" (*Druzes,* p. 104). For Hodgson, "Al-Darazi's name clearly was used simply because he was the first in the public eye," and he notes that "the term *Durziyya* (or *Daraziyya*) applied generally to all the Ḥākim-cult circle in Egypt and included those of Syria by a natural extension. The story of al-Darazī's Syrian mission may well stem from someone's attempt to account for the subsequent presence of Druzes . . . in Syria" ("Al-Darazi and Hamza," p. 6). For other theories of the derivation of the term *Druze,* see Abu-Izzeddin, *Druzes,* pp. 29–32.

25. Marshall G. S. Hodgson, "Durūz," *The Encyclopaedia of Islam* (Leiden: E. J. Brill, 1965), vol. 2, p. 632.

26. al-Najjar, *Druze,* p. 135.

come a Christian monk after Christ appeared to him in a vision chastising him for having persecuted Christians. The thirteenth-century Christian chronicler Abu Salih relates that al-Hakim left his ass and groom near Hilwan, a few miles south of Cairo, and "went alone into the inner parts of the desert and never returned." Baron Silvestre de Sacy, quoting the almost contemporary account of Severus of Eshmounain, gives a very similar account of the imam's disappearance. Nejla M. Abu-Izzeddin, however, in her recently published study of the Druze and their religion, cites "recently uncovered manuscripts [which] reveal that Ḥākim departed east, to Sijistān in eastern Iran on the border of India," where he lived for many years and continued to communicate with his followers. With al-Hakim gone from the scene, Hamza immediately went into hiding, and the new caliph, al-Zahir (1021–1035) instantly "denied any claim by his ancestors to divinity and threatened those who adhered to such a belief with eradication by the sword."[27] True to his word, al-Zahir ruthlessly persecuted followers of the new faith of Druzism and succeeded in wiping them out in nearly all their strongholds, from Cairo as far north as Aleppo. Those who survived were found principally in southern Lebanon and Syria, especially the Wadi al-Taym region on the slopes of Mount Hermon, and in the Jabal al Aʿla region west of Aleppo.

For six years following al-Hakim's disappearance the Druze leadership remained in hiding. But with the waning of active persecution, Hamza wrote to Bahaʾ al-Din instructing him to pursue the *daʿwa* and spread the faith. According to Abu-Izzeddin, "Bahāʾ al-Dīn resumed the proselytizing work, composing epistles and dispatching missionaries, and carrying the responsibility of the *daʿwa* in the absence of the imām."[28] Like Jesus, al-Hakim had assured his followers that he would return in the lifetime of the generation that knew him, and Bahaʾ al-Din clearly expected the return of the mahdi at any moment.[29] As the years passed, however, al-Hakim's return, like that of Christ, was gradually postponed until the end of time itself.[30]

27. See Hitti, *History of the Arabs,* p. 621; Assaad, *Reign of al-Hakim,* pp. 190–91, 183ff.; Abu Salih, *The Churches and Monasteries of Egypt and Neighboring Countries,* edited by Alfred Butler (Oxford: At the Clarendon Press, 1895), p. 154; Silvestre de Sacy, *Exposé de la réligion des Druzes,* 2 vols. (Paris: Imprimerie Royale, 1838), vol. 1, p. ccccxvi; Abu-Izzeddin, *Druzes,* pp. 105ff.

28. Abu-Izzeddin, *Druzes,* pp. 105ff.

29. *Ibid.*

30. This postponement did not prevent periodic appearances of millennialism among the Druze, as among Christians. A. C. Inchbold, writing of Syria at the turn of this century, reported that the Druze were waiting for the reappearance of al-Hakim nine hundred years after his disappearance to usher in "their consumation of happiness" (*Under the Syrian Sun,* London: Hutchinson and Co., 2 vols., 1906, vol. 1, p. 74). Laurence Oliphant refers to al-Hakim's reappearance while discussing the Druze belief that he had gone to China and that large numbers of Druze live there. "According to the Druses, however, who deny his notoriously bad character, he did not die, but was translated, and his soul went to China, whither it has since been followed by the souls of all pious Druses, who are supposed to be occupying in

In the meantime, Baha' al-Din, who had been given the title of *al-muqtana* (literally, the imam's deputy) by Hamza to implement the *da'wa* in the imam's absence, began the important work of codifying the religious teaching (*tawhid*) of Druzism and nurturing the faith among those who had survived al-Zahir's persecution. In some cases force was required, particularly in the Wadi al-Taym, where the leadership of one Sukayn, though popular, was at odds with the tawhid. Baha' al-Din turned first to peaceful diplomatic methods, including the sending of a mission led by his niece, Sitt Sarah (who is venerated to this day as a sage and peacemaker). When these failed, he resorted to dispatching a group of followers to destroy Sukayn and his key supporters. This done, he remained as the leading force in the Druze faith until his death. During the sixteen years (1027–1043) in which Baha' al-Din actively pursued the missionary *da'wa* to gain converts, the various epistles, 111 in total, composed by al-Hakim, Hamza, and Baha' al-Din himself, were collected and arranged in six books, the so-called Druze Canon, or *al-Hikmat al-Sharifa* (the Noble Knowledge). The style of these epistles reflects the esotericism of the faith, so that even if copies were to fall into alien hands, as they have done on several occasions over the centuries, the true meaning of their contents would not be easily discernible to the uninitiated reader.[31] The last of these epistles is dated 434 / 1042, and in the following year the call was formally ended, twenty-six years after it was first proclaimed by Hamza in Cairo. After this no new adherents were to be accepted into the faith.

According to Druze tradition, Hamza, who was still in hiding in Cairo, left and journeyed to "the land of the Chinese oases,"[32] where he joined up with the caliph al-Hakim, who continued to send mystic meditations (in the Greek sense of *mystikos,* or secret) to Baha' al-Din as late as 439 / 1047.[33] From this date until the appearance fifty years later of the Crusaders on Syrian soil in 1097, the Druze all but disappear from the stage of history, to reappear only briefly from time to time until their rise as a major political force in the Levant following the Ottoman conquest in 1516. Having survived the initial wave of persecution launched immediately after al-Hakim's disappearance, under Baha' al-Din's leadership the Druze were bound together into a tightly knit society by the *tawhid.* After 1043, a closed

---

large numbers certain cities in the west of China, and preparing for the great event which the Druses believe to be now impending" (*The Land of Gilead, with Excursions in the Lebanon,* New York: D. Appleton and Co., 1881, p. 319).

31. "Esotericism serves to endow scriptures with subtle inner meanings that are different from literal or 'apparent' meanings. It also involves the deliberate disorganization of arguments, the use of vague metaphors, and the discussion of apparently trivial subjects while actually treating important issues. As a consequence, even when non-Druze have gained access to Druze scripture it has not been of great concern to the Druze because only the initiates of the religion can understand the actual meaning of the text." Alamuddin, *Crucial Bonds,* p. 12.

32. Abu-Izzeddin, *Druzes,* p. 107. See also Chap. 3, *n.* 17 below.

33. *Ibid.,* p. 105.

and secretive community, they effectively blended into the Levantine landscape as yet another religious cult that had aimed for universal acceptance but survived as a reduced remnant that kept very much to itself, refusing to share its beliefs with the various neighboring religious communities that to this day make up the religious patchwork that is Mount Lebanon.

2

The Origins, Religious Tenets, and Traditions of the Druze

Whatever the origins of the term *Druze* (various of which will be discussed later in this chapter), to the members themselves they are *Muwahhidun,* or Unitarians, believers in absolute monotheism. The word in Arabic is taken from the root *WHD,* meaning to be one, and their faith itself is the *tawhid,* from the same root, which expresses the oneness of God.[1] They also refer to themselves as the peo-

1. "The essence of their doctrine is a strict and uncompromising unity of the Deity. The absolute oneness of the Godhead admits of no attributes distinct from His essence" (Abu-Izzeddin, *Druzes,* p. 111). Al-Najjar quotes from epistle thirteen of the Druze Canon to illustrate this core concept of Druzism: "Our Lord, sanctified by His name, is neither ancient nor eternal, for the two are created and He is their creator. His identity cannot be visualized by fancy or physical organ and cannot be determined by opinion or comparison. . . . He resides in no known place for He would then be restricted to that definite place and out of all other places; nor can it be said that any place is outside His presence for that implies lack of power; nor is He first for a first must be followed by a last; nor is he last

ple of the *Banu al-Maʿruf* (the Sons of Beneficence), from the Arabic *al-Aʿraf*, or those who help others.[2] Although their theology as expressed in their sacred writings assembled during the period 1017–1043 reflects much of the extremist Isma'ili Shi'ism out of which the movement grew, its actual relationship to Islam is historical only.

The tenets of the faith have been held in secret since the closing of the *daʿwa* in 1043 and shared by only a small number from among the community in each succeeding generation known as the *ʿuqqal* (singular *ʿaqil* [m.] and *ʿaqila* [f.]), or "the enlightened," which from the earliest days included women in its ranks.[3] The remainder, known as the *juhhal* (the ignorant or noninitiated), as members of a secret cult protected the secrecy and sanctity of their religion through their loyalty to one another. Although not permitted access to the six holy books or to knowledge of the mysterious secrecies of their contents, the uninitiated were not without a religion but were given a simplified outline of their faith in the form of a strict code of moral and ethical behavior.

It was often held by European writers on the Druze that because the bulk of the Druze community was uninitiated into the secrets of their religion they held none at all and in consequence had no morals. In 1736 John Green wrote in *A Journey from Aleppo* (pp. 18–19) that "it may even be said that they [the *juhhal*] have no Religion and consequently live in a Course of Libertinism, which they believe is permitted them." The late eighteenth-century French visitor to the Druze Mountain, Count Volney, is impressed in his *Voyage en Syrie et Egypte* (vol. 2, p. 76) by the "Druze spirit of social solidarity" but speaks of their "indifference for religion, which forms a striking contrast with the zeal of Mahometans and Christians." Druze children, he reports, "are neither taught to read the Psalms like the Maronites, nor the Koran like the Muslims; the shaykhs barely know how to write a letter." A much earlier visitor, the Spanish Jew Benjamin of Tudela, who traveled within a few miles of the Druze territories at the time of the Crusading kingdoms (mid-twelfth century), was even more specific about Druze "libertinism": "This nation," he writes of the Druze in his *Itinerary* (vol. 1, pp. 61–62), "is very incestuous; a father cohabits with his own daughter,

---

for a last must be preceded by a first; nor is He visible for that suggests invisible, nor is He invisible for He would then be shadowed by the visible. I cannot say that He is life or soul for He would then be like his creatures and subject to addition and subtraction. . . ." (*Druze*, pp. 122–23). (For a contradictory view of absolute unitarianism as embodied in the Druze faith see chap. 2, *n.* 17 below).

2. Assaad, *Reign of Al-Hakim*, p. 158.

3. The *ʿuqqal* are in turn divided into two classes, "those who have passed the simple test of trust and can be permitted to know some elementary facts of religion" and "those well founded in the knowledge and mysteries of their religion" (Iliya F. Harik, *Politics and Change in a Traditional Society: Lebanon, 1711–1845* [Princeton: Princeton University Press, 1968], pp. 25–26. The higher class of *ʿuqqal* are known as *al-ajawid* (the righteous).

and once every year all men and women assemble to celebrate a festival upon which occasion, after eating and drinking they hold promiscuous intercourse." In actual fact, the uninitiated Druze, especially the women, have always striven to live just as moral and circumspect a life as the enlightened, the major difference between the two being the considerable time the latter devote to scriptural study, by which they gain the wisdom that earns them their respected status in Druze society.[4]

The beliefs and characteristics that set the Druze apart from Muslims are many. Their faith is an exclusive one, and the secrecy of its theology has served to reinforce communal separateness. Since the closing of the *daʿwa* proselytizing has been forbidden, so that in theory at least no new members have been admitted since 1043. One cannot convert to Druzism; one is born to it.[5] A non-Muslim belief shared in part with the Alawis and Yazidis is the Far Eastern concept of the transmigration of souls (*tanasukh* in Arabic). The Druze believe that the number of all souls of believers and nonbelievers was fixed and limited at the Creation. Thus when a Druze dies, another Druze is born. The soul of the former enters the body of the latter instantly by a system of metempsychosis. The stern Islamic message of the Day of Judgment (*yawm al-din*) does not exist in the Druze faith in this form. "Souls do not die to be resurrected nor do they sleep only to be awakened. Judgement Day in the sect's book is the end of a long journey in repeated reincarnations for the full development of the soul."[6] Unlike the teaching of Islam the Druze faith promises not a paradise full of earthly delights but rather a beatific vision of the Holy One, with hell being the failure to achieve this ultimate goal of the just man.[7] The Druze exclude predestination, a cardinal Islamic concept. "They believe that God gave man intelligence to choose and act and to try to modify society and environment within God's all-embracing plan and cosmic purposes."[8]

Male circumcision, universal among Muslims, is not ritually practiced

4. Not all visitors shared the Druze community's reverence for the *ʿuqqal*. The early nineteenth-century English traveler, John Madox, let slip his personal anticlericalism when he observed that "the second, or inferior class of Druses are called Djahels, or ignorant, not being admitted, or at least but slightly so, within the mystic pale. They eat, drink, smoke, and laugh, like good fellows; they have no affectation of superior sanctity, and are, in my opinion, much the wiser of the two. We find imposters everywhere, and, I suspect, the initiated Druse is one of the species" (*Excursions in The Holy Land, Egypt, Nubia, Syria &c., Including a Visit to the Unfrequented District of the Hauran*, 2 vols., London: Richard Bentley, 1834, vol. 2, p. 184).

5. This exclusion of converts has not apparently prevented small numbers of outsiders from becoming accepted as Druze at various times since 1043. One of the two leading Druze political clans in Lebanon, the Junbalat family, is considered to be of relatively recent Kurdish origin, having come to Mount Lebanon from Aleppo in the early seventeenth century (see Salibi, *History of Lebanon*, p. 10). The other clan, the Arslans, trace their ancestry to the Arab Lakhmid princes of al-Hira in sixth-century Mesopotamia (see Abu-Izzeddin, *Druzes*, p. 142).

6. Al-Najjar, *Druze*, p. 117.

7. *Ibid.*, pp. 117–19.

8. *Ibid.*, p. 109.

among the Druze, although it is quite commonly undertaken, particularly in urban centers, for reasons of hygiene. There is no ceremony of circumcision as a rite of passage such as exists in many Muslim societies as, for example, in Turkey and among the tribes of Arabia. ("La circoncision chez les Bedouins est l'occasion de fêtes bruyantes. Au Djebel [Druse] on ne la fête pas."[9]) If a male Druze is not circumcised as an infant (and this does occur in villages where children are often born at home with only a midwife in attendance), it is unlikely that the operation will be performed later. I have been assured by males of one Druze family who grew up in a remote Druze village in Lebanon during the late 1950s and early 1960s that whenever an itinerant *mutahhir* (ritual circumciser) made his appearance, the uncircumcised boys of the village would hide in the hills until he left, just in case their parents might be tempted to engage his services.

Polygamy, while permitted to Muslims, is forbidden to Druze, along with concubinage and temporary marriage (*mutʿa*), which are likewise a feature of traditional Islamic society. Nor is divorce for a Druze the easy matter it is for a Muslim, and a Druze woman can initiate the proceedings (something that may theoretically take place in Islam but rarely does). Druze women, moreover, have always had the right to own property and to dispose of it freely, unlike their Muslim sisters.[10] Both Abu-Izzeddin and Aharon Layish attribute this very nontraditional Islamic view to the grandfather of al-Hakim, the Fatimid caliph al-Muʿizz al-Din Allah, who "enjoined contenting himself with one wife and thereby anticipated by a thousand years the modernists of the school of Muhammad ʿAbduh."[11]

The *shariʿa,* or code of Islamic law that governs the life of all religious Muslims, was interpreted allegorically by Hamza and his followers, and the binding character of its commands and prohibitions denied.[12] Thus in Druzism the so-called five pillars of Islam[13] are not ritually observed or even

9. Narcisse Bouron, *Les Druzes: Histoire du Liban et de la Montagne Haouranaise* (Paris: Editions Berger-Levrault, 1930), pp. 292, 299, 300. The origins and practice of male circumcision in Middle Eastern society very likely predate Judaism's covenant of Abraham. Although deeply ingrained in Muslim tradition (exceptions having been found, however, by Wilfrid Thesiger in his study of *The Marsh Arabs,* London: Longmans, Green and Co., 1964), circumcision as a religious duty is nowhere to be found commanded of the faithful in either the Qurʾan or in the *Hadith* (sayings of the prophet Muhammad). Most Copts and Armenians follow the practice, but other Christians, notably those of the Byzantine tradition and the Maronites, do not.

10. Abu-Izzeddin, *Druzes,* p. 230.

11. *Ibid.*

12. H. A. Hirschberg in A. J. Arberry, ed., *Religion in the Middle East,* 2 vols. (London: Cambridge University Press, 1969), vol. 2, p. 335.

13. Prayer at five specific times daily facing Mecca; public witness that there is no God but Allah and Muhammad is the final prophet; almsgiving; fasting from sunrise to sunset during the month of *Ramadan;* and pilgrimage to Mecca during the prescribed month at least once in the believer's lifetime (unless health or finances prevent it). To these the Shia sects add a sixth and seventh pillar: *jihad* (Holy War against the infidel) and *imam* (adherence to the authority of the spiritual leadership of the community).

acknowledged.[14] Instead of praying five times a day toward Mecca as the prophet Muhammad commanded, the Druze regard prayer in the allegorical sense of "association of one's soul with the unity of God."[15] For them, as Makarem states, prayer "developed into prayer as a constant state of being."[16]

Instead of five pillars, Hamza substituted the seven duties (*al-shurut al-sabʿa*), which all Druze are required to observe:

> Recognition of al-Hakim and strict adherence to monotheism.
> Negation of all non-Druze tenets.
> Rejection of Satan and unbelief.
> Acceptance of God's acts.
> Submission to God for good or ill.
> Truthfulness.
> Mutual help and solidarity between fellow Druze.

In the first rule Arberry states: "Recognition of al-Ḥākim also requires belief in Ḥamza and the four ministers below him." Abu-Izzeddin sets this rule forth as "belief that the doctrine of unity was preached in every age," thus accounting for the many streams of religious tradition that are found in Druze theology. As J. W. Hirschberg (author of the article on the Druze in Arberry, *Religion*) states, "the Druze concept of the Deity combines almost all notions current at the time of its emergence. Besides Jewish and Christian beliefs, we find Gnostic, Neo-Platonist and Persian elements, and all this under the flag of strict monotheism." Abu-Izzeddin likewise acknowledges this multiplicity of antecedents:

> The Druze faith is founded on the Qurʾān as interpreted by the propagator of the *daʿwa*. It accepts the Old and New Testaments as divine books, in line with the attitude of Islam towards the two earlier monotheistic religions. It reaches beyond the traditionally recognized monotheisms to earlier expressions of man's search for communion with the One. Hence its reverence for Hermes, the bearer of a divine message, for Pythagoras, the ascetic sage who rose to the heavens and came back to preach the unity of the Godhead, for the divine Plato,

14. While no Druze is required to practice any of the five pillars, individual Druze do observe the Ramadan fast or make the pilgrimage to Mecca. James Silk Buckingham, who visited the Jabal al-Druze in the early 1820s, noted that "though the Druses dislike the Mohammadans generally, and entertain no tenet in common with their faith, yet . . . many of them have been so infected with their customs, as to keep the fast of Ramadān with as much rigour as the most orthodox follower of the Arabian prophet" (*Travels Among the Arab Tribes Inhabiting the Countries East of Syria and Palestine*, London: 1825, pp. 246–47). The great feast, the *ʿid al-Adha*, or sacrifice, that takes place at the conclusion of the annual pilgrimage (*al-hajj*) is a major holiday for the Druze community—the one major tangible link between Druzism and traditional Islam, probably adopted to protect the Druze from persecution, as permitted by *taqiya* (see Bouron, *Les Druzes*, p. 287).

15. Makarem, *Druze Faith*, p. 96.

16. *Ibid.*, p. 77.

> and for Plotinus, the influence of whose system is clear in the Druze Scriptures. The faith sponsored by Ḥākim was preached to Muslims, specifically to Ismāʿīlīs whom Ḥamza calls *muqaṣṣira,* those who lag behind, i.e. having passed from *ẓāhir* [outward form] to *bāṭin* [inner truth], from *tanzīl* [literally, "revelation," or following the outward form of divine revelation] to *taʾwīl* [carrying the inner interpretation of revelation to the extreme of denying the literal sense which is the outer law—see Abu-Izzeddin, *Druzes,* p. 103], failed to go beyond *taʾwīl* to the ultimate goal, *tawḥīd* [pure unitarian religion]; for Islam (*ẓāhir*) is the door to *īmān* (*bāṭin*), and *īmān* is the door to *tawḥīd.*[17]

The duty of truthfulness in matters of religion applies only to the relation of Druze with each other. Toward non-Druze, strict secrecy is required, and to protect himself and his family in times of mortal danger presented by religious persecution a Druze is permitted outwardly to deny his faith—the Shia principle of dissimulation, or *taqiya* (from the root *WQY,* meaning to guard, preserve). Unlike the Shia, the Druze place no religious virtue on martyrdom. And while they are respectful of other religions and immensely courteous toward members of other faiths who come peacefully into their midst, they hold by tradition that a harsh judgment of varying severity awaits all non-Druze.

Popular Druze tradition relates that "the Shi'a deserve fifty curses, the Sunnis forty, the Christians thirty and the Jews twenty." This tradition certainly reflects contemporary reality, the aberrations of the civil war in Lebanon notwithstanding. To my knowledge, the origins of Druze contempt for the Shia is not spelled out anywhere but probably stems from the fact that the Fatimid Shia establishment out of which Druzism emerged refused to accept the new interpretation of unitarian faith and ruthlessly suppressed it throughout most of their empire. The proximity of most Druze to Twelver Shia villages in southern Lebanon for centuries doubtless reinforced this contempt, since the Shia of the Jabal ʿAmil have traditionally formed the lowest level of society in the region, being composed almost entirely of landless, illiterate peasants living in the poorest of surroundings on the least desirable land. Christians come second best, a view reflected in the fact that the Druze, if they live in villages with non-Druze Arabs, are far more likely to share their surroundings with Christians than with Sunnis. They virtually never do with Shia. The fact that the Jews are the least condemned might account for the relatively good relations the Druze in Israel enjoy with the Zionist government, as opposed to the generally hostile attitude Israelis hold toward Muslim and Christian Arabs in their country. Rabbi Benjamin of Tudela, although critical of the Druze for their supposed licentious habits, observed that "the Druses are friendly towards the Jews." However, the "Catechism of the Druze" explicitly states the punishments reserved for those "who deny

17. Arberry, *Religion,* vol. 2, p. 338, and Abu-Izzeddin, *Druzes,* p. 117.

our Lord": "They shall be reduced to servitude, and shall undergo severe tortures, and sufferings continually. In the ears of everyone of them shall be fastened ear rings of a black substance which in summer shall burn them like fire, and in winter shall freeze them like snow. Their covering shall be a cap made of the skin of the hog, and they shall toil under our yoke, like bulls and asses. The same punishment shall be inflicted, but more lightly, on the Christians."[18]

An additional feature of the Druze faith is its Neoplatonic doctrine of periodical manifestations of the Universal Intelligence (*al-ʿAql al-Kulli*) emanating from the Creator. In the Isma'ili system these manifestations occurred in the persons of Adam, Noah, Abraham, Moses, Jesus, Muhammad, and, finally, the seventh imam, Muhammad ibn-Ismaʿil. In the Druze faith they are reduced to the status of prophets, and the predecessors of Hamza ibn ʿAli as the incarnation of the *ʿaql* included Shuʿayb (Jethro) at the time of Moses and Salman al-Farisi, a companion of the prophet Muhammad.

For the Isma'ilis each manifestation of the Universal Intelligence revealed the Divine Spirit more completely, and in the person of the imam-caliph al-Hakim, "the true believers in God's message experienced the utmost light they could endure."[19] In him the true knowledge of God was divulged, "free from all ritualistic impositions and free from all dogmatic obligations, whether literal or allegorical."[20] Druzism, therefore, separates itself from Islam irrevocably by declaring that the revelations of al-Hakim contain the ultimate truth, not those of the prophet Muhammad.[21]

Though the Druze do not observe the Muslim commandment of ritual prayer five times daily, they do conduct simple services of worship on Thursday evenings at a place for seclusion and prayer called a *khalwa* (meaning a place of retreat) or a *majlis* (a meeting place, or conference room), the latter term according to Layish reflecting *taqiya* because of its purely secular connotation.[22] Every village with a modest Druze population has such a building, usually "an austere hall, without architectural embellishments and without furniture, except small lecterns to lay books on during meditation."[23] During

18. Asher, *Tudela*, vol. 1, p. 62; de Sacy, *Réligion des Druzes*, vol. 2, pp. 640–41, English translation in *Foreign Quarterly Review* 57 (1842): 189–93.

19. Makarem, *Druze Faith*, p. 77.

20. Arberry, *Religion*, vol. 2, p. 338.

21. Assaad, *Reign of Al-Hakim*, p. 163.

22. Layish, *Marriage*, p. 14. Nura Alamuddin draws a slightly different distinction between the two: "The *majlis*, which is a place where all Druze may come and pray, and the *khalwi* [sic], a private area for the initiates to sit, pray, and meditate. Villagers wishing to pray come to the *majlis* on Thursday evening, a time the Druze use for their religious observances because the Call started on that day of the week in 1017 and because traditional Islam designates Friday as the day of worship." In her footnote to the preceding she adds, "For Muslims a new day begins at sunset rather than at midnight. Thursday evening in the West is early Friday for them." *Crucial Bonds*, pp. 32, 107.

23. Arberry, *Religion*, vol. 2, p. 344. Bouron notes that "rien n'est plus nu, rien n'est plus triste, rien n'est plus froid qu'une salle de 'medjles' Druze. . . ." (*Les Druzes*, p. 285).

the first part of the service community affairs are discussed in the presence of all who wish to attend—including the *juhhal,* who have to leave when prayer, study, and meditation begin.[24]

The religious leadership of the community is in the hands of the *shuyukh* (*shaykhs*) or religious elders (*masha'ikh al-Din*), the chief of which in a given area is the *shaykh al-ʿaql*. In Lebanon this office is held by Muhammad Abu-Shaqra, whose residence is at Baʿdaran in the Shuf mountains.[25] Syrian Druze have traditionally looked to the leading *shaykh* of Qanawat, a small, entirely Druze town built on a foundation of spectacular Roman ruins a few miles northeast of al-Suwayda'. At present there are three *shuyukh* in the Jabal al-Druze of southern Syria who hold the title of *shaykh al-ʿaql,* residing in Qanawat, al-Suwayda', and Sahwat al-Balata respectively. The present *primus inter pares* of this pontifical trio is generally recognized as Husayn Jarbuʿ of al-Suwayda', in view of his own personal leadership qualities and the importance of his residence in the only Druze settlement that can truly be called a city. He maintains an office at the newly built *majlis* of ʿAyn al-Zaman to the left of the main highway as one enters al-Suwayda' from the south.[26] In Israel the office of spiritual head of the Druze has for several generations been hereditary in the Tarif family of Julis in western Galilee.[27]

These spiritual leaders and the *shaykhs* and judges under them administer Druze civil law in matters of marriage, divorce, and inheritance. The *Masha'ikh al-Din* are held in high esteem by the faithful, and pilgrimages are often made to shrines built on sites where notably pious elders used to retire to pray. Such a shrine is known by the *taqiya* term *mazar* (plural *mazarat*), meaning simply a place one visits or as a *maqam* (pl. *maqamat*), which refers specifically to the tomb of a saint or a sacred place. Examples include the *khalawat* of Qanawat in Syria, Bayyada above Hasbayya in the Wadi al-Taym of southeast Lebanon (site of the principal Druze theological school), al-Nabi Ayyub above Niha in the southern Shuf district, and al-Nabi Shuʿayb in eastern Galilee, adjacent to the Horns of Hattin, site of the great Crusader disaster in 1187.

To become a *shaykh,* the would-be initiate must undergo many years

24. Arberry, *Religion,* vol. 2, p. 344.

25. During the early days of the Junbalat-Yazbaki rivalry in the eighteenth century there were two *shuyukh al-ʿaql* in Lebanon, one for each faction. According to Iliya Harik, writing in 1968, this "is a division which persists to this day" (*Politics and Change,* p. 26); the division between the two factions does indeed persist, but there is only one *shaykh al-ʿaql* in Lebanon.

26. An exception to Bouron's observation of almost sixty years ago (*n.* 23 above), is the new *majlis* of ʿAyn al-Zaman in al-Suwayda'. Although not completely finished it is very large indeed, with a grand courtyard, expansive *diwan* (reception area) and offices. Outside the entrance to the area reserved for prayer is a small bird cage containing a species of dove whose cry, uttered at the same time it makes a gesture with its head that resembles praying, sounds to the ears of Arabic-speaking visitors like the invocation "*Ya Karim*" ("O Noble One," referring to God). The atmosphere at ʿAyn al-Zaman is anything but "bare, sad, and cold."

27. Layish, *Marriage,* pp. 12–13.

of study and close scrutiny by the *ʿuqqal*. Many who begin the undertaking fail to fulfill the rigid requirements for membership and fall irrevocably back into the ranks of the *juhhal*. As Philip Hitti wrote half a century ago,

> To the high rank of enlightened *ʿuqqāl*, no one can aspire whose character has not marked him [or her] as one entirely trustworthy and capable of extreme secrecy. Before admission, however, he [or she] must be subjected to a rigorous process of long trial and probation. Then follows the ceremonial rite of induction. This secret ceremony has been witnessed and described by only one or two outsiders throughout the whole history of the Druze religion.
>
> Once admitted to the favored rank, the Sheikh begins to wear a heavy white turban, and abstains from gaudy colors, swearing and obscene language. His deportment becomes dignified and reserved. Under no condition is he thereafter to touch alcoholic liquor or to smoke. He may even refrain from eating at the table of a wealthy man or government official lest something of the money used in buying the food might have been illegitimately acquired.[28]

According to W. B. Seabrook, the rather eccentric traveler who wrote his account of the Druze at the same time as Hitti produced his controversial 1928 study (and who was undoubtedly one of the sources Hitti used in attempting to unravel the more mysterious of the sect's alleged secret practices), the ceremonial rite of induction resembles the celebrated bouts of self-denial attributed to the early Christian monks of Egypt, with temptations proffered in the form of delicious food and seductive women that the initiate must ignore.[29] My own experience and study, however, would lead me to discount such speculation as sensationalist exaggeration.

Though the *ʿuqqal* probably make up less than one-fifth of the Druze, their presence in any Druze town or village is a dominant one, like that of "fairy-tale kings," as the British author Colin Thubron, writing in the late 1960s, described them.

> The distinctive [white] fez and long black aba, once the simplest vestments in the Mountain—for the "uqqal" was [sic] forbidden to dress gaudily—are now the most flamboyant. But their wearers train them-

28. Philip K. Hitti, *The Origins of the Druze People and Religion* (New York: Columbia University Press, 1928), pp. 42–43. Such is the reserved demeanor of both male and female initiates that they do not customarily shake hands with visitors, but rather acknowledge their presence with a visual greeting.

29. William B. Seabrook, *Adventures in Arabia Among the Bedouins, Druses, Whirling Dervishes and Yazidee Devil-Worshippers* (London: George C. Harrap and Co., Ltd., 1928), pp. 199–201. Seabrook was an eccentric American adventurer of dubious scholarly qualifications. His wife, Marjorie Muir Worthington, was quoted in her obituary in the *New York Times* (Feb. 18, 1976) as having described him as "a fine, intelligent and lovable man, with a touch of genius as well as madness."

> selves in stateliness and reserve. They answer questions circumspectly, or merely gesture with princely condescension. Any form of strife goes against their religious convictions. They neither smoke nor drink. Some refuse to see a doctor in their illness and this, at least in Baaklin [Baʿqlin, a Druze town in the central Shuf mountains], has preserved them into senility.[30]

Sharing the leadership of the community with these religious leaders are the traditional political figures, the *mashaʾikh al-zaman,* who belong to the religiously uninitiated. Politically the *juhhal* dominate the *ʿuqqal* (perhaps in the sense, to cite a rough Western parallel, that the Commons dominate the Lords in the British Parliament), and the religious leaders generally defer to their secular political counterparts in all matters affecting the community except purely religious ones.

The aspects of the Druze that most intrigued visitors from the West were their origins and secret practices. Little is known of the people who accepted the call to the Druze faith in the early eleventh Christian century other than that they were probably already adherents of Isma'ili Shi'ism. Their racial background is obscure. Hitti credits them with some Arab blood via the Banu al-Tanukh, an Arabian Bedouin tribe that emigrated from eastern Arabia in the third century A.D. to the Syrian coastal mountains by way of al-Hira, the Arab client state of the Sassanid Persian empire in Mesopotamia. But he is more inclined to view them as a combination of Persian and Kurdish elements. "Racially, therefore, the Druze people were a mixture of Persians, Iraqis and Persianized Arabs, and were thereby admirably fitted for the reception of the Druze dogmas and tenets of belief."[31] It is generally accepted that there were influxes of Persians and Kurds into the area now occupied by the state of Lebanon at frequent intervals throughout the first centuries of Islamic domination, and it is most likely that this movement of populations from the east would have accelerated during a period of Shia ascendancy, since the heartland of Shia Islam has always been southern Mesopotamia. Nevertheless, Hitti has been criticized for underestimating the Arab and Arabicized Phoenician/Aramaic stock that was particularly dominant in the more remote regions of the Lebanon mountains.

An Israeli author of works on the Druze, Gabriel Ben-Dor, makes a sweeping dismissal of the whole matter with the curious statement that the racial origins of the Druze are "completely irrelevant and uninteresting . . . the argument over actual racial origins appears trivial."[32] Such an approach, it should be pointed out, falls in line with Israeli government policy, which is aimed at separating the Druze from the rest of the Arabs and convincing

30. Colin Thubron, *The Hills of Adonis* (London: Heinemann, 1968), p. 69.

31. Hitti, *The Origins of the Druze,* p. 23.

32. Gabriel Ben-Dor, *The Druzes in Israel* (Jerusalem: The Magnes Press, Hebrew University, 1979), p. 45, *n.* 42.

them (and anyone else who will listen) that they are somehow a race apart. But any serious observer must acknowledge the obvious fact that the Druze are Arab not only by language and culture but also in large part by racial origin. This is certainly the overwhelming view of the Druze themselves. Individual Druze are often physically similar to each other, and this is to be expected in a group of people who have married for nearly a thousand years only within their own relatively small community, with no admitted admixture of alien bloodlines. These similarities are, however, less dominant than one would expect under the circumstances.

As for the name *Druze,* it derives according to most scholars from that of the heretical missionary al-Darazi. Abu-Izzeddin acknowledges this (see chapter 1, *n.* 23), but she points out that they were also called *Hakimiya* and *Tayamina* in early accounts, the first term meaning followers of the caliph al-Hakim, and the second referring to the Wadi al-Taym, the major Druze center. There are, however, other theories of interest that have been advanced by travelers, scholars, and Orientalists at various times in the past several hundred years. The most picturesque, if the least plausible, is a tradition stemming from the Crusader days that portrays the Druze as descendants of a French Comte de Dreux, who disappeared in the mountains of Lebanon at the end of the thirteenth century following the fall of the final Latin outpost of the Outremer in 1291.

> Some writers pretend that a Count of Dreux in the Time of the Croissades, having been defeated by Saladin, his Soldiers fled into the Mountains, and there intrenched themselves: that afterwards multiplying, they built Habitations, and took the name of Druses in Memory of their Chief.[33]

The seventeenth-century traveler George Sandys does not mention Count de Dreux by name but alludes to the same general account.[34] The eighteenth-century visitor Richard Pococke carries the tale even further by attributing to the Druze an English ancestry, though he later acknowledges that some sources believe it to be French.[35] Not all European travelers, how-

33. Green, *Journey from Aleppo,* p. 14.

34. George Sandys, *A Relation of a Journey Begun in A.D. 1610,* 6th ed. (London, 1670), p. 164. ". . . the Druses: the remainder of those French-men which were brought into these parts by Godfrey of Bulloign, who driven into the Mountains above, and defending themselves by the advantage of the place, could never be utterly destroyed by the Saracens. At length, they afforded them peace and liberty of Religion; conditionally, that they wore the white Turbants, and paid such Duties as the natural Subject. But in tract of time, they fell from the knowledge of Christ, nor thoroughly embracing the other [Islam] are indeed of neither."

35. Richard Pococke, *A Description of the East &c.,* 2 vols. (London, 1745), vol. 2, p. 94. "If any account can be given of the original of the Druzes, it is that they are the remains of the Christian armies in the holy war; and they themselves now say they are descended from the English." A footnote adds, "Some say, they are descended from the Franks, whom Godfrey of Bulloign brought with him to the holy war; and that Feckeridine pretended to be related to

ever, were willing to accept so romantic a story. The French aristocrat Constantin-François Chasseboeuf, Comte de Volney, writing just before the French Revolution, dismisses the Comte de Dreux theory on the very sound observation that no trace of any European language, let alone French, remained in use among them.[36] Certainly no one today takes this fable seriously, but it does reflect the view that the Druze were sufficiently unique as a group to inspire a common foreign ancestry that would explain why they differed from their neighbors in so many respects.

A far more plausible Crusader connection is that the Freemasonry of the West developed as an offshoot of Druzism via the Crusaders returning home with some knowledge of the esoteric tenets of the Unitarian community with which they had had more than passing contact for almost two centuries (the Druze having served occasionally as guides and even allies against the common Muslim enemy). Many visitors from the West and assorted Orientalists have made a Masonic-Druze (or earlier Shia) connection, among them Hitti, referring to the Isma^cilis and their Qarmatian precursors, and H. V. F. Winstone, with his reference to "the Druses . . . whose customs and precepts seemed strangely to have much in common with Freemasonry." The similarity between the Druze Star, symbol of the five *hudud* (dignitaries), and the Eastern Star of the female Masonic order is one curious example. This star, which appears as an emblem of Druze identity, is encountered everywhere the Druze congregate. It is seen atop the new khalwa at al-Suwaydaʾ in the Jabal al-Druze and is embossed on the letterhead of the American Druze Public Affairs Committee. It contains five sections, each with a different color corresponding to a specific dignitary. "To the hierarchy of the superior *ḥudūd* in the organization built by Ḥamza, cosmic ranks were attributed. Ḥamza was the personification of the Universal Mind or Intelligence (*al-ʿAql*) [green]. Next in rank was Ismāʿīl al-Tamīmī, the Universal Soul (*al-Nafs*) [red]; after him came Muḥammad b. Wahb al-Qurashī, the word (*al-Kalima*) [yellow]. The fourth and fifth, Salāma al-Sāmurrī and Bahāʾ al-Dīn are respectively the Right and Left Wing, also called the Antecedent [blue] and Follower [white]." The Druze flag, created by an assembly of religious and secular leaders the day after the proclamation of an autonomous Jebel Druze state by the French on April 5, 1922, contained the

---

the house of Lorrain." By the time of Bishop Pococke's visit, the Druze were already searching for an ally against the French-supported Maronites, which accounts for their claiming English descent.

36. Volney, *Voyage*, vol. 2, p. 41. ". . . car un société retirée dans un canton séparé où elle vit isolée, ne perd point son langage. Cependant celui des Druses est un Arabe très-pur, qui n'a pas un mot d'origine Européene."Abu-Izzeddin asserts that this "amusing notion" first appeared while the *amir* (prince) Fakhr al-Dîn II was on his state visit to the duke of Tuscany (1613–1618), but she gives no source for this theory (*Druzes*, p. 187). Bouron states that the amir's Medici visit simply strengthened a story circulating since the fifteenth century. Pope Paul V himself arranged an audience to receive "this descendant of Godfrey de Bouillon, dispossessed like his ancestors by the infidels" (Bouron, *Les Druzes*, p. 116).

five colors, green, red, yellow, blue, and white in that order, in horizontal stripes. A newer version of the flag, as seen on the wall of the entrance to the *mazar* of al-Nabi Shuᶜayb in Galilee, puts the green of Hamza in a triangle at the left (see Plate 22), with the four colors of the remaining *hudud* arranged in order at the right. I have likewise seen the five colors painted (in equal vertical stripes) on the front bumper of large trucks, obviously of Druze ownership, traveling on the highways of northern Israel.[37]

The "Catechism of the Druzes" as related by Baron de Sacy offers an entirely different origin of the term *Druze*. In the ninth of a series of questions by which young Druzes were supposedly instructed in the rudiments of their faith the catechumen is asked: "The name of Druze, from what thing is it derived?" His reply is: "From the letters [*dāl, rā, jīm : dāl, rā, jīm, tanwīn* and *khā, rā, jīm : khā, rā, jīm, tanwīn:*] for they *went out from* all people and *arranged themselves in order* under the laws of our Lord Hakem, &c."[38] This explanation is yet another attempt to account for the very separate status of the Druze with respect to the communities that surround them.

Other authorities, supposedly quoting Druze sacred writ and tradition, present different interpretations of the term *Druze*. Two versions are given by Colonel Charles Henry Churchill, an Englishman who lived for twenty years in Mount Lebanon during the upheavals that followed the collapse of the Shihabi dynasty and the Egyptian occupation of 1841–1842, and who wrote four volumes of memoirs shortly before and after the Druze-Christian massacres of 1860:

> Some of the Ockals [*ᶜuqqal*], if questioned as to the reason of their being called Druses, will say that the name is derived from the Arabic word "Durs," which signifies "clever, industrious," and that they have been thus called, on account of their deserving in an eminent degree those epithets. Others will maintain, that it is derived from the Arabic word "Turs," or shield, and that they are called the Druses or the Shields, because in the time of the Crusades, they were selected by Nouradeen and Saladin, to watch and defend the line of coast from Beyrout to Sidon.[39]

The eighteenth-century English traveler John Green, writing of his trip from Aleppo to Damascus (via Mount Lebanon), arrived at an entirely different derivation:

37. Hitti, *History of the Arabs*, pp. 443, 445; H. V. F. Winstone, *Leachman: "O.C. Desert"* (London: Quartet Books, 1982), p. 110; Abu-Izzeddin, *Druzes*, p. 104; Bouron, *Les Druzes*, p. 394, app. 6.

38. de Sacy, *Réligion des Druzes*, English trans. in *Foreign Quarterly Review* 57 (1842): 190.

39. Charles Henry Churchill, *The Druzes and Maronites under Turkish Rule from 1840 to 1860* (London: Quaritch, 1862), p. 115. We recall that the Druze fought with and served the interests of the Crusaders as well, depending upon the circumstances (see *n*. 37 above).

> Was one to judge by their Books, its likely their Name is a Corruption of the *Arabic* Word *Darz* (t), which signifies the Suture or Seam, where the two Parts of the Skull join that form the whole. For it must be observed, that their Authors frequently allude to the perfect Union that is between the two Parts of a Man's Skull, in order to enforce the Union which ought to reign in the Members of the Nation, for their Security against Enemies; and constant Uniformity in the Practice of Customs, Rules and Ceremonies. From this Comparison so often repeated in their Books, we may, therefore, conclude, that this Nation took their Name from the Word *Darz,* being at first called *Darz,* or in the plural *Daruz* (v), as who should say, Men that preserve Union and Uniformity among them; and from these *Arabic* Words is come by Corruption the Name *Druses,* which sticks by them.[40]

This explanation relates closely to the most common assertion that the Druze take their name from the heretic al-Darazi, whose name in Arabic means the tailor, from the verb *daraza,* to sew, stitch. The plural of the word *darz* (seam, hem, suture) is *duruz,* which is the identical spelling in Arabic of Druze (the plural in this case of *durzi*).

A very recent theory, expounded by the eminent contemporary Christian Lebanese historian, Kamal Salibi, is that the name *Druze* came from the tribe of the Banu Darriza, "who inhabited the vicinity of Mecca sometime before Islam and probably migrated to Syria."[41] To a question for which there is no universally accepted answer, this suggestion is as plausible as any of the earlier guesses that have preceded it.

Perhaps because of the secrecy of their rites, the Druze have been accused by their neighbors of many peculiar and dissolute practices, among them incest and communal sexual rituals[42] and the worship of a golden calf. If incest were ever practiced it certainly has never been authenticated, though it has been persistently asserted by various writers—beginning with Rabbi Benjamin of Tudela in the twelfth century—possibly because of the Druze practice of marrying within the extended family up to and including first cousins (see Chapter 5 below) with no noticeable hereditary detriment. The persistent rumor of calf worship is just as persistently denied by the Druze themselves. All three of the contemporary Druze writers on the subject of their faith, al-Najjar, Makarem, and Abu-Izzeddin, avoid the matter entirely,

40. Green, *Journey from Aleppo,* pp. 14–15. But he notes, "As it is certain that this nation bore the same Name before the Time of the Croissades, their Origin is more ancient than either that which they give themselves, or other authors ascribe to them," thus adding his voice to the theory of Conder (see *n.* 50 below) that they in fact antedate their appearance on the stage of history.

41. Sally Ann Ethelston and Matthew Manzella, *Lebanon 1984: 21 Experts Give Their Views* (Washington, D.C.: Georgetown University Center for Contemporary Arab Studies, 1984), p. 4.

42. See *n.* 4 above.

although al-Najjar does make a passing reference to the existence of gossip and rumor surrounding Druze practices that have grown up as a result of their secrecy (see footnote 57 to this chapter). Hitti devotes only one page to the question in his study, while Seabrook spends slightly more time delving into it in a popular and unscholarly fashion without drawing any defensible conclusions.[43]

The earlier writers, however, were particularly fascinated by the story and considered it to be a crucial feature of the Druze religion that might link it to pagan practices of the ancient Phoenicians. Among the first to relate the rumor was Pococke, who assures us of the calf's existence and alludes to phallic idols as well.

> I was indeed told, that by some accident, the statue of a calf had been seen in their retired places; but if the information of one, who pretended to have discovered some of their secrets, is to be depended upon, they have a small silver box, closed in such a manner as not to be opened, and many, even among them, know not what it contains; they pay a sort of worship to it; and he said he was informed, that there were in these boxes the images of the nature of both sexes.[44]

Hitti, writing nearly two centuries later, was even more convinced of the existence of such effigies, although he tended to give more credence to Seabrook's interview with an unnamed Druze *shaykh* than is perhaps merited.[45]

> That there is jealously guarded and hidden from the uninitiate eye, in one of their leading places of seclusion (*khalwah*), of which there are about forty in the Lebanon, some gold figure of a calf or bull inside of a silver box has been almost ascertained beyond doubt. A high Druze sheikh has practically admitted in a recent interview the existence of such a box [and here Hitti makes a footnote reference to Seabrook's study].[46]

John Green, who wrote his travel account from Aleppo to Damascus a decade before Pococke, alleges the statue to be of Hamza, whom he refers to as the great Druze legislator.

> There are but two Villages which have the Honour (to speak in the Language of the *Druzes*) to possess the Statue of their great Legislator, namely *Baclim* and *Fredis* [Baᶜqlin and Firaydis] which are situate in the Mountains, and the Places where the Chiefs of the *Durzi* have their Residence.

43. Seabrook, *Adventures in Arabia,* pp. 180ff.

44. Pococke, *Description of the East,* vol. 2, p. 94.

45. The *shaykh* in question was "a Druse who had apparently read everything in comparative religion from Frazer's *Golden Bough* to Reinach's *Orpheus.* I spent an evening with him alone." Seabrook, *Adventures in Arabia,* pp. 196–99.

46. Hitti, *The Origins of the Druze,* p. 49.

> The Statue of their Legislator, according to their Account, ought to be of Gold or Silver; they shut it up in a Wooden Box, and never take it out, but to appear in their solemn Ceremonies, when they address their Vows to it, in order to obtain their wishes; imagining that they speak to God himself; so great is their Veneration for this Idol.[47]

Assuming that the calf image does exist, there are three interpretations offered by scholars as to its function in Druze worship. The first theory is that of de Sacy, who proposes that the calf is the emblem of Iblis, or Satan, the enemy and rival of al-Hakim:[48]

> . . . and here he quotes the words of the sacred books, which charge the calf as the enemy of Hakem, and declare it to be Eblis, or Satan. Hamza, and Boha-eddin, his coadjutor, repeatedly speak of the worship of calves and buffaloes as symbolical of false religions, opposed to Unitarianism, which we conceive to have been the real mystery of all antiquity. . . .[49]

The second theory is that of Lieutenant Colonel C. R. Conder, who in observations written at the turn of this century concluded that the idol is "a relic of older paganism" which the Druze kept hidden "only to treat with insult and contempt."[50] Many who know the Druze would like to cling to the romantic idea of this noble and exotic people as a remnant of the great Phoenician race that has hidden its true identity under the guise of pseudo-Islamic secrecy for centuries.[51]

The third explanation is that the effigy is the image of the discredited missionary al-Darazi, whom the Druze faithful are encouraged to revile. Colonel Churchill, among others, asserts that Hamza, outraged at the attempts of his emissary to take control of the movement, denounced him as "'Satan,' the 'Rival,' the 'Calf.' . . . This bodily Calf is no other than

47. Green, *Journey from Aleppo*, pp. 19–20.

48. de Sacy, *Réligion des Druzes*, vol. 1, p. 232. The earl of Carnarvon in his *Recollections of the Druses of the Lebanon* (London: John Murray, 1860), p. 57, equates Iblis with "a relic of the old Egyptian superstition which had honoured the bull Apis."

49. *Foreign Quarterly Review* 57 (1842): 185–86.

50. C. R. Conder, *The Latin Kingdom of Jersualem, 1099–1291* (London: Committee of the Palestine Exploration Fund, 1897), p. 234. Bouron concurs, saying that "if certain images of the calf have persisted in their practices, it is because, long ago, the calf—reminiscent perhaps of the 'golden calf' of the Israelites—was for them, the image and spirit of evil. . . ." (*Les Druzes*, p. 284).

51. William H. Worrell, *A Study of Races in the Ancient Near East* (New York: D. Appleton, 1927), p. 106. Druze "religious exclusionism is probably the continuation of a racial one which may be Canaanitish-Aramaeni." Harold Armstrong in his *Syria and Turkey Reborn* (London: The Bodley Head, 1930), p. 4, saw the Druze as the old Hivites of the Bible who inhabited "Hermon in the Land of Mizpeh [Lebanon]" (Joshua 3:11, 19).

Darazi, whom he [Hamza] holds up to ridicule by that expression."[52] The earl of Carnarvon also subscribes to this solution:

> Travellers in the Lebanon have said, and it was long believed, that in the secret conclaves of the Druze worshippers, the image of a golden calf was produced either as the visible emblem under which the divinity of Hakem was adored, or as a relic of the old Egyptian superstition which had honoured the bull Apis. But modern research has set many of these fancies at rest. The fact of the production of the image was and probably is true, but the inferences drawn from it are incorrect. That figure represents neither Hakim nor Apis; it is rather the monument of detestation and contempt in which the memory of the innovator Darazi is held.[53]

None of these three theories, nor that of Seabrook (which is in many respects a combination of them all),[54] can be substantiated, and I am not about to speculate on this aspect of the Druze faith that has intrigued so many earlier observers but is in fact not especially relevant to the total picture of their belief. There is no doubt that the image of the calf as Satan does exist in their religious writings, as seen in epistle sixty-two of the Canon, quoted by al-Najjar, according to which those who fail to achieve the beatific vision of the Holy One at the last day, "those who worshipped the calf [Satan] by a life of mendacity and perjury," are condemned to "remain forever in their evil bailiwicks in consequence of their infractions."[55]

Only one person to my knowledge has claimed to have seen the legendary golden calf in this century and that was Francis A. Waterhouse, a former French Legionnaire who wrote about his experiences in Syria during the Druze Rebellion of 1925–27 in a highly sensational and suspect narrative entitled *'Twixt Hell and Allah*. According to Waterhouse he and a comrade were led by an old Druze man and a naked lad through a hole in the ground (near "the humble Druse village of Tell ——" in the Jabal al-Druze) to a

52. Charles Henry Churchill, *Mount Lebanon: A Ten Years' Residence from 1842 to 1852, Describing the Manners, Customs, and Religion of Its Inhabitants with a Full and Correct Account of the Druse Religion*, 3d ed., 3 vols. (London: Saunders and Otley, 1853), vol. 2, pp. 112, 114.

53. Carnarvon, *Recollections*, pp. 55–56.

54. "You will permit me to go much farther back than Hakim. A golden calf was the first symbol of God that the Israelites set up and worshipped after their flight from Egypt. Before that the bull, the cow, and the calf, both here and in Assyria, Babylon, and Egypt, were symbols of divinity. I will suggest that your Hakim adopted, incorporated into his new religion, this symbol, already, perhaps, adored by many of his converts. I will suggest that the Druses first looked upon it as an emblem; that they worshipped it idolatrously and were denounced by their prophets; that they have retained it secretly to this day, not as an object of idolatry, but as the image or symbol originally intended. I might even risk going so far as to suggest that among the Druses, as among all peoples, there may be groups who confound the material emblem with the spirit behind it. He [the shaykh] smiled and said, 'Well, it's an ingenious theory.' And that was all." Seabrook, *Adventures in Arabia*, pp. 198–99.

55. Al-Najjar, *Druze*, pp. 118–19.

subterranean cavern where they were allowed to view "the most monstrous effigy that ever beggared imagination."

> Towering above our heads on a rough stone dais stood this beast, two long forelegs supporting a grotesque body surmounted by a hideous head in which scintillated two large green stones for the eyes. The beast was graven in solid gold and we stood dumb in wonder, wet with the sweat of fright, gazing . . . gazing at the Golden Calf of Baal.[56]

Whether this is imagery drawn from the Baal worship of the Aramaeans, the Hebrew tale of Aaron and the golden calf in the wilderness of Sinai, the ancient Egyptian source from which the Jews took their model, or has an altogether unknown provenance is not likely to be resolved until the Druze initiates themselves choose to reveal it or demolish it altogether. Al-Najjar concludes that the time has come for this to be done. By maintaining absolute secrecy the sect may have ensured its survival, but it also has invited unfair criticism and allegations of every sort: "gossip, rumor, [and] blind speculation."[57] Addressing the final sentence of his book to his own community, al-Najjar insists that "the reason behind the Secret Code is now definitely gone—its edifice is dilapidated and rust eats at the hinges on its door."[58] It is now twenty years since this challenge was laid at the doorstep of the *mashaʾikh al-din*. Two academic studies by Druze authors (Makarem and Abu-Izzeddin) have appeared since then, and each has been of considerable interest and full of scholarly revelation. But not all the questions have been addressed, let alone answered.

56. Francis A. Waterhouse, *'Twixt Hell and Allah* (London: Sampson Low, Marston & Co.: n.d. [ca. 1930—the inscribed presentation is dated "Christmas, 1931"]), pp. 132, 136. The entire tale is related in Waterhouse's chap. 7, "The Worshippers of Baal," pp. 128–42.

57. Al-Najjar, *Druze,* pp. 118–19.

58. *Ibid.*

Part II

Social Structure, Customs, and Demography

3

The Druze in the Social Fabric of the Middle East

It is hardly surprising that over the course of nearly a millennium of living apart a community as closed and tightly knit as the Druze should have developed a number of unique social patterns and characteristics. What is often overlooked, however, are the equally numerous traits they have in common with their Christian and Muslim Arab neighbors. All Levantine Arabs have a heritage of widely varied racial strains, and though little can be definitely ascertained as to the racial origins of the Druze (see pages 24–28 above), they certainly have many contrasting blood lines. Apart from the obvious pool of tribal Arab genes, it is highly likely that both before and after the official closing of the community there were infusions of Persian, Kurdish, Turkish, Byzantine, and even European blood (via the Crusades). In recent generations leading members of both the Arslan and Junbalat families have married into families of Circassian descent. The rich racial background is clearly evident in the many fair-haired, blue- or green-eyed children one finds in a Druze village, whether it be in Lebanon, Syria, or Israel,[1] as opposed to the rarity of such features among their Maronite Christian counterparts, who are almost invariably black-haired and dark-eyed.

As a consequence there are no clearly distinct physical characteristics that would mark a Druze, even though some members of the community sincerely believe that they can tell another on sight.[2] Unlike the Greek Orthodox from the Kura district with their characteristically prominent noses or the Maronite with their pointed skulls and broad countenance, the Druze do not fit into any convenient anthropological category. Despite the shared traits and cultural similarities that do exist, however, it cannot be stressed too strongly that Druze ties with neighboring communities have been and remain formal and primarily at the leadership level. The average Druze *jahil* has little social contact with non-Druze, even in the same village. The sense of separateness that is at the core of Druze beliefs about themselves and the secrecy of their religion, which must be hidden from all outsiders, has served to keep them very much apart. Therefore Druze interaction with other communities, states, and political ideologies (except for the leadership and highly educated elite, about 1 percent of the male population) is minimal to nonexistent. This situation is of course changing as more Druze emigrate, travel and work abroad, and seek higher education. But such exposure has tended thus far to influence only the individuals themselves, not the outlook or internal life of the community. When a Druze who has been exposed to an alien way of life returns to live in a Druze environment, he does not advocate changes in the accepted system but conforms to age-old ways and makes a conscious effort to avoid non-Druze manners.

The characteristic that most travelers have noted over the centuries about the Druze is their high standard of healthy good looks in both men and women. Typical of nineteenth-century visitors making this observation

1. The Druze of Galilee are locally noted for their fair hair and complexions accompanied by blue, green, or grey eyes, especially those in the villages of Yirka, Julis, and Abu Sinan. A popular tradition ascribes this both to Crusader blood and the influence of soldiers from Napoleon's army during the siege of nearby Acre (ʿAkka) in 1799. The English writer and traveler Colin Thubron, who visited Lebanon in the late 1960s, observed that many Druze there "have a glint of yellow hair which is unknown among the Maronites. The children stare up through startling grey eyes, and a few of the women, who are beautiful, are fair as harvest" (*Hills of Adonis*, p. 67). When I visited the Druze villages of the Jabal al-Aʿla for the first time (June 1985), I was struck by the number of villagers at Qalb Lawzah who were as blond and fair as Scandinavians. My companion at first thought they were Swedish tourists strolling through the magnificent sixth-century Byzantine church that dominates the hilltop settlement.

2. In his final book, *I Speak for Lebanon* (London: Zed Press, 1982), p. 36, Kamal Junbalat asserted that "even their faces are different. If there is one Druse in a crowd of 20, it will always be easy to pick him out." Such a belief in the ability of one member of a specific group to recognize another is not confined to the Druze. In traditional Arab society it is widely held that "blood identifies itself" to members of tribe, clan, or family otherwise unknown to each other.

were Gray Hill, who described the Druze men of Mount Carmel as "fine, handsome, pleasant-looking," and Laurence Oliphant, who said of their daughters, "I don't know that I ever remember in the same number to have seen a larger proportion of pretty women."[3] Such paeans to the comeliness of the Druze were usually accompanied by praise of their virtues—particularly their hospitality, for which they are justly renowned. Freshfield found them to be "a people of patriarchal manners and genuine patriarchal hospitality."[4] Gertrude Bell considered all Druze to be gentlefolk because of their decorum.[5] Oliphant, if not totally convinced of their honesty toward outsiders, was still very impressed by their sober and industrious character.[6] The inveterate twentieth-century traveler, Freya Stark, also had (grudgingly) complimentary observations to make about their hospitality and manners, though she did object to their "keeping the women as such absolute inferiors."[7]

The majority of the Druze today are still the hardy, independent, and prosperous farmers living in small towns and villages of fewer than ten thousand inhabitants that earlier visitors described. In Lebanon they are primarily dependent upon their olive groves and fruit orchards, carefully nourished on intricately terraced hillsides.[8] In the Jabal al-Druze they are more often wheat farmers, though recently planted orchards of cherry and apple trees now dot the slopes above al-Suwayda' and Qanawat. Most families grow their own vegetables and fruit, bake their own bread, and live for the most part on a vegetarian diet with meat served only on special occasions.[9] The

3. Gray Hill, *With the Beduins: A Narrative of Journeys and Adventures in Unfrequented Parts of Syria* (London: T. Fisher Unwin, 1891), p. 93, and Laurence Oliphant, *Haifa, or Life in Modern Palestine* (New York: Harper and Brothers, 1887), p. 146. Oliphant continues, however, that "if they are pretty, they are also a heartless lot." The only European traveler observing the Druze who found them "physically repulsive" was Charles Colville Frankland (*Travels to and from Constantinople,* 2 vols., London: Henry Colburn, 1829, vol. 2, p. 115). I would agree with Colin Thubron, who noted that as he moved from the Christian villages of the southern Lebanese coast to the Druze heartland of the Shuf "the long visages of the desert, receding from heavy noses, had disappeared. The Druse faces were broad and short, often pale-skinned, handsome, with stubborn chins" (*Hills of Adonis,* p. 67).

4. Douglas W. Freshfield, *Travels in the Central Caucasus and Bashan* (London: Longmans, 1869), p. 51.

5. Gertrude Bell, *The Desert and the Sown* (New York: Dutton, 1907), p. 102.

6. Oliphant, *Haifa,* p. 89. He describes the Palestinian Druze as "fairly honest" and as having "their own notions of morality to which they rigidly adhere." *Ibid.*

7. Freya Stark, *Letters from Syria* (London: John Murray, 1942), pp. 146–47. Her visit to the Jabal al-Druze was made in 1928.

8. All Druze villages are located on the slopes or tops of hills and mountains. Apart from the obvious reason of defense, this gives proximity to their hilltop shrines and *khalawat*. Also, the Druze would collect the dung from their livestock during the winter months and pile it outside the village, from where the rains would carry it to fertilize the fields below; as well as being the mark of good husbandry, this had its sanitary benefits.

9. A typical village meal may include olives, mountain bread (thin, almost transparent unleavened circular loaves), eggplant, cauliflower, and chickpeas flavored with onions, garlic,

village life described by Volney in the late eighteenth century has not changed greatly, except for the acquisition of electricity and telephones (and there are still many Druze villages without one or both) and regular bus and taxi communications with the principal urban centers. The women, except some in the cities, still wear the traditional blue or black dress with the *mandil,* a diaphanous white head covering. This also used to cover the *tantur,* or horn, sometimes as much as two feet high, that was commonly worn by both Druze and Maronite women until well into the nineteenth century. Captain Charles Frankland of the Royal Navy who visited Mount Lebanon in the late 1820s described it as "perhaps the most singular headdress in the world . . . a long silver or wooden horn about twelve or fourteen inches in length, shaped something like a speaking trumpet. . . . Over this unicorn-looking instrument, the veil (of white muslin or calico if Christian, and black if Druse) is thrown, which closing across the face, at the will of the wearer and falling down the shoulders behind, has not altogether an ungraceful appearance."[10] Most *juhhal* have abandoned the *shirwal* (the baggy pants brought tight at the ankles), though they can still be purchased in shops off the Street Called Straight in Damascus, and the red-and-white or black-and-white checkered *kufiya* is still a common sight among the men working their fields. The *ʿuqqal* of course still wear the traditional mountain costume.

In his everyday speech the Druze is easily recognizable by the use of the *qaf,* a strong gutteral "k" sound that is found in classical Arabic (transliterated into English as "q") but is dropped altogether or altered to "j" or hard "g" in nearly all other Arab colloquial dialects.[11] The pronunciation of the letter *dad,* the velarized "d" sound peculiar to Arabic (transliterated into English as "ḍ")[12] is likewise retained in a form very close to the classical, unlike in most dialects, where it has lost its unique sound. Outside the

---

and *tahina* (sesame oil), rice, burghul (dried cracked wheat), or potatoes, salad (made of tomatoes, cucumber, parsley, and other herbs, flavored with olive oil and lemon), yoghurt, and seasonal fruit. In villages where there is no butcher shop, animals are slaughtered only occasionally, and the meat usually consumed the same day. The basic cooking ingredients are olive oil, made from one's own olives pressed locally, and *samna* (clarified butter) or sometimes animal fat. Lamb is the favored meat (along with kid), followed by chicken (now more often frozen, imported rather than raised locally) and beef. Pork is frowned upon, but not with the vehemence of Muslims. Most educated *juhhal* of my acquaintance do not object to eating it. Sheep, goats, and cows are slaughtered by slitting their throats in *halal* (acceptable Muslim) fashion.

10. Frankland, *Travel,* vol. 2, pp. 20–21. Viscount Castlereagh, writing twenty years later in his *Journey to Damascus,* 2 vols. (London: Henry Colburn, 1847, vol. 2, p. 242), describes the horn in detail and takes great exception to the filth it produces among the women who wear it (and rarely, if ever, remove it in order to wash their hair). He notes with some relief that the custom of wearing it appeared to be confined to the older women by this time.

11. Christian villagers in Druze parts of the mountain will also use the *qaf* in their speech. Certain phrases in polite formal speech are also unique to the Druze and serve as another means of communal identification. See Junbalat, *I Speak for Lebanon,* p. 36.

12. Arabs refer to their language as the *lughat al-dad* (the language of the letter *dad*), because it is a consonant that exists in no other modern language.

community, the Druze of Beirut or Damascus as well as visitors from the mountains may consciously drop the *qaf* and other characteristics of village speech either to avoid identification or to appear more sophisticated, but at home it is automatically reemployed, and to drop it is to invite peer criticism for putting on airs.

Unlike Muslims and Christians who are frequently identifiable by their first or family name (or both), the Druze are more often than not given names that could be either Christian or Muslim. Previously, men were frequently given Muslim names like Mahmud, Husayn, ʿAli, or even Muhammad, but this practice is no longer as common as it was even a generation or two ago. A Druze boy is now more likely to be called Samir, Salim, Fuʾad, Fawzi, Samih, Wasif, Amin, or Suhayl, names of no particular religious significance and ones often borne by Christians, especially Greek Orthodox, and Muslims. The same is true for Druze girls, among whom names of Muslim religious significance (such as ʿAʾisha and Fatima, the wife and the daughter of the prophet Muhammad) have all but disappeared in favor of neutral, even Christian, ones.[13] Few family names are predictably Druze, aside from Arslan, Junbalat, and al-Atrash.[14] Nearly all others have Christian or Muslim branches, often both. And in Lebanon during the past ten years not having an immediately identifiable name has been a distinct advantage, since being easily recognizable by one's religion could cost one's life at the wrong checkpoint.

In the realm of popular religion it is still the accepted procedure for men and women to gather at the village *khalwa* (or *majlis*) every Thursday evening where, after the *juhhal* are dismissed the *ʿuqqal* conduct their prayer and study. The *khalawat* also serve as schools where Druze children are instructed in the basic tenets and outward beliefs of their faith. The Druze frequently visit their shrines located on the tops of mountains or on hillsides, and at some such as al-Nabi Shuʿayb there are annual religious festivals that attract thousands. At the tomb of the holy man or woman or the prophet to whom the *mazar* (or *maqam*) is dedicated, they pray quietly, leave small gifts of food and money, and take away small bits of colored cloth as votive tokens of divine blessing to be kept at home or in the family automobile. Families will also come for extended stays to sacrifice animals in fulfillment of a vow, or simply to have picnics or a quiet weekend. The Druze, like Muslims and

13. A Lebanese Druze family of my acquaintance named one of its sons in memory of a Christian friend with an identifiably Christian name, and it was several weeks before villagers came to pay their respects to the mother and infant (normally attended to as soon as the mother can receive them). When a generation later a granddaughter in the same family was given a Christian name, village resistance had weakened and there was no discernible consternation.

14. Christians and Muslims with the family name Atrash (which means deaf in Arabic) do exist. The current mayor of the predominantly Christian town of Bayt Sahur near Bethlehem on the West Bank is Yuhanna (John) Atrash. Arslan is a common Turkish Muslim surname (meaning lion). I know of no Christian or Muslim Junbalats.

some Arab Christians, frequently wear talismans around their necks that contain bits of sacred writing consecrated by a *shaykh*. Although the Druze faith has no tradition of monasticism, it was not uncommon in times past for exceptionally devout members of the community to become hermits and, like their Christian counterparts, to be sought out for instruction and advice.[15]

The belief in *tanasukh* (transmigration of souls) is firmly adhered to, and stories are common even today of young people appearing in a village claiming to be the reincarnation of a departed member of the community. The conviction that they will be reborn after their death has made the Druze formidable fighters, much as the belief of Muslims that if they die as martyrs in a *jihad* (holy war) they will pass directly to heaven has made possible the suicide missions of the Shia against the Israelis in southern Lebanon and against the Iraqis in the Ayatollah Khomeini's war of revenge (*tha'r*). The Druze war cry, "Who wishes to sleep in his mother's womb tonight?" reflects a sincere conviction strongly held.[16] An incident reported in the January 12, 1987, issue of the Arabic-language Jerusalem daily *al-Quds* illustrates how deeply individual Druze subscribe to their belief in a previous and future life. A Druze member of the Israeli Defense Force (IDF), Muhammad Zayd Salim, was convicted of desertion despite his unique defense that in a previous incarnation he was a Syrian soldier who was crushed to death by an Israeli tank and therefore could not bear to be near one in his present life. The Tel Aviv military court that tried him was obviously not willing to accept reincarnation as a defense, but most Druze would doubtless have accepted Salim's argument as demonstrating sufficient mitigating circumstances.

Given the firm popular adherence to this distinctive belief that separates the Druze from both Christians and Muslims, one wonders, therefore, why the five-hundred-man delegation of *shaykhs* and community notables accompanying Walid Junbalat to the funeral of assassinated Lebanese prime minister Rashid Karami on June 3, 1987, chanted (according to Nora Boustany in her special report to the *Washington Post* of the following day, p. A31): "Walid has come to bid you farewell and ask you to greet Kamal" (his father). As if to emphasize their point, the procession bore posters showing Kamal Junbalat shaking hands with Karami. Surely the late Kamal had been immediately reincarnated in the bodily form of another Druze according to Druze belief, and even more surely the Druze and Muslims share no common afterlife. Such a manifestation must, therefore, be regarded as either a purely

15. See Abu-Izzeddin, *Druzes*, pp. 224–25, for an account of the most famous of these hermits, Shaykh al-Fadil Muhammad Abu-Hilal (died 1640).

16. Lady Hester Stanhope, the English eccentric who spent most of her adult life on the edge of the Druze country near Jun, wrote in 1838 that "the Druze army . . . does not at present exceed two-thousand five-hundred men; but each man of that two-thousand five-hundred is worth twenty." *Memoirs of the Lady Hester Stanhope, as Related by Herself in Conversations with Her Physician* [Dr. C. I. Meryon], 3 vols., London: Henry Colburn, 1845, vol. 3, p. 310, quoted in Abu-Izzeddin, *Druzes*, p. 221.

theatrical display of support for the deceased, who had been an ally of Kamal Junbalat in the 1958 civil war, or a sarcastic reproach to the Syrian leadership (the Alawis likewise believe in reincarnation), whom the Druze hold responsible for Kamal's murder.

Many Druze believe that large numbers of their community are to be found elsewhere, especially in China. Indeed, reincarnation in China is considered the greatest blessing that God can bestow on the departed. In popular folk belief it is viewed as the location of paradise, which would go a long way toward explaining why propaganda publications of Communist China were so popular in Shufi villages, at least during the decade of my periodic residence there. Where this belief originates is unclear. Conder cites a Druze tradition that "El Hākem would re-appear, leading an army from their Holy Land in China, to which the good Druze was carried by angels when he died."[17] The Islam correspondent of the *Economist,* in an article on the Druze (July 23, 1983, p. 49), made several references to this belief, which the Druze officially deny. In a letter published a month later (August 20, 1983, p. 4), the secretary of the Permanent Bureau of Druze Institutions in Beirut, ʿAfif Khidr, took exception to the many statements in the article and emphasized that "the Druzes do not believe in any paradise in China. This is a myth and a joke." It is an interesting coincidence, however, that the Syrian ambassador to the Peoples Republic of China in the early and mid-1970s was a Druze, Jabir al-Atrash, nephew of Sultan. If the China paradise connection is a joke, it is one that many Druze accept as true.

I have also heard simple Druze peasants express the belief that many Druze exist in such countries as Turkey, Greece, Iran, and Russia, whereas in fact few if any do. The only corroboration I have seen in print for those supposed to be in Turkey is by Kamal Junbalat, who makes mention in *I Speak for Lebanon* (p. 27) of sixty thousand Druze in "Southern Turkish Anatolia." Although upward of half a million Arabic-speaking Turkish citizens live in the provinces adjacent to the Syrian border, to my knowledge they are all Muslim, with the exception of the Greek Orthodox of Antioch (Antakya) and Mersin and the Syrian Orthodox around Mardin. As with so many rural peoples of the Middle East, their concept of the world is a very parochial one, centered around their own village, and knowledge of life outside its narrow confines is often vague to nonexistent. It should come as no surprise, therefore, that myths of lost or long-separated pockets of the faithful should persist in such an environment of isolation and ignorance of life beyond the community's own everyday frame of reference.

Although life for the average village Druze revolves around his immediate and extended family, to whom frequent and formalized visits are a prominent feature of daily life, social contact with the whole village or even district does occur regularly. Apart from the weekly meetings on Thursday

17. C. R. Conder, *The Latin Kingdom of Jerusalem, 1099–1291* (London: Committee of the Palestine Exploration Fund, 1897), p. 234.

evenings at the *khalwa,* or *majlis,* there are the larger religious celebrations at the various *maqamat* throughout Druze territory, as well as marriages and funerals. Weddings usually involve small gatherings, but funerals are community events that draw participants from miles around. Every Druze village has a *mawqaf* (literally a stopping place), generally a small crude amphitheater of cement or stone rows of seats, where hundreds, even thousands, can gather to remember the departed and extend condolences to his or her family. It is not necessary to be related to the deceased or even to have known him well; when a respected community or religious leader dies, an appearance by all who knew of him is expected, either personally or by proxy. Funeral arrangements are made immediately after death, and ceremonies are held the next day at the latest. Announcements are made in the deceased's village and often in villages where he was known (in earlier days by public crier but now most often by a loudspeaker attached to the mayor's rooftop). The body is washed and dressed in the finest clothes. At the funeral ceremony women lament in the traditional Arab style (though not to the extent common at Muslim funerals), and acquaintances recount stories of the departed's virtues. Interment of the body is above ground usually just outside the village, with monuments ranging from the very simple to the large and elaborate in the case of wealthy and prominent personages.

Marriage celebrations can also be quite extensive, but this depends upon the means of the families involved, since food and drink in large quantities are expected by the guests. At such festivities the dishes served are copious and extravagant, and unless there are too many disapproving *shaykhli* personages present, *ᶜaraq,* wine, and other spirits may be served. Many Druze *juhhal* distill their own *ᶜaraq,* and its consumption, though frowned upon, is frequently indulged in, though far more often by men than women. Marriage festivities also serve a useful community service by providing one of the few occasions on which young men and women may mix socially and eye each other as prospective husbands and wives.

Although Druze women traditionally enjoy a truly privileged status of equality or near equality with men, in the matter of female chastity there can be no compromise. A young woman is expected to be a virgin at the time of her marriage and to remain faithful to her husband throughout her whole life.[18] In earlier days, when Druze women wore the *tantur,*[19] if the groom found his bride unchaste on the wedding night, he would simply

18. Such chastity is not, so far as I know, expected of Druze men. Although the opportunities for young men to experience premarital sex in a Druze environment are rare (as in all traditional societies), they do occur. Likewise, homosexual activity by teenage boys with each other and with older men, even if severely frowned upon and never discussed, does take place, though perhaps not with the frequency encountered in other Mediterranean societies. Indeed, nothing of a personal physical or sexual nature is ever brought up in conversation in a Druze household, especially with elders present. Even to tell a slightly off-color anecdote is considered an unpardonable breach of manners.

19. See *n.* 10, above.

return the headdress to the bride's father to announce the murder of an unsuitable wife who was a disgrace to her family. A woman's honor (*ᶜird*) is the single most important factor in Druze family life, and its defilement is the greatest humiliation that can befall it. According to Layish, "virginity of the bride is a condition of the performance of marriage, and female chastity is a condition of its integrity."[20] If a woman's dishonor becomes public knowledge it is the responsibility of her father or brother to take appropriate action, and it is not unknown even today for a Druze woman who has shamed her family to be murdered by her nearest male relative. "Women, especially unmarried women, are shut up at home and debarred from social contacts outside the family; needless to say, extra-marital sexual relations are strictly forbidden to them. An offence against this prohibition may, in accordance with customary norm, entail violent sanctions, including death and grievous bodily harm, in addition to religious and legal sanctions."[21]

The pressure of the community is such, however, that few Druze women have the opportunity to blacken their honor, and even if given the chance few would. "Sobriety, gravity, decorum are qualities expected of, and admired in [Druze] women."[22] A firm counterbalance to these austere social demands, however, are the legal rights of Druze women, which far exceed those of Muslims and equal those of Eastern Christians. As has already been noted, Druze women have enjoyed equal religious status with men since the earliest days of their faith, and many reach the status of *ᶜaqila*. No figures are available for the number of *ᶜuqqal* and *ajawid*, let alone the distribution by sex, but my personal opinion would be that probably two-thirds to three-quarters of the Druze religious initiates are men, so that it would be twice to three times more likely for a man to seek admission to the secrecies of his religion than for a woman to do so. Though women attend meetings at the *khalwa*, they are relegated to a special section, just as women are in mosques and in some Eastern Christian churches. Druze holy women, though not as frequently encountered as their male counterparts, are far from unknown. Beginning with Baha al-Din's niece, Sitt Sarah, through the present day, individual Druze women have achieved the aura of greatest sanctity within their community.[23]

20. Layish, *Marriage*, p. 21. In Israel Druze judges have forced the government to waive the requirement for Druze women's photographs on official documents, such as identity cards, and have objected to their being attended by male doctors or to having autopsies. Having one's picture taken or going to a cinema is considered by many conservative Druze as shaming a woman's honor. Yet it is becoming increasingly common for women to leave their homes in the company of other women to enjoy modern society's more innocent pleasures, such as films, lectures, or shopping.

21. *Ibid.*, p. 107. In 1965, a Druze woman thought to be a prostitute had her throat slit by her brother in broad daylight on the Beirut airport road. Her head was then severed and taken in triumph to Amir Majid Arslan's palace in ᶜAlayh. The Yazbaki leader summoned the police and disavowed the act, but the murderer was given a light sentence in accordance with Lebanon's traditional Mediterranean leniency for crimes of passion.

22. Abu-Izzeddin, *Druzes*, p. 234.

In the secular world as well individual women have risen to positions of political importance, notably the mother of Fakhr al-Din, Sitt Nasab. Sitt Hubus Arslan dominated her prominent clan in the early nineteenth century (like her contemporary counterpart, the *amira* Khawla) "to the exclusion of several Arslan amirs qualified to occupy the position."[24] The daughter of Shaykh Bashir Junbalat, Sitt Nayfah, ruled Hasbayya in the Wadi al-Taym as a widow during the time of the 1860 massacres, protecting Christian women and children in her home, and later established the principal Druze religious shrine, Khalawat al-Bayyada, above the town. Finally, in this century, the mother of Kamal Junbalat, Sitt Nazira, known popularly as "the veiled lady of Mukhtara," led the Junbalat clan after her husband's assassination in 1921 until her young son was in a position to assume full responsibility in 1943.

Druze women have always had the right to own property and to dispose of it freely.[25] There has always been a significant number of literates among Druze women, and today literacy is almost universal for those under age twenty-five. Most Druze girls, however, do not go beyond the basic six years of elementary education, and their presence in high school was discouraged until recently by early marriage and a traditional distrust of coeducational schools. A substantial number of Druze women now attend secondary school, and a small but growing group go on to university or higher training for professions such as teaching and nursing. By tradition the social life of the Druze woman, particularly in the village, remains very restricted. It is still the exception for a woman to hold a full-time job, and then rarely outside her village, though in a city like Beirut Druze women do serve as headmistresses. Layish notes that "the proportion of Druze women in the labour force is very small."[26] In the words of one prominent Druze spokesman for the religious establishment in Israel,

> A woman must live secluded in her home; she is responsible for the

23. Layish, quoting Salman Fallah, notes that "Fāṭima al-Ṣāliḥ of Kafr Sumayʿ has reached senior religious rank and is considered a saint, whilst her *khalwa* is a place of pilgrimage for religious leaders from all localities," and that an octogenerian woman, "Umm Nasīb has been in charge of religious affairs, the *khalwa* and the *waqf* in that village for over fifty years and is highly esteemed by religious functionaries" (*Marriage,* p. 20). The English traveler John Green (*Journey from Aleppo,* p. 17) noted two and a half centuries ago that "the women are reckoned to be better instructed in their religion than the men."

24. Abu-Izzeddin, *Druzes,* p. 231. Princess Khawla is a Junbalati by birth. Intermarriage between the Junbalats and Arslans for reasons of political reconciliation has occurred several times in this century.

25. *Ibid.,* p. 230.

26. Layish, *Marriage,* p. 22. This would probably change quickly if small industry were attracted to Druze villages whose economy is now almost entirely based on farming. In July 1985 Druze Knesset Deputy Zaydan ʿAtsha urged the government to take steps in establishing factories in Arab settlements with meagre work opportunities (see *Report on the Palestinians under Israeli Rule,* July 1985, p. 11).

> household and the upbringing of the children; she must serve her husband; she must not work away from home; she must not move more than one kilometre from her village unescorted; a woman's going out into the street alone at night is an act of wantonness; she must not pay visits to town (except to see a doctor if necessary), nor go shopping in the market, nor participate in outings, amusements or sports activities; she must not wear jewelry or other ornaments or make up her face so as to hide her natural colour; she must not dance, sing or play instruments such as a lute, violin or harp.

Quoting the great fifteenth-century Druze holy man and sage, al-Amir al-Sayyid al-Tanukhi, he concludes, "Women are all nakedness (*ʿawrāt*) and all nakedness should be covered."[27] Even so cosmopolitan a figure as the Druze man of letters, Shakib Arslan, who lived for more than twenty years in Europe, declared in an article that appeared in the Cairo weekly *al-Shura* of April 23, 1930, that "mixed dancing should continue to be banned because it involved holding close, and 'holding close is the first stage of fornication.' "

Marriage is expected of all Druze women and at a relatively early age. It is usually preceded by an engagement period of about two years and is traditionally forbidden under the age of fifteen. Most village girls have become engaged by the age of seventeen and are married well before they reach twenty-one.[28] The generally accepted minimum age for marriage under Druze religious law is seventeen for the bride and eighteen for the groom, though until recently marriages at much younger ages were common.[29] Still, the median age for Druze women at marriage in Israel at least has remained virtually the same throughout this century, ranging between 17.7 and 19.7 years, as it has for men (a range of 21.6 to 23.1).[30]

Marriage partners are usually chosen from eligible young people within the same village, and frequently within the same extended family up to and including first cousins. According to Israeli statistics, more than one-third of Druze marriages were endogamous, with the proportion generally higher the younger the couple (when there was probably less choice offered to the bride) and in smaller, more remote (and usually more traditional) villages. The endogamy rate was, for example, 56 percent at Jathth and nearly 50 percent at three other conservative villages, al Buqayʿa, Hurfaysh and

27. Layish, *Marriage,* p. 21. The English word *nakedness* is a euphemism. *ʿAwrat* literally means *genitals.*

28. *Ibid.,* p. 25 (see also his table I, p. 37); 76.7 percent of Israeli Druze women marry by age twenty-one and 95.5 percent by age twenty-nine.

29. Druze religious law, according to Shaykh Kamal Muʿaddi, permits marriage of a girl of fifteen under compelling circumstances, e.g., if she is cut off from her family and has no support or is threatened with ill-treatment, provided there is medical evidence that she is physically fit for marriage.

30. *Ibid.,* see table IV, p. 43. A significant disparity in age between the bride and groom is rare.

Yirka. An anomaly was the Druze community of al-Rama (one-third of a predominantly Christian, chiefly Greek Orthodox town), where there was not a single endogamous marriage during the period of Layish's study. He was hard put to explain this, pointing out that although this village is one of the most Westernized in Israel, the Druze population is not small (well over one thousand) and is ringed by half a dozen nearby Druze settlements, so that there should have been no difficulty in arranging interclan unions.[31] Most families prefer to marry their daughters to cousins or at least to members of the clan to preserve property and a better knowledge of family background. Even the prospect of money is not an attraction for the more traditionally minded. Layish, quoting Salman Fallah, who has written extensively about his own Druze village of Kafar Sumayᶜ, has observed that "they prefer a poor relative to a wealthy stranger."[32]

A certain amount of wealth is a necessary consideration, however, since a dowry (*mahr*) agreed on in advance is a legal prerequisite to a Druze marriage. Article twenty-four of the Lebanese Druze Law of 1948 provides that dowry is an obligation of the husband toward the wife, and although a marriage can theoretically take place without one, it is unheard of for a Druze woman to leave her family without a substantial financial guarantee. The amount of the dowry varies greatly depending on the families involved and often includes property as well as cash. With the increased number of Lebanese Druze working abroad, particularly in Saudi Arabia and the Gulf, since the civil war began in 1975, the ability of many to pay large amounts for a bride has significantly increased the average demand.

At a conference held at the *Maqam Sayyidina al-Khidr* in Kafar Yasif on January 15, 1969, attended by numerous *shaykhs,* the Druze leadership in Israel tried to limit to five thousand Israeli pounds the expenses of the engagement, the *jihaz* (the wife's requirements), clothing and bedding, the dowry, and the cost of the wedding feast (*zifaf*). Likewise, the Lebanese *shaykh al-ᶜaql* "recently campaigned to limit the amount a *mahr* should reach."[33] The rapid deterioration of Israeli currency since then and the generally increasing prosperity of the Druze community have long since made this recommendation irrelevant. But it does reflect a concern within the community that the increasingly excessive dowries, demanded and paid as a symbol of bourgeois status, ignored the traditional principle that the dowry should be uniform for rich and poor and "of an amount everyone can af-

31. *Ibid.,* p. 6. To illustrate the communal pressures normally favoring endogamous marriages, Layish cites a case where a woman already engaged to a relative was required to break off the engagement when another man suddenly appeared who was "nearer to her agnatically and consanguineously" (*ibid.,* p. 27, quoting *Majallat al-Akhbar al-Durziya* [*Bulletin of Druze News*] 3, nos. 3–4 [1968]: 37–40; also Gabriel Baer, *Population and Society in the Arab East* [London: Routledge, 1964], p. 65).

32. Layish, *Marriage,* p. 63.

33. *Ibid.,* p. 95, and Nura S. Alamuddin, *Crucial Bonds,* p. 47.

ford,"[34] which in general created a situation of economic hardship at the outset and thus discouraged rather than promoted marital happiness. One of the reasons for the popularity of marriages between Israeli men and Druze women from the newly occupied Golan Heights after the 1967 war (and from Lebanon after the 1982 invasion) was the significantly smaller dowries expected there in comparison with the Druze villages of Mount Carmel and Galilee.

The primary reason for marriage is of course children—in particular, heirs. Like all Middle Eastern societies, the Druze prefer sons to daughters, especially in the case of the first born. As sons are considered an asset, socially and economically, large numbers of them (particularly in rural areas) are a blessing. If one has daughters initially, one keeps having children until there are sons. Either way this leads to large families. An average Druze family has five or six children, sometimes as many as ten or twelve. The fact that polygamy is illegal makes a wife's fertility paramount in a successful marriage; failure to bear offspring, sons in particular, is a legitimate and not infrequent cause for divorce.

Official statistics, all but unknown outside Israel, indicate that the Druze live birthrate is close if not equal to that of Muslims and higher than that of Christians and Jews. David Yaukey's study *Fertility Differences in a Modernizing Country* conducted in Lebanon during the late 1950s, showed the live birthrate among Druze in Beirut to be slightly less than for Sunni or Shia Muslim families but considerably higher than among Christians.[35] The Israeli Census Bureau of Statistics' projection of population up to 1993 shows the Druze rate of reproduction to be 3.5, as opposed to 4.07 for Muslims and only 1.64 and 1.47 for Christian Arabs and Jews respectively.[36] Thus the Druze share of the non-Jewish population in Israel as reported in the 1983 census, while 9.58 percent of the total, was 9.95 percent of the same popu-

34. Layish, *Marriage,* p. 91. The amount of dowry (and the proportion of money to kind or property) varied considerably from village to village, as did the question of prompt and deferred dowry, it being quite common to agree in advance that a certain portion, nearly always less than half (except in one village, Mughar), would be paid at a later date, usually after marriage. The advantage for the woman is that if it is "a considerable amount, it deters the husband from rash or arbitrary divorce and in this sense is a stabilizing factor in family life," since he is obliged to pay it even if his wife dies, in the latter case to her legal heirs (*ibid.,* pp. 82–83).

35. The live birthrate for Sunni, Shia, and Druze women of Beirut cited in the Yaukey study was 6.45, 6.83 and 6.17 in that order, as opposed to only 3.63, 3.81, and 3.65 for Maronite, Eastern Catholic, and Orthodox women in the same city (David Yaukey, *Fertility Differences in a Modernizing Country* [Princeton: Princeton University Press, 1961], p. 29, and Betts, *Christians in the Arab East,* p. 84). In the villages, the birthrates were much less disparate between Muslims, Druze, and Christians.

36. Down slightly from the birthrate of the years 1972–75 (4.3 for Muslims, 3.7 for Druze, and 2.0 for Christians). The overall fertility rate in those years was seven children for Druze women, eight for Muslim women, less than four for Christian, and only three for Jewish women (Layish, *Marriage,* p. 16).

lation group under the age of five years (Christians, though making up 13.69 percent of the overall total were only 9.34 percent of the under-five group, less in actual numbers than Druze children of that age range).[37]

Although there has indeed been a small decline in the Druze reproductive patterns established earlier in this century, it should be noted that the decline has been general throughout the Middle East, where almost universal education and a passing familiarity at least with secular values from the West are common. The logic of having fewer children and being able to care for them better has not been lost on the rising generation of Druze couples, particularly the growing number of those who have studied and worked abroad. Exposure to twentieth-century reality has without doubt weakened some aspects of Druze traditional life, in particular the influence of the *ʿuqqal* in community affairs. Egon Mayer in his study of a Druze village in Galilee in the early 1970s came to the conclusion that successful *juhhal* were increasingly looking to members of the secular community for advice rather than to the embodiment of traditional wisdom, the *shaykh:*

> . . . the *ʾuqâl* [sic] have been relegated to a social niche of relative irrelevance. Because their knowledge is not only obscure and mysterious but secret as well—and they are sworn to keep it as a secret—they have been superseded by two local school teachers, a handful of students, and minor governmental functionaries as the repositories of socially useful "wisdom."[38]

In other areas of social life, especially marriage, change has been very slow in coming. Few young Druze question the role of their family in arranging (or at least helping to arrange) suitable matches, and deviation from the family choice is relatively rare. As Nura Alamuddin has noted, "given the massive socioeconomic transformation which has taken place in Lebanon . . . , the basic nature of Druze marriage patterns shows a truly remarkable resilience."[39] Mayer observed in his mythical village of Bayt Shabab (in actuality Bayt Jann) that while "most of the young men agreed that they felt restricted by the traditional rules concerning courtship and marriage, yet they all agreed that they had little interest in marrying outside of the village."[40]

37. *The 1983 Census of Population and Housing* (Jerusalem: Bureau of Statistics, 1985, vol. 7, table I, p. 19). The total Israeli Christian population was 94,157, of which 10,071 were under age five; the Druze total was 65,861, of which 10,725 were under age five.

38. Egon Mayer, "Becoming Modern in Bayt al-Shabâb," *The Middle East Journal* 29 (Summer 1975): 289–90.

39. Alamuddin, *Crucial Bonds,* p. 85. Despite the fact that most Druze cling strongly to their marriage traditions, they must surely be bemused by the behavior of their leader, Walid Junbalat. Although his marriage to a non-Druze Circassian was in the tradition of both his own family and that of the Arslans, his recent reported marriage to a second, non-Druze (Muslim) woman, also married, without benefit of divorce on either side, is without doubt a violation of Druze law that no amount of equivocating can disguise.

40. Mayer, "Becoming Modern," p. 286.

Such marriages of course do take place, and have done so increasingly since Mayer's study was made. There are many recent examples of marriage outside the community as well. Although the Lebanese Druze Law of 1948 makes no reference to disparity of religion as an impediment to marriage, Druze religious law strictly forbids the marriage of a Druze man or woman to a non-Druze.[41] The reasoning behind this is obvious, since the existence of the community, especially as it does not permit proselytization, is threatened by marriage outside the faith. In Lebanon the Druze courts will not register a marriage of a Druze to a non-Druze, so the only alternative is conversion to another religion.

If marriage is contracted outside Lebanon then the union is looked upon as invalid, and any children are technically considered illegitimate. Nevertheless, in Israel at least, offspring from marriages of Druze men to Jewish, Christian, Bahai, or Muslim women (the marriage of a Druze woman to a non-Druze man is almost unheard of)[42] are recognized as following the religion of their father.[43] In Syria, where secular law applies, the question does not legally arise. Still, marriage outside the community is probably rarer there than elsewhere, because of the relative isolation and concentration of most Syrian Druze in one geographical area with only an insignificant presence of other religious communities. It was here that I found the most resistance to the idea of marriage to a non-Druze partner—and much concern over the fact that Walid Junbalat had taken a half-Sunni Circassian wife. There is of course a strong family tradition for this. Walid's mother, May Arslan-Junbalat, daughter of the Arab nationalist, Prince Shakib Arslan, was herself half Circassian, since her mother, Salima al-Khass, was born in Russian Circassia. Moreover, Shaqib's mother was also Circassian, his father Prince Hamud having broken "with Druze custom by marrying a Circassian woman."[44] The ancestry of Walid Junbalat, therefore, is fully one-half Circassian, and his children are three-quarters so.

Such marriages are the easiest to dissolve, since under Druze religious

41. An acquaintance of mine from the prominent Taqi al-Din family and his Italian Catholic wife were both formally converted to Shia Islam in the late 1960s in order to marry in Lebanon, since she could not become Druze and marriage to a non-Druze was forbidden to him under Lebanese law.

42. A notable exception was the late sister of Marwan Hammadi, Nadia, a well-known woman of letters who was married to Ghassan Tuwayni, Greek Orthodox publisher of *al-Nahar* and former Lebanese ambassador to the United Nations. It has been pointed out to me, however, that this family was already mixed, their mother having been Christian. Likewise, Kamal Junbalat's grandmother was a non-Druze. William L. Cleveland, *Islam Against the West: Shakib Arslan and the Campaign for Islamic Nationalism* (Austin: University of Texas Press, and London: Al Saqi Books, 1985), p. 5.

43. Layish, *Marriage,* p. 108.

44. His political spokesman, Marwan Hammadi, is also married outside the community to a French Catholic. Many Druze are of the impression that some sort of dispensation was given in these cases by the Druze courts. This is not true, and their marriages are not valid under Druze law.

law they never took place. Otherwise divorce (*talaq*) is, compared with the Muslim procedure, fairly difficult to obtain and must be based on a relatively few, traditional grounds. As I mentioned earlier, the most frequent is the failure of the wife to bear children, especially sons. Here a Muslim woman is at an advantage, in that her husband can take a second wife and maintain the first if he wishes. A Druze man, if he wants heirs, is obliged by his religion's strict insistence on monogamy to divorce his first wife, however much affection he might have for her, in order to take a second that may bear him sons.[45] Other causes of divorce include disobedience, immodest behavior (proven adultery is guaranteed grounds), and mental or some other chronic illness that makes normal sexual intercourse impossible.[46] For the wife's part she has recourse to divorce on the last-mentioned grounds as well, plus such causes as impotence, nonsupport, and desertion or prolonged absence.[47]

Once agreed upon and registered with the Druze courts in Lebanon or Israel or the civil courts in Syria, divorce under Druze religious law is absolute and irrevocable.[48] The marriage cannot be reinstated, nor are the partners allowed to meet under the same roof ("even if separated by many partitions").[49] If a woman is divorced through her own failings the husband is permitted to reclaim the dowry and other marriage expenses, but in most cases the Druze follow the custom of compensating the divorced wife for her "exertions" (*atᶜabuha*), a benefit that is particularly important for the older divorcée who has few prospects of remarriage and does not or can not return to her father's house and expect other support in her old age. As Layish notes, "the custom of making compensation [money, accommodation, kind] for the wife's 'exertions' is rather frequent, and is voluntary, a matter of good will, not a legal right."[50]

Such a tradition ties in closely with the most celebrated Druze custom of all—hospitality—for which they are known not only in name (as the *Banu al-Maᶜruf*) but in deed. Nearly all European visitors to the Druze country have made much of Druze generosity and munificence, but such outward displays of hospitality go beyond the traditional Bedouin Arab custom of cordially receiving the foreign guest. Nearly all Druze villages have one or more *mudafat* (singular mudafa), or guest houses, where visitors, not nec-

45. There are known cases of Druze converting to Islam so that they can remain married to their first wife and still take a second spouse (similar instances have occurred in Christian, even Maronite, families). In the event that the man does so without the approval of the wife, however, she has grounds for divorce; Layish cites just such a case (*Marriage,* p. 236).

46. *Ibid.*, pp. 138–40.

47. *Ibid.*, p. 141. Article 40 of the Lebanese Druze Law provides "that if the husband lacks sexual power (ᶜ*unna* or impotence) the wife may apply for dissolution when it has been medically proven that the defect is incurable" (*ibid.*, p. 172).

48. *Ibid.*, p. 181.

49. *Ibid.*, pp. 181–82.

50. *Ibid.*, p. 194.

essarily strangers, are regularly lodged. Often these are endowed by a wealthy family (in the Jabal al-Druze they are nearly all gifts of the Atrash) or simply maintained by the community out of religious and communal duty. Behind such outward displays of hospitality is the classical Arab concept of *muruʾa,* the guiding principle of chivalry, knightly virtue, and sense of honor that governs Druze behavior.[51]

Like the Muslims, the Druze have an extensive system of *awqaf* (singular *waqf*), or endowed properties, for religious and/or charitable use. Such property is given in wills by pious Druze for such purposes as the establishment and maintenance of a *khalwa* or *mazar,* including payment of pensions to the religious functionaries who look after them, and to the needy members of the community. Most of the *waqf* property is administered privately and is usually kept in the hands of specific families through heredity.[52] Like many closely knit, largely rural religious groups in the West (such as the Mennonites and the Mormons), the Druze look after their own community's orphans, widows, and destitute. A Druze beggar is unknown. If for some reason the extended family cannot look after one or more members in need of assistance, means of sustenance will be found within the larger community.

In the realm of education the Druze have consistently outpaced all non-Christian Arab groups. The requirements for induction into the ranks of the *ʿuqqal* have guaranteed that a substantial minority of both men and women would be literate at any given time (although illiterates are admitted after having memorized the holy texts), and the Druze were among the first to take advantage of the opportunities offered by the American mission schools established in Lebanon and Syria during the nineteenth century. The Israeli census of 1961 showed that fully one-half of the Druze population was literate (49.6 percent), as compared with 37.9 percent of the Muslim community and 76.1 percent of the Christian. Among women the rate was substantially lower than that of the men (26.8 percent as opposed to 72.9 percent), but still twice that of Muslim women (14.4 percent). Of the Druze women under the age of thirty, close to half (40.5 percent) were literate, as were nearly all (89.6 percent) of the men.[53] Subsequent censuses of 1972 and 1983 have registered impressive gains toward almost universal literacy in the Israeli Druze community, and many women now complete secondary school and pursue a university education.[54]

The 1960 census in Syria (the last to break down statistics by religious

51. Hanna Ghosn, "Village Welfare," *The Arab World* 1, no. 1 (1944): 94.

52. *Ibid.,* p. 14. In 1959 the Druze Division of the Ministry of Religious Affairs created a Druze Endowments Committee to certify wills and endowments; "the certificates were to be used as evidence in land settlement proceedings, and in courts (*ibid.,* p. 5).

53. *Israeli Census of Population and Housing, 1961,* publication no. 17, table XXXIX.

54. See *n.* 26 above. Druze women are now to be found in all faculties at universities in Lebanon, Syria, and Israel, but it is still very uncommon for a Druze girl to be allowed to leave home to attend university abroad.

grouping) showed that the non-Christian population of the Suwayda᾿ (Jabal al-Druze) governate[55] enjoyed an overall literacy rate of 37 percent, compared with a countrywide figure of 29.2 percent (the highest non-Christian literacy rate for any governate apart from Damascus and Aleppo cities).[56] Although no literacy figures exist for Lebanon by religious community, a study conducted at the same time as the Israeli and Syrian censuses, *Le bilinguisme arabe-français au Liban* by Selim Abou, in which some ten thousand rural Lebanese were interviewed, showed that the Druze ranked consistently above both Sunni and Shia Muslims (but below all Christian groups) in their rate of literacy, and among the non-Christian women interviewed only the Druze registered a literacy rate of more than 50 percent (as did those from every Christian community).[57]

Though still a largely rural people, the Druze are far from exclusively so. Many of the younger members of the community have left their villages for larger urban environments, both in the Middle East and abroad, to further their education and establish businesses. Long gone are the days when Hitti could assert that "in the lists of the leading merchants of Aleppo, Damascus, Beirut and Sidon, one would search in vain for a Druze name."[58] The Druze are today encountered at the highest levels of Lebanese and Syrian commerce, including banking, trade, small businesses, and transportation services. The former president for many years and principal shareholder of Middle East Airlines was a Druze, Najib ʿAlam al-Din, and throughout much of the airline's existence a large percentage of the personnel, including the pilots, have been Druze.[59] Druze students in American universities are just as likely to major in business administration or economics as their Muslim and Christian countrymen, though many tend to favor engineering or a combination of the two. In Saudi Arabia and the Gulf States, Druze men are prominent members of the local business community, particularly in American and European firms, which find them to be especially hardworking and trustworthy.

55. The 1960 Syrian census broke down statistics by Christian, Muslim, and Jew only; Druze and Alawis were considered for statistical (and political) purposes to be Muslim. As the Muslim population of the Jabal al-Druze is insignificant (less than 2 percent), the non-Christian figures can be taken as applying to the Druze inhabitants.

56. *The 1960 Census of Population and Housing* (Damascus: Ministry of the Interior, 1962), quoted in Robert Betts, "The Indigenous Arabic-Speaking Christian Communities, p. 462.

57. Selim Abou, *Le bilinguisme arabe-français au Liban* (Paris: Presses Universitaires, 1962), p. 101 (table XIV). Of the Druze women interviewed (147), 59.2 percent were literate, as compared with 49.6 percent of the Sunni and 15.5 percent of the Shia women. The Druze figure was higher even than that of the Maronite women (of the 3,320 interviewed, just 57.7 percent were literate). Only Greek Orthodox (65.1 percent) and Greek Catholic (62.6 percent) women enjoyed a higher literacy rate.

58. Hitti, *Origin of the Druze*, p. 5.

59. The current president of Middle East Airlines is Salim Salam, son of Sunni Lebanese politician, Sa᾿ib Salam.

In recent years a significant number of Druze have joined the ranks of the intelligentsia, and many are now found on the faculties of high schools and universities throughout the Middle East. There are Druze poets and writers, prominent among them Samih al-Qasim, a young Druze Palestinian poet from the mixed Druze-Christian town of al-Rama in Galilee.[60] In the earlier years of this century, a leading literary figure in the Arab world was the Druze prince Shaqib Arslan, who was known as "the prince of eloquence" (*amir al-bayan*) and chosen in 1938 as president of the Arab Academy in Damascus.[61] The field of journalism includes Druze contributors in Lebanon, Syria, and Israel. Walid Junbalat's principal spokesman, Marwan Hammadi, was for years a leading editorialist with Beirut's most highly regarded daily, *al-Nahar* (owned by his brother-in-law, Ghassan Tuwayni), and in Israel Rafiq Halabi became a nationwide celebrity in the early 1980s as the leading reporter for Arab affairs in the West Bank and the Gaza Strip for state-controlled Israeli television.[62] In the world of music individual Druze have made names for themselves both in the Western classical tradition (such as the pianist Diana Taqi al-Din), and, more prominently, in the sphere of traditional Middle Eastern music. One of the most celebrated and best-loved exponents of *al-ᶜud* (the lute) in the traditional Oriental style in recent times was the late singer and composer Farid al-Atrash (1916–1976), whose sister Amal, known as Ismahan (1917–1944), established herself in the late 1930s as a singer and cinema star—and was reputedly a mistress of King Faruq of Egypt before she died in a mysterious road accident that many people at the time believed to have been murder.

But such incidence of glamour and fame are not the norm, and they certainly do not reflect the kind of life that the Druze religion encourages its members to follow, though when they do they are not considered any the less of a Druze for it. Many Druze were delighted when President Ronald Reagan appointed Mrs. Archibald Roosevelt (née Salwa Shuqayr, the elder

60. Sarah Graham-Brown, "The Poetry of Survival," *Middle East* no. 22 (Dec. 1984): 43–44. The Druze share the Arabic-speaking peoples' love for poetry, and their own tradition is rich with a variety of images and ideas. Unlike the poetry of the Bedouins and the pre-Islamic anthologies in general, the poetry of the Druze excludes love songs, favoring themes like the love of God and of one's native countryside (see Nadia Tuéni, "La poésie chez les Druzes," in *Nadia Tuéni: La prose (oeuvres complètes)*, Beirut: Dar an-Nahar, 1986, p. 123). The popular extemporaneous poetic art form known as *al-zajal,* though enjoyed by the *juhhal,* is usually frowned upon by the more serious-minded of the community as unworthy of God-fearing *muwahhidun*.

61. Cleveland, *Islam,* p. 13. Ironically his son, Gharib, educated mostly in Europe, never learned Arabic (*ibid.*, p. 84). Also ironically, Prince Shakib himself was refused Lebanese citizenship by the French (ostensibly because he waited too long to apply in terms of the 1923 Treaty of Lausanne), and he traveled for the rest of his life on a Saudi Arabian passport (*ibid.*, p. 65).

62. See Shimon Weiss, "A Traitor in Everybody's Eyes," *New Outlook* 23 (Aug. 1980): 38–39); also *Newsweek,* Jan. 4, 1982, p. 61. In the latter article, Halabi's Druze affiliation was not mentioned, only that he was an Israeli Arab.

daughter of Druze emigrants from the Matn district of Lebanon) as the State Department's chief of protocol in 1982. A diligent and accomplished diplomat, Ambassador Roosevelt is in the long tradition of Druze women who have risen to prominence in public affairs through commitment to service.[63]

Such virtues are unlikely to change, no matter how extensive the exposure to the liberal, even permissive, attitudes introduced from European and American cultures. The communal pattern of strong family (though increasingly centered on the nuclear rather than the extended),[64] personal diligence, self-reliance, and a strong sense of moral probity still pervades Druze life today, and there is little that would lead one to foresee any substantive alteration. There is nothing in the Druze faith that would breed the kind of fundamentalist fanaticism that pervades much of the Islamic world today. In fact, most Druze fear this groundswell of Muslim supremist intolerance as much as Arab Christians do. They are quite content to live side by side with the modern world and profit from its economic, medical, and technological advantages. But few of them find in Western culture anything that they would substitute for their own society and communal code of behavior. Although seemingly restrictive to those looking in from the outside, the Druze community is not regarded by its members, not even the women or the young, as something to escape from.

The reasons for this deeply felt loyalty even among those who do not consider themselves to be especially (or at all) religious can be found in the very strong sense of community in which the Druze are instructed as children, the division of the sect among those for whom religion is important and those who are content to let others be concerned with such matters, and the customs and traditions, which though strict are logical, not unreasonably demanding, and (certainly to a greater extent than those of Islam) flexible. Finally, there is a strong sense of pride in being a member of such a unique community whose history, exclusivity, and high ethical standards have earned them the respect, or at least the cautious fear, of their Christian, Muslim, and Jewish neighbors. To be a Druze is to be an heir to a thousand years of honorable history—and to a tradition that is unlikely to yield under the external pressure of the changing times or to succumb to internal forces desirous of "modernization."

63. *International Herald Tribune*, Feb. 24, 1983, back page. Her mother, Mrs. Najla Shuqayr (Showker), from a prominent Druze family of Arsun in one of the northernmost Druze settlements in Lebanon, emigrated to the United States after graduating from high school in order to marry an earlier Druze emigré who had established a business there. Once her children were grown she earned an M.S. degree in linguistics from Georgetown University and recently retired from the faculty of modern languages at East Tennessee State University.

64. See Layish, *Marriage*, p. 19: "there can be no doubt that the Druze extended family is disintegrating more rapidly than it did in the past and is gradually being replaced by the nuclear family."

4

Druze Demography in the Twentieth-Century Middle East

The total population of Druze throughout the world probably approaches one million. Except for Israel, which collects statistics with European precision, population figures are inexact. In Lebanon there has been no census since 1932, and although there were government estimates as late as 1956 that broke down the population by confessional groups, they were considered by most to be weighted in favor of the Christian communities, who were a bare majority in the 1932 census and by popular consensus had slipped to something less than 40 percent of the population by the outbreak of the civil war in 1975. In Syria there were government estimates until the mid-1950s and a census in 1960 that counted (or undercounted) Christians separately but lumped all other groups except Jews with the Muslim majority. A not too generous projection, however, based on analyses of past statistics and the various estimates of scholars and other knowledgeable individuals (some within the Druze community) would give the Druze some 390,000 adherents in Lebanon (out of a total population of nearly four million), 420,000 in Syria (out of a population rapidly approaching twelve million), 75,000 in Israel (inclusive of nearly 15,000 Syrian Druze in the Golan district), 15,000 in Jordan, and a maximum of 80,000[1] elsewhere (mostly the Americas, Australia, and West Africa).[2]

The oldest and until recent times the largest concentration of Druze in the world is found within the borders of the Republic of Lebanon. The 1932 census counted 53,334 Druze out of a total population of 793,392, or 6.72 percent.[3] Although the Druze themselves felt they had been undercounted and that they in fact made up closer to 10 percent of the total, the French mandate figures did accurately reflect the distribution of Druze throughout the country. Only 2 percent (1,318) of Druze were found in the capital city of Beirut itself, which was roughly half Sunni Muslim and half non-Maronite Christian (chiefly Greek and Armenian Orthodox, with a small smattering of other sects). A few old Druze families such as al-Rawda had been established in the capital for generations, principally in the picturesque seaside quarter of ʿAyn al-Maraysa—until the 1960s a warren of narrow streets and lovely old Arab-style homes below the American University, and in the vicinity of the Druze community center midway between the Hamra business district and the Muslim area of Corniche al-Mazraʿa (al-Musaytba).

Virtually all the remaining Druze were settled in six of the eighteen subdistricts (*aqdiya*ʾ, or judicial jurisdictions, singular *qada*ʾ, usually spelled *caza* in English and French) of the four provinces (*muhafazat*) that made up the country exclusive of Beirut city. There they lived in small towns and villages for the most part exclusively theirs, though mixed Christian and Druze communities were not infrequently encountered. Very few Druze lived side by side with Muslims, and then only with Sunnis, never Shia. The same applied in Syria and Palestine. These six subdistricts contained 51,375 Druze out of a total population of 217,344 (which included 119,886 Christians and 45,655 Muslims), or 23.64 percent of the total (versus less than 7 percent countrywide) amounting to 96.33 percent of all the Druze in Lebanon. (See Table 1 in the Appendix for the 1932 confessional distribution in the six

1. Estimate of the American Druze Public Affairs Committee.

2. Another comprehensive estimate is given by Laurent and Annie Chabry in *Politique et minorités au Proche-Orient* (Paris: Editions Maisonneuve et Larose, 1984) on p. 191 as follows: 350,000 Druze in Syria, 300,000 in Lebanon, 35,000 in Israel, and 10,000 in Jordan. In view of the known 1983 figure of 53,956 Druze in Israel proper (65,861 if the Golan is included), figures for the other countries are also likely to be underestimated.

3. In addition to the resident population, an additional 159,571 Lebanese abroad were classified as citizens but not counted for purposes of the sectarian distribution of political offices. Of these Lebanese resident abroad only 4,863 (3.05 percent) were Druze; well over half (57.20 percent) were Maronites.

subdistricts.) Apart from the small concentration in Beirut (1,318), only a handful (641) were found elsewhere in the country.

In subsequent years the Lebanese government released occasional estimates to update the 1932 census figures, but as the government was Maronite dominated, it was widely acknowledged that these figures were adjusted to show a continued and even increasing Christian majority. Thus the last such official estimate released in 1956 showed Christians enjoying a slightly larger total percentage of a population that had nearly doubled. The Druze figure in that year was put at 88,131 out of a total of 1,416,520, or 6.22 percent, a net decline of half a percentage point since 1932. Of the 1956 total of 402,508 persons reported to be living in these *aqdiya*ʾ the Druze numbered 85,324 (21.2 percent), Christians 242,281 (60.19 percent), and Muslims 74,676 (18.55 percent). (See Table 2 in the Appendix for the 1956 confessional distribution in the six subdistricts.) The Druze in the Beirut community had nearly doubled to 2,457, while those elsewhere had shrunk by half to only 350. Overall, a net percentage decline was registered in all the subdistricts except al-Matn, which had the smallest of the Druze concentrations. In the *qada*ʾ of Bᶜabda , which included the largely Shia southern suburbs of Beirut, the Muslim and Christian population was seen as increasing at a far faster rate (90.86 percent and 91.41 percent respectively) over the preceding quarter-century, as opposed to 73.54 percent for the Druze. The Druze themselves believed the figures to be inaccurate, and what unofficial figures are available from roughly that period (such as Yaukey's survey)[4] bear this suspicion out. Joseph Chamie's more recent study, however,[5] claimed that recent trends had lowered Druze birthrates in Lebanon considerably, leaving them with a projected annual growth on the basis of his statistics of only 1.8 percent, exceeded by all other major groups (Shia—3.8 percent, Sunni—2.8 percent, Catholic Christian—2.0 percent) except the Orthodox Christians, who had a rate of 1.7 percent.[6]

This survey, though, does not jibe either with official figures for the Druze in Israel or my own observations. In late 1975, during the peak of the fighting in the first year of the civil war in Lebanon, the daily *al-Nahar* (Greek Orthodox owned) published unofficial figures supposedly based on government statistics showing Muslims and Druze to number 2,008,000 out of a total population of 3,207,000. The Druze figure was 348,000 (or 10.95 percent) of the total.[7] Countrywide totals only were given, so there is no way of comparing district figures with earlier official and semiofficial results. Although the *al-Nahar* figures were very disconcerting to the Christian establishment (Maronites were listed as numbering only 496,000, or

4. See chap. 3, *n.* 35 above.

5. Joseph Chamie, *Religion and Fertility—Muslim-Christian Differentials* (London: Cambridge University Press, 1981), p. 85.

6. *Ibid.*, p. 85.

7. *al-Nahar,* Nov. 5, 1975.

15.47 percent, rather than the 29.91 percent claimed in the 1956 official estimate), they were, given their reputable provenance, as accurate as any could be. Population figures published in the New York *Times* on February 6, 1984, numbered the Druze at 350,000 out of a total of 3,350,000 (10.45 percent) and the Maronites at 580,000 (or 17.31 percent), slightly better than the *al-Nahar* figures of nine years earlier so far as the latter were concerned, but nowhere near the Shia, almost universally recognized as having replaced the Maronites as Lebanon's major sect (970,000, or 30.25 percent in *al-Nahar* and one million, or 29.85 percent, in the New York *Times*). (See Table 3 in the Appendix.)[8]

The Druze 10 percent of the population was now neatly contained in very large part within the borders of the "Druzistan" established by the Druze militia in the aftermath of the Israeli withdrawal after 1982. They and the Maronites of "Marunistan" to the north were the only Lebanese sects to enjoy the security of their own confessional canton. The Maronite canton, however, does not by any means contain all the country's Maronites. Between one-third and one-half of the total community live under Syrian occupation in northern Lebanon (the bailiwick of former President Sulayman al-Franjiya, blood enemy of the Gemayels since the murder of his son Tony by the Phalangists in 1978), the Biqaʿ Valley, and the ʿAkkar district northeast of Tripoli, not to mention those in the Druze canton and in the SLA enclave along the Israeli border (including the large village of ʿAyn Ibil, home of the Maronite patriarch, Antoine Cardinal Khuraysh). The other principal communities had even smaller geographical bases or none at all.[9]

8. The *Times* gave no source for its estimate; also, it included Armenian Catholics in the Armenian Orthodox figure rather than the figure for the Greek and Other Catholics as in the *al-Nahar* estimate. The *Times* did not include figures for the smaller groups of Christians, i.e., the Syrian Orthodox, Nestorians, or Protestants, which probably do not exceed the figure of fifty thousand quoted by *al-Nahar*; Alawis from Tripoli and the ʿAkkar district (for whom I have never seen an estimate); Jews (no more than a few hundred remaining, down from a peak of some six thousand to seven thousand before 1948); and of course Palestinians, who never figure in Lebanese population statistics. They are nearly all Sunnis except for a handful of Christians, mostly Orthodox, living in Dubayya refugee camp near Juniya. All but several thousand of the Palestinian Christian refugees of 1948–49 obtained Lebanese or some other nationality in the decade following. The total number of stateless Palestinians in Lebanon is approximately three hundred thousand.

9. The Shia of southern Lebanon have established a quasi-autonomous Islamic republic under *Amal* paramilitary forces in the wake of the Israeli withdrawal, with a capital of sorts at Tyre (Sur), and have maintained their own small urban enclave in West and South Beirut with Syrian support (the arrival of fifty tanks in late July 1985, as a gift from the Syrians substantially strengthened their position there). The Shia of the northern Biqaʿ Valley were in Syrian occupied territory, while others lived under SLA control in the south. The Armenian Orthodox were nearly all in Kataʾib-controlled East Beirut and its suburbs, including Antilyas, seat of the Armenian Orthodox patriarch of Cilicia (Sis). A few still lived in predominantly Muslim West Beirut. The Sunnis had no autonomy at all, living in West Beirut under *Amal* or Druze Militia control (since the latter forces wiped out the Sunni paramilitary group, the *Murabitun,* in April 1985), in the Druze canton in towns of the Shuf foothills such as Barja and Shahim, and in Tripoli,

The strip of land linking the southernmost Druze villages of the Shuf (Batir and Niha) with those on the other side of Mount Lebanon in the Wadi al-Taym included of necessity part of the Lower Litani River Valley with its mixed Christian and Shia Muslim population—although the Shia had been substantially diminished by fighting and the depopulation of whole villages, especially since 1982. In contrast, the Druze had not suffered the permanent loss of any of its settlements, and many that had previously been mixed with Maronite and Greek Catholic Christians were now exclusively Druze. Only in the area north of the Beirut-Damascus highway and in SLA-occupied Hasbayya were Druze settlements found outside the military protection of Junbalat's forces. In al-Matn, Druze were found only as minority communities in four towns and villages, notably al-Matayn, where they are half the population. The northernmost Druze town is Salima in Bʿabda subdistrict (just south of the border with al-Matn), the site of a massacre by Phalangist forces in 1976. Other principal Druze settlements north of the highway are ʿAbadiya, Raʾs al-Matn, Qurnayyil, and Arsun. Six smaller villages with Druze majorities are also found here, and five other settlements such as Hammana have substantial Druze minorities.

The ʿAlayh subdistrict contains fifteen towns and villages (including the resort town of ʿAlayh itself) that are predominantly Druze. Many (such as ʿAytat) were seriously damaged in the massive shellings of September 1983 that took place between Druze militia forces and the Lebanese Army for control of the Suq al-Gharb ridge and crossroads, and they have been only partially resettled. Principal Druze settlements in this subdistrict are Shuwayfat, ʿAramun, Bishamun, and Baysur. Before the civil war the Shuf subdistrict contained thirty-one exclusively or predominantly Druze towns and villages, notably Baʿqlin, Baruk, and al-Mukhtara, almost all located in the eastern two-thirds of the *qadaʾ*. The Christian villages along the coast and lower foothills were forcibly evacuated in May 1985, so that only small pockets of Christians remain, principally at Dayr al-Qamar. In the Wadi al-Taym region both the towns of Rashayya and Hasbayya retain their Druze majorities and are surrounded by twenty-one Druze villages.

The Druze in Syria have been effectively cantonized since independence. According to the official government estimate of 1956, the last to be published, 81.5 percent of Syrian Druze lived in the Suwaydaʾ province (which coincided with the boundaries of the autonomous Jabal al-Druze established by the French Mandate), where they made up 88.18 percent of the population (102,017 out of a total of 115,687).[10] According to French Man-

---

the ʿAkkar and the Biqaʿ being under Syrian control. The Greek Orthodox were almost all within the Syrian sphere (Tripoli, the al-Kura district south of it, the ʿAkkar, and the Biqaʿ), as were Greek Catholics in their principal center at Zahlah in the central Biqaʿ, with others in the Druze canton, in *Amal*-controlled Tyre, and the SLA cordon sanitaire, including Jazzin.

10. Out of a total population of 4,025,165, the Druze numbered 125,063, or 3.11 percent. Of this number, 102,017 were found in al-Suwaydaʾ province, 20,771 in Damascus province, and 2,167 in Aleppo province, with a scattering of 108 elsewhere in Syria.

date statistics of 1927 (quoted in Bouron's study) the autonomous Jabal contained 117 settlements, of which 66 were entirely Druze in population, 43 were Druze in majority with Christian and/or Sunni minorities, two were exclusively Christian, four had large Christian majorities with small Druze and/or Sunni minorities, and one had a Christian plurality with substantial minorities of both Sunnis and Druze.[11]

In my visits to al-Suwayda' and its environs between 1975 and 1985 I confirmed to my own satisfaction that the distribution and proportions have been largely maintained since these statistics were published in 1927. There has definitely been a significant movement of rural Christians to the growing city of al-Suwayda' itself, and from there to Damascus and abroad. It is very doubtful that the Christians constitute 10 percent of the province's population today. Their seven villages still exist, even prosper, and in Kharraba and ʿAnz there are several new churches, some still under construction. A Greek Orthodox bishop of Basra and the Hawran has his seat in Suwayda', and while his tiny black basalt cathedral is hardly imposing, the present incumbent, Bishop Samaha, most certainly is.[12]

Actual population figures for the Jabal al-Druze are not available and are difficult to estimate. The last actual census was taken in 1960 during the three-year union of Syria and Egypt under Nasser's United Arab Republic (1958–1961), and it showed the population as having declined since the 1956 estimate by 20 percent to only 92,011. Of these 5,109 were Christian and the rest (86,902) were classified as Muslim. The census also indicated a substantial emigration from the countryside to the provincial capital. From a large village of 4,753 inhabitants in 1927, al-Suwayda' had grown to 18,154 in 1960, nearly a fourfold growth at the same time the province itself had less than doubled in population (from 49,674 to 92,011). Christians in par-

11. Bouron, *Les Druzes,* pp. 411–13. The exclusively Christian villages were Kharraba and Asliha, population 715 and 237 respectively. Two others, Jubayb (now part of the Hawran province) and Darah had Christian majorities of 407 and 293 and Sunni minorities of 26 and 34 respectively; Hit had a Christian majority of 284 and a Druze minority of 182; Samma registered a Christian majority of 370 with Sunni and Druze minorities of 66 and 21 respectively. ʿAnz near the Jordanian border had a Christian plurality of 327, with Druze and Sunni minorities of 227 and 204. More than half of the province's Christians (2,633 out of 4,699 in 1927) lived in these more or less exclusive rural concentrations, only one of which, Hit, was located in the Jabal proper (near Shaqqa in the northern part of the mountain) the others being found on the Hawran plain west of al-Suwayda', but just within the governate's boundaries. Of the rest, 1,299 lived in nine larger Druze towns and villages such as al-Suwayda', Salkhad, Shahba, and Shaqqa, totaling 14,803 inhabitants (13,389 Druze, 218 Sunni, and 10 other), and the remaining 767 in twenty-three smaller settlements with a total population of 8,339 (all Druze, except for 159 Sunnis in five of the settlements).

12. A native of Dhur al-Shuwayr in the Matn district of Lebanon, the bishop was raised a Greek Catholic but converted to Orthodoxy. Though for many years he held close ties with the Soviets and the Syrian-controlled branch of the Palestinian military forces, *al-Sa'iqa,* he cast the deciding vote in the 1979 synod that elected the present patriarch, Ilyas Hazim, former bishop of Latakia and a member of the pro-American faction within the clergy of the Antiochene Patriarchate.

ticular were attracted to the prosperity and security of the growing town, where their numbers grew from a mere 136 in 1927 to nearly one thousand (968) in 1960 (from less than 3 percent of the total population to more than 5 percent). When I first visited al-Suwayda' in 1975 its population was variously estimated at between twenty-five thousand and thirty-five thousand. Ten years later I heard figures as high as 150,000, which may be inflated but not enormously so; certainly a population of between seventy-five thousand and one hundred thousand is the case today, and a higher figure is not out of the question. The population of the province could be as high as four hundred thousand, of which not more than twenty thousand are Christian and five thousand Sunni Muslims, reflecting the threefold growth of Syria's population since 1956 (to nearly twelve million, from 4,025,165).

In addition to the major concentration of Druze in the Suwayda' *muhafaza,* another twenty-five thousand to thirty thousand are found in villages of Damascus province on the eastern slopes of Mount Hermon (exclusive of the four Druze villages under Israeli occupation since 1967), Damascus city proper, and the Ghuta,[13] and another thirty thousand to forty thousand in the remote Jabal al-Aʿla west of Aleppo in the hills overlooking the former Syrian province of Alexandretta, Turkish since 1939. Centered around the prosperous market town of Qirqaniya are a dozen Druze settlements such as Qalb Lawzah, built amid magnificent ruins of sixth-century Byzantine churches, much as the Druze villages of the Jabal al-Druze have grown up among the formidable remains of late Roman cities.[14]

The small Druze population of Jordan is for the most part the product of emigration from Lebanon and Syria for political and economic reasons. The only Druze settlement is in fact an extension of the Jabal al-Druze at al-Azraq oasis in the Syrian desert northeast of ʿAmman. This picturesque patch of greenery where Sultan al-Atrash sought refuge on more than one occasion, is actually two settlements, the one Circassian and the other Druze. According to the census of 1964, the Druze section had a population of only 209, but most recent accounts report a community of some two hundred families, which would indicate a population of fifteen hundred to two thousand, mostly dependent upon the local salt industry and livestock grazing.[15] The most recent Druze arrivals are concentrated in the capital area, especially its northeastern suburbs of al-Zarqa and al-Rusayfa.

13. The 1956 estimate counted 20,771 Druze in Damascus province, most of them in villages on the Hermon slope, and in the Ghuta. Only 1,198 were found in the city of Damascus proper.

14. Syrian government estimates always indicated a tiny Druze presence in the Aleppo district (1,601 in 1943 and 2,167 in 1956). Hirschberg, in his essay on the Druze in Arberry, *Religion,* estimated the Druze in the Aleppo district to number ten thousand (vol. 2, p. 330, *n.* 1). Kamal Junbalat shortly before his death cited a figure of twenty thousand Druze in the Jabal al-Aʿla (*I Speak for Lebanon,* p. 27).

15. See Christine Osborne, *Jordan* (London: Longman, 1981), pp. 113–14, and Bryan Nelson, *Azraq, Desert Oasis* (Athens, Ohio: Ohio University Press, 1974), p. 54.

In Israel the Druze population has grown substantially since independence in 1948. The British Mandate of Palestine census of 1931 counted only 9,148 Druze out of a total non-Jewish population of 861,211, or a mere 1.06 percent of the total. In 1972 the Israeli census showed the Druze to have increased fourfold to 36,563, or 7.93 percent of the total Israeli Arab population of 460,982. By 1983 this number had grown to 53,956, and the 11,905 Syrian Druze under Israeli control and annexed to Israel proper in 1981 brought the total to 65,861, or 9.58 percent of non-Jewish Israelis.[16] Apart from the Golan Heights, all this growth has taken place within the eighteen Druze settlements, sixteen in Galilee and two on Mount Carmel, that have been in existence for centuries.[17] In fourteen of these the Druze are a majority; according to the 1983 census they numbered 46,470 out of a total population of 54,224. The rest of the inhabitants were principally Christian (4,842), with a smaller number of Muslims (2,871), forty Jews, and one "other." In the four remaining settlements, where they were a minority, the Druze numbered 6,319 out of a total of 33,024 (of which 12,712 were Christian and 13,976 Sunnis, plus seventeen Jews). Only 1,167 Druze lived elsewhere in Israel for reasons of work, military service, or marriage outside the community. All but two of the eighteen settlements stretch in a roughly contiguous belt across northern Israel, from the hills immediately overlooking the Sea of Galilee (Mughar) in the east to the edge of the coastal plain (Abu Sinan) in the west. The other two villages (ʿIsifiya and Daliyat Karmil) are located on the eastern slope of Mount Carmel just south of Haifa.

Tables 4 to 8 in the Appendix list the population of the Druze settlements in Galilee and Mount Carmel, beginning with the figures cited by Guérin in his survey of the villages of Galilee published in 1880 and continuing with the figures reported by the Israeli censuses of 1961, 1972, and 1983. The Druze share of the total population of these eighteen settlements has remained remarkably constant since 1961, having been reported as

16. The total non-Jewish population of Israel was reported in the 1983 census as 687,623 out of 4,037,620, or 17.03 percent. Of these, 526,639 (76.59 percent) were Muslim, 94,157 Christian (13.69 percent), 65,861 Druze (9.58 percent), and 966 Other (0.14 percent). Twenty-two years earlier the non-Jewish population had totaled only 247,134 (exclusive then of both East Jerusalem and the Golan Heights), of which 170,830 were Muslim (69.12 percent), 50,543 Christian (20.45 percent), and 24,282 Druze (9.83 percent); Others totaled 1,479, or 0.60 percent.

17. The Druze presence in Galilee dates back with certainty to the time of Fakhr al-Din II (early seventeenth century), possibly earlier. M. V. Guérin, *Description géographique, historique et archéologique de la Palestine,* 2 vols. (Paris: L'Imprimerie Nationale, 1880), catalogues every village in detail. He notes all of today's sixteen Druze settlements except ʿAyn al-Asad, the smallest of the Galilean Druze villages, and gives sectarian population proportions that more or less coincide with the contemporary distribution; major changes appear only in Abu Sinan, which had no Muslims; al-Rama, which was mentioned as half-Druze (rather than less than one-third today) and half Orthodox Christian, with no Muslims; and Kafar Yasif, where the tiny Druze community of today—3.5 percent—was not mentioned at all by Guérin and the Christians outnumbered Muslims 5:1, rather than less than 1.5:1 today. (See Table 4.)

60.36 percent in that year, 60.43 percent in 1972, and 60.51 percent in 1983. It should be noted, however, that the Christians, who were twice as many as the Muslims in 1961, barely had a majority of the non-Druze population by 1983. This is typical of the pattern elsewhere in the country.[18] No major changes were noted in the overall Druze distribution, except the village of Abu Sinan, where a Druze majority of 50.19 percent in 1961 was reduced to a minority of 32.41 percent in 1972 and 29.89 percent in 1983 because of a huge increase in the Muslim population between 1961 and 1972 (668 percent), while the Christian and Druze communities increased normally (by 58.5 percent and 46.5 percent respectively).

The reason for this change was the settlement of Muslims from other areas within the village borders, but in general the Muslims in Galilee have shown remarkable growth rates. In the town of Shafa ʿAmr their growth of 98.18 percent between 1972 and 1983 resulted in a percentage decline of the total population among both Christians (whose numbers grew by 41.68 percent) and Druze (39.18 percent); the Muslims are probably the majority by now. Also in Mughar, al-Rama, and Kafar Yasif the Sunni population grew far more rapidly than either the Druze or the Christian communities there. Despite these internal fluctuations, which reflect population movement rather than actual birthrate, Druze growth in these settlements and in the country as a whole has been consistent, and their share of the total population of the eighteen settlements is slightly higher now than it was in 1961, despite a 126.5 percent growth in their total population (from 38,516 to 87,248).

Since Israeli independence there has not been any trend for Druze to exchange the traditional environment of their villages for life in the larger urban centers of Jerusalem, Tel Aviv, or Haifa, just as Damascus and Beirut hold little attraction for their Syrian and Lebanese coreligionists. And while al-Suwaydaʾ qualifies as a city in terms of population, its atmosphere is decidedly that of an overgrown village, and there is no evidence of traditional values having broken down in the process of urbanization. Many of the city dwellers are in fact farmers who commute to their prosperous fields on the Hawran plain in new cars rather than aging donkeys. The rural ethos still prevails and is unlikely to change in any of the areas of Druze concentration, no matter how large their settlements grow.

Of the Druze living outside the Middle East, the largest communities are in North and South America, with smaller groups in Australia, West

18. Christian numbers have been declining relative to Muslim since 1948, when Christians counted 21.3 percent of the non-Jewish population. By 1964 this had dropped to 20.5 percent, and in 1972 and 1983 to 17.6 percent and 13.7 percent respectively. The population projection of the Israeli Central Bureau of Statistics for 1993 estimated that Christians will number 120,000, or only 11.5 percent of the non-Jewish population; Muslims are projected at 80.8 percent and the Druze at 7.7 percent (down nearly two percentage points from the 1983 census; but since this projection was published before the 1981 incorporation of the Golan, it did not take into consideration the additional thousands of Druze living there).

Africa, and Western Europe. All are emigrants from their parent Middle Eastern communities, particularly Lebanon. The American Druze Women's Committee, in an information packet distributed in the spring of 1984, estimated the Druze population in the United States to be twenty-seven thousand, "most of them descended from the great wave of immigrants who arrived in the early 1900's."[19] The majority settled in small towns across the country and adopted a very low religious profile. Many became at least nominally Christian (invariably mainline Protestant, usually Presbyterian or Methodist). An amusing, though highly exaggerated story published in the *Economist* recently claimed that many Druze changed their family names to Scottish ones in order to assimilate more quickly and easily.

> Thus the many Druzes who have emigrated to North America have for the most part become Presbyterians. And since quite a few Druze names begin with the syllable *Mak,* easily changed to *Mc,* many of the seemingly Scottish elders of the Presbyterian church in America hail not from the Grampians but from Jebel Barouk or Jebel Druze.[20]

Most did not abandon their Druze heritage, however much they may have conformed to the new society in which they now found themselves. They faithfully sent remittances back to their families in Lebanon and often arranged marriages with young women from their own home village. They have maintained their own community relations in America for many years, but it was not until the Lebanese crisis after 1975 brought the word *Druze* to the front pages of American newspapers, particularly after 1982, that the American Druze Public Affairs Committee (ADPAC) was formed to educate the public, and especially the media and politicians (though ADPAC is now in abeyance, pending the formal establishment of a Druze lobby in Washington). The American Druze Society holds an annual convention. Two publications deal with Druze affairs in the United States and abroad.[21] Although there are as yet no official Druze places of worship in America,[22] there are at present five *shaykhs* in the country who can be contacted for spiritual advice.

But for most Druze in America, and for the majority in the Middle East, the purely religious aspect of their tradition is secondary to their commonly held ties of culture and society. As Kamal Junbalat stated in his final

19. Information packet published by the American Druze Women's Committee, April 1984, p. 4.

20. *Economist,* July 23, 1983, p. 49.

21. *Our World* and *Our Heritage,* both quarterlies that cover issues and topics of interest to the Druze of an international and domestic American nature respectively.

22. The first Druze religious center in the United States was tentatively established in Annandale, Virginia, a suburb of Washington, D.C. But because of zoning difficulties and problems of politicization within the Druze community, it has been moved to Los Angeles.

work, *I Speak for Lebanon,* "rather than religion, it is our social relations, our mores and our culture which link us to one another and distinguish us from the non-Druses. This shared sense of community and morality has more in common with nationalism and a rather vague sense of nationhood than with religious sectarianism."[23]

23. Junbalat, *I Speak for Lebanon,* p. 36.

Part III

Modern History

5

The Growth and Gradual Decline of Druze Power in Greater Syria, 1516–1914

Sources in either Arabic or European languages referring to the expansion of Druze power in the central and southern regions of Mount Lebanon prior to the establishment of the Maʿn dynasty in 1516 by the Ottoman conquerors of Egypt and the Levant are few and contradictory. The principal Arabic source is the genealogical register of the Arslan family, who with their related clan the Buhturis (both belonging to the Banu Tanukh tribe) served as rulers of southern Lebanon and its Druze population from the rise of Druze power until the coming of the Ottomans. At its height in the mid-fifteenth century, the Tanukhi emirate (*Imara* in Arabic) extended from Tripoli in northern Lebanon to Safad in Galilee.[1] Not all the population was by any means Druze, but from the earliest days of the *daʿwa* they had dominated the region of the Wadi al-Taym on

1. Abu-Izzeddin, *Druzes,* p. 166.

the slopes of Mount Hermon, from which they gradually spread northward into the Shuf district and, by the sixteenth century, into the districts of Kisrawan and al-Matn north and east of Beirut.

The Maronites were confined to the extreme northern areas of Mount Lebanon around Bisharri, Ihdan, and the Wadi al-Qadisha (the Holy Valley), where their patriarch lived in the monastery of Qannubin. The Sunni population dominated the coastal towns of Tripoli, Beirut, Sidon (Sayda'), and Tyre (Sur), intermixed with the substantial Greek Orthodox (and latterly Greek Catholic) population whose presence dated from the earliest days of Christianity. The Maronites were frequently subjected to persecution by the Mamluk rulers of Cairo (the Sunni heirs to the Isma'ili Fatimids who, following the collapse of the Ayyubi descendants of Saladin in 1250, ruled Egypt and Syria until the coming of the Ottomans in 1516),[2] but the Druze were left to themselves so long as their ruling families were loyal to the Mamluk sultan and gave lip service to Sunni Islam.[3] They were an exclusively rural people. With the exception of their amirs (*umara'*) who maintained properties in Beirut where they sometimes resided with their coreligionist retainers, the Druze were found entirely in the villages tucked safely away in the foothills and heights of Mount Lebanon, approaching the exposed position of the Mediterranean coast only at Shuwayfat, the early seat of the Arslan family, perched on a rocky promontory overlooking Beirut.

By the time the Crusaders arrived in Syria the Druze were firmly entrenched in the region, with smaller communities surviving elsewhere in Syria, notably the Jabal al-Aʿla to the west of Aleppo, and the Ghuta, or Plain of Damascus. They periodically fought against the lords of the Outremer but were equally at odds with the Crusaders' Muslim enemies and the Isma'ili Shias (the famous Assassins of the Crusader period), since their obvious priority was the protection of their community against whoever threatened its security. With the final defeat of the European Christian principalities in 1291 by the Mamluks of Cairo the Druze passed under an unbroken role of Sunni authority from Cairo (until 1516) and Istanbul that lasted, at least officially, until 1918.

2. After the collapse of the Crusader states in 1291, the Maronites who had supported them and become Catholics under the aegis of their own uniate church were attacked in their mountain fastness by the Mamluks, who laid waste much of their territory and forced many to flee to Cyprus (then still under Crusader rule), where some five thousand still live. A Maronite see still exists from this time, although its bishop resides near Beirut and the majority of his faithful are in Lebanon.

3. Abu-Izzeddin cites many examples of cooperation between the Mamluk sultans and the Druze amirs, including the presence of "a valiant representative, the amīr Zayn al-Dīn Ṣāliḥ ibn ʿAlī," in one of history's decisive battles at ʿAyn Jalut (the Spring of Goliath) near Nazareth in 1260, where the combined forces of Islam defeated the Mongol armies for the first time, halting their advance, saving the region from certain devastation, and leading to the conversion of the Mongol nation to the Muslim faith, despite previous near-successful efforts by Christian missionaries from both East and West. Abu-Izzeddin, *Druzes,* p. 157.

When the Druze had to contend seriously with this authority during its first few centuries, they adopted many outward forms of Sunni Islam, a religious compromise permitted them by their doctrine of dissimulation (*taqiya*). During the reign of the Tanukhi prince al-Sayyid (1417–1479), "the most deeply revered individual in Druze history after the *hudud* [the five dignitaries, see Chapter 2, *n.* 37] who founded and propagated the faith,"[4] new mosques were built and existing ones repaired in the Druze villages, the *zakat* (alms) collected, and the Qur'an taught and memorized.[5] Deference to the rule of orthodox Islam continued under the amirs of the Maʿn family, who replaced the Tanukhi princes following the Mamluk defeat at Marj Dabit near Aleppo in 1516 by the armies of Sultan Selim the Grim (died 1521) and the subsequent extension of Ottoman authority over all of Syria, Egypt, and the Holy Cities of Arabia.

The Maʿn family, originally from the Rabiʿa tribe of Bedouins, had emigrated to the Shuf district from the region between the Tigris and Euphrates in Upper Mesopotamia known as al-Jazira during the early Crusader period. According to Abu-Izzeddin the Shuf was then a desolate country (though no source is given for this statement),[6] and after "the Maʿns were welcomed by the Tanukhs with whose help they built houses and gave up tent life . . . [it] became covered with villages."[7] The Maʿn family established itself in the town of Baʿqlin, today the largest Druze town in Lebanon. There is little reason to suspect that the Maʿn family followed the Druze religion before coming into its sphere. As in the case of the Junbalat family that appeared during the latter years of Fakhr al-Din II's reign (circa 1610), how they came to be accepted as members of a religious cult that does not permit conversion poses a serious threat to the theory that the Druze community has remained intact since the closing of the *daʿwa* in 1043.[8]

By officially recognizing a Druze amir (prince), Qurqmaz ibn Yunis al-Maʿni, as ruler of the region of the Shuf and southern Lebanon in 1516, the Ottoman sultan gave new authority to the old established tradition of granting the Druze autonomy to rule themselves so long as the distant authority of the Sunni caliph (now called *sultan*) was recognized. The early

4. *Ibid.*, p. 172.
5. *Ibid.*, p. 173.
6. *Ibid.*, p. 179.
7. *Ibid.*
8. Gabriel Ben-Dor, while noting that the Junbalats "were accepted as Druzes" (*Druzes in Israel*, p. 10), acknowledges that "we do not know how they were able to accomplish this" (*ibid.*, p. 47). More than likely they simply proclaimed themselves members of the community (Druze settlements after all did exist in the Aleppo region), and for political reasons they were accepted by the *masha'ikh al-din* and the community. Kamal Junbalat, in *I Speak for Lebanon* (pp. 26–27), admits that "we are not exactly sure when we first converted to the Druse faith," but, citing the Druze presence in the Aleppo hinterland since the beginning of Druzism, believes it to be "quite probable that our ancestors were already Druses when they were living in the Aley region."

years of Ottoman domination, however, saw several clashes between the local authority and the central. The second Maʿnid prince, Fakhr al-Din I, was summoned to Damascus in 1544 and murdered by the Ottoman governor (*wali*) there; his successor, ever wary of coming into the presence of the sultan's authority, died a fugitive, leaving two very young sons, the elder of which, Fakhr al-Din II (who ruled from 1590 to 1633), was the greatest of the Druze rulers of Mount Lebanon and is traditionally accepted as the founder of the first autonomous Lebanese state.

According to Hitti, the young Druze prince was taken under the wing of the Maronite al-Khazin family, who protected him from would-be Turkish assassins. This accounts for the favoritism he showed Christians, especially Maronites, throughout his long reign, permitting them to move southward and establish themselves in the previously exclusively Druze regions of Kisrawan and al-Matn.[10] Abu-Izzeddin, however, dismisses this story as having been "invented in the nineteenth century,"[11] though again she gives no source to support this statement. According to her, the care of Fakhr al-Din and his brother, Yunis, passed to their maternal uncle, a Tanukhi prince, and their mother, "a remarkable woman [who] brought them up."[12]

As the ruler of Mount Lebanon, Fakhr al-Din II worked to achieve the threefold ambition ascribed to him by Hitti: "building a greater Lebanon, severing the last link in the chain that tied it to Constantinople, and setting it on a path of 'modernism' and progress."[13] In all three he achieved considerable success, facilitated by the rapidly declining power that afflicted the Ottoman Porte following the death of Sulayman the Magnificent in 1566. The authority of the sultan had diminished markedly by the time the young Ma'nid prince came into his rightful inheritance, and he was able to fill the resulting power vacuum with the force of his own personality and ambition.

Fakhr al-Din inherited a princely fiefdom that covered most of what is today southern Lebanon, including the Shuf, an area that at the time came under the authority of the Ottoman governor of Damascus. One by one Fakhr al-Din annexed the districts adjacent to his, beginning with Sidon and Beirut. The sultan Ahmad I (1603–1617) was distracted for most of his reign by wars with the Habsburgs at one end of his dominions and the Persians at the other. Moreover, another ambitious figure, Ali Janbulad, ancestor of the modern Druze family of Junbalat, had asserted himself in the province (*vilayet*) of Aleppo, carving out a substantial fiefdom stretching from Adana in Cilicia to Hama in central Syria. Fakhr al-Din cleverly allied himself with Janbulad against the common Ottoman enemy, including the Turkish governors in Damascus and Tripoli, thus facilitating the growth of the Druze

9. Abu-Izzeddin, *Druzes,* p. 180.
10. Philip Hitti, *The Near East in History* (New York: Macmillan, 1961), p. 451.
11. Abu-Izzeddin, *Druzes,* p. 180.
12. *Ibid.*
13. Hitti, *Near East,* p. 451.

domain. By the time the sultan was able to defeat Janbulad in 1607,[14] Fakhr al-Din was well on his way to consolidating his power.

By 1610 the Ma'nid rule extended from the Dog River (Nahr al-Kalb) north of Beirut, south to Mount Carmel (Haifa in present-day Israel), and as far inland as Tiberias on the Sea of Galilee. Fakhr al-Din soon added the fertile Biqaᶜ (Bekaa) Valley between the Lebanon and the Anti-Lebanon mountains and extended his sway deep into the Syrian desert as far as Tadmur (Palmyra), where a castle he built still dominates the ancient oasis and surrounding desert landscape. According to Hitti, possession of the Biqaᶜ gave him sufficient revenues to build an efficient army.[15] He strengthened the agricultural base of his economy by promoting new sources of income, notably the silk worm; thousands of mulberry trees were planted on the mountain slopes. Along with the traditional olive groves, fruit orchards and vineyards nourished for centuries on the carefully terraced hillsides provided Lebanon with the basis of its prosperity into the twentieth century. *Caravansarais* (inns for travelers) were built, roads improved, and fortresses established to ensure the safety of commerce and trade.

Fakhr al-Din encouraged contacts with Europe, particularly Italy, and granted capitulations (trading privileges) identical to those negotiated by the Ottoman sultans with Western nations since the early sixteenth century. In 1613, however, the sultan Ahmad I, freed briefly from his external conflicts, combined forces with those of his governor in Damascus and marched against the Druze ruler. According to Hitti, "prudence dictated withdrawal from the scene."[16] Sending his mother to Damascus as a pledge of his loyalty, Fakhr al-Din undertook a visit to the Medici grand duke of Tuscany, Cosimo II, a principal European trading ally, remaining in Florence for five years as a state guest. Here he strengthened his ties with Tuscany and other Italian and European states and observed firsthand the benefits that post-Renaissance Europe had to offer his land and its people.

During this period he resisted attempts by the Catholic church to achieve his conversion, all the while keeping the external appearances of faithful adherence to Sunni Islam. A mosque and *muʾadhdhin* (muezzin, he who calls the faithful to prayer from the minaret of the mosque) were maintained, and the fast of Ramadan observed.[17] In 1618, judging correctly that the local political scene was ripe for his return, he sailed to Sidon, resumed his authority, and quickly added Tripoli and much of Palestine and Transjordan to his fief, thus prompting a second attempt by the governor of Damascus to curtail his power in 1623. This campaign was a total failure. The governor's forces were annihilated, and the governor himself was captured. The sultan had no choice but to recognize Fakhr al-Din as "Lord of Ara-

14. Abu-Izzeddin, *Druzes,* p. 184 (quoting J. De Hammer).
15. Hitti, *Near East,* p. 451.
16. *Ibid.*
17. Abu-Izzeddin, *Druzes,* p. 189.

bistan."[18] Now free of external political threats, he invited engineers, architects, and irrigation and agricultural experts from Tuscany to come to Lebanon to introduce those techniques he had so admired in Italy. He also permitted European (mostly French) Catholic missionaries to settle in Lebanon and undertake their educational and religious work.

Religious tolerance, always a characteristic of Ma'nid rule, became the most remarkable feature of the remaining fifteen years of Fakhr al-Din's reign. Although he continued outwardly to profess Islam[19] and at the same time secretly to convince the Druze of his adherence to the *tawhid,* he extended unprecedented liberties to Christians and is said to have been baptized by his Capuchin physician.[20] Abu-Izzeddin notes that "the Maronites were the principle [sic] beneficiaries of his tolerance. . . . It is in his reign that they began to emigrate in large numbers to south Lebanon."[21] Lebanon prospered as never before, and the seeds of its future development and Westernization were firmly planted.

But a new and stronger sultan, Murad IV (1623–1640) was unwilling to tolerate autonomous Ma'nid power in his empire. The last of the great fighting Ottoman rulers, who actually led his troops into battle and added Baghdad and Iraq to his domains, he ordered his governors of Damascus and Cairo to take action against the Druze amir. Fakhr al-Din's appeal to Europe for aid went unheeded, and in 1633 he was led captive to Constantinople, where he was strangled in 1635 along with two of his sons.[22]

18. Hitti, *Near East,* p. 451.

19. Abu-Izzeddin, *Druzes,* p. 193; "he built mosques at his own expense, attended prayers during Muslim feasts, and had *ʿulamāʾ* (learned men of religion) at his court. He often subsidized the pilgrimage to Mecca, and on one occasion stipulated that his son should be the commander of the pilgrim caravan (*Amīr al-Ḥajj*)."

20. Hitti, *Near East,* p. 452. Christian baptism of male children has traditionally been practiced by leading Druze families for centuries. It does not imply conversion but rather a politically motivated manifestation of *taqiya* in some cases and a good-luck charm in others (e.g., when previous male infants have perished). Bouron cites the example of the baptism of Sultan al-Atrash's second son in 1924 after the death of his first (*Les Druzes,* p. 282, *n.* 1, and p. 299).

21. Abu-Izzeddin, *Druzes,* p. 192.

22. *Ibid.*, p. 199. Richard Knolles, *The Turkish History from the Original of that Nation, to the Growth of the Empire &c.*, 2 vols., 6th ed. (London, 1687), considers the principal cause of Fakhr al-Din's execution to be the sultan's objection to his nonadherence to Islam. "The Plea against him was managed especially by the Pasha of Tripoli, who alleged, that he was an Enemy of the Mahometan Law, destroyed the Moschs . . . that he openly favoured the Christians, suffering them freely to build Churches in his Country. . . . [The Pasha] taking the Mufti on their side accused him of many crimes, and more particularly that he was a Christian, and an Apostate from the Mahometan faith. This point of Religion so sensibly touched the Grand Signor, that he resolved to condemn him in a manner Solem and Extraordinary" (vol. 2, pp. 21, 23). A popular folk tradition among the Druze holds that Fakhr al-Din escaped from his Turkish captors by hiding in the caves above the Jazzin escarpment near Batir in the southern Shuf, a feat made possible by his diminutive size. Hitti repeats a famous story of his being so short that if an egg were to drop from his pocket it would not break (*Lebanon in History,* London: Macmillan, 1958, p. 381).

The Ma'nid line continued until the end of the seventeenth century, but an intense power rivalry began to develop almost immediately between the so-called Yamani and Qaysi factions within the Druze princely families. These two terms refer to a rivalry that appeared very early in Islamic history during the days of the Umayyad dynasty (661–750), between a southern-Arabian (Yemeni) tribe related to the ruling caliphs and the northern-Arabian *Qays* tribe who opposed them. Periodic struggles between these two factions disrupted the entire caliphate from Spain in the west to Sind (Pakistan) in the east, which lay the groundwork for the Umayyad collapse in 750. The fighting continued sporadically for generations, much like that between the Guelphs and Ghibellines in late medieval Italy, but by the time of Fakhr al-Din the terms had simply become convenient sobriquets that opposing forces adopted in an attempt to lend legitimacy to their quest for power.[23]

The Maʿn family were of the Qaysi persuasion. Their leading rivals, the ʿAlam al-Din clan were Yamani partisans. When the last Ma'nid amir died in 1697 without male issue, an assembly of Druze elders and *shaykhs* chose a member of the Shihab family, Bashir, to succeed him. The Shihabs were the traditional princes of the Wadi al-Taym, related to the Ma'nids by marriage, who traced their lineage back to the noble Quraysh family of Mecca from which the prophet Muhammad descended.[24] For a century and a half (1697–1842) "the Shihabis maintained, through a feudal hierarchy of princes and shaykhs, the two principles of home rule and hereditary succession."[25] But the Shihabs were also Qaysis, and the Yamani faction immediately began to resist their accession to power in 1697. When the first Shihabi ruler died in 1707, his successor, Haydar, had to face a full-fledged rebellion led by the Yamani forces of the ʿAlam al-Din princes. A major battle between the two groups took place at the village of ʿAyn Dara in the Shuf in 1711, resulting in a total victory for the Shihabs and their Qaysi allies. This was to have extensive repercussions for the Druze community over the next century and a half.

The immediate result was a wholesale depopulation of the Druze districts as thousands of Yamani loyalists fled to the eastern Hawran region of southern Syria still known as al-Lijaʾ (the Refuge), a volcanic wasteland virtually uninhabited since Byzantine times, and to the unpeopled hills beyond that overlooked the vast expanse of the Syrian desert to the east. Here, amid ruined Roman cities on hillsides strewn with black basalt boulders, the

23. Kamal Salibi remarks, with characteristic understatement, that the rivalry "had long outlived accurate genealogy" (*History of Lebanon,* pp. 6–7).

24. The Shihabs are still a political force in Lebanese politics and affairs, though they are no longer Druze. Most have become Maronite Christians, but there is a Sunni Muslim branch as well. The third president of the Lebanese Republic was Fuʾad Shihab (1958–1964), a Maronite Christian who was more frequently referred to as *amir* (prince) rather than by his official title of *raʾis* (president).

25. Hitti, *Near East,* p. 452.

Yamani refugees established a new Druze center under the leadership of the al-Hamdan family, who by the mid-eighteenth century had been replaced as the leading Druze clan in Syria by the more numerous al-Atrash (in English, the deaf), a position they have held until the present day.

In the wake of those Druze abandoning their ancestral homes came Maronite Christian settlers who began to move south in substantial numbers, joined by Greek Orthodox and Greek Catholics from the interior of Syria, establishing themselves in districts that had previously been largely Druze. By the end of the eighteenth century the Druze had become a distinct minority in the region of the mountain that used to bear their name but had now reverted to its biblical title, the goodly mountain, Lebanon [*Jabal Lubnan*]. The name Druze Mountain survived, however, in Syria, where it came to be applied to the hilly (though hardly mountainous) region in which the Yamani Druze survivors of ʿAyn Dara had settled and begun to eke out a precarious living on the small patches of fertile soil that underlay the thick covering of volcanic stone.

In order best to represent their religiously varied subjects, the Shihabs were ambiguous in their own beliefs, often appearing to embrace all three of the leading faiths, Druzism, Maronite Christianity, and Sunni Islam. The fourth ruling prince of the Shihabi line, Mansur (1754–1770), converted to Maronite Christianity shortly after coming to power, and by the beginning of the nineteenth century the Druze branch of the family had died out, "finally setting the seal to the Druze decline."[26] Other Druze families followed suit, and those remaining loyal to their faith continued to suffer unhappily from division and internecine struggles. The Yamani-Qaysi rivalry had largely subsided with the exodus of most Yamanis to the Hawran after 1711, although one group of Yamani supporters, the Arslan clan of Shuwayfat, remained in the ancestral fiefdom that had been theirs since the earliest days of the Druze faith. A new rivalry developed between two *shaykhli* clans, the Junbalat and Yazbak, over the succession to the ruling emirate after the death of Milhim Shihab in 1754. The Junbalats were the victors in this initial confrontation,[27] but the rivalry continued to divide the Druze community intermittently, and often bitterly, up to recent times.

The rise of the Junbalat family is certainly one of the more interesting developments in the Druze history of the past two centuries. Originally linked to the Druze through the alliance between Ali Janbulad of Aleppo, who was of Kurdish origin, and the amir Fakhr al-Din II, the Janbulads were offered sanctuary in Mount Lebanon following their suppression by the Ottomans in 1607. How they came to be recognized as Druze and rose to political prominence has never been explained, and no Druze author has addressed this issue. They apparently gained acceptance in the community by marriage into the Tanukhi clan and conformity to Druze practice. By the

26. Salibi, *History of Lebanon,* p. 14.
27. See Abu-Izzeddin, *Druzes,* p. 203.

middle of the eighteenth century the leading member of the family, Shaykh Ali Junbalat, had become the most prominent chief of the mountain, enjoyed a reputation of piety, and was inducted into the ranks of the *ᶜuqqal*.

By the early part of the nineteenth century the Junbalats were more powerful than the Shihabs in men and money,[28] and a serious rivalry developed between the amir Bashir II (1788–1840) and the leading Junbalat, also named Bashir. A *shaykh* like his father, Bashir wasted no time in proclaiming his challenge to the century-old Shihabi political dominance. Among other things he built a family palace at al-Mukhtara, the traditional Junbalat family seat, which according to Colonel Churchill succeeded in "even outvieing and outshining" the amir Bashir's residence at Bayt al-Din.[29] The feud came to a head in 1825 when the amir Bashir, assisted by troops supplied by the Turkish governor of Acre (ᶜAkka) in Palestine, defeated the Junbalatis at the battle of al-Simqaniya near al-Mukhtara. Bashir Junbalat was taken prisoner and strangled in prison at Acre. With his disappearance from the scene the Druze entered a period of serious decline as the Shihabs seized Junbalat holdings, instituted large-scale confiscations of the properties of Druze *shaykhs*, forced sales of land, and generally impoverished many families, some of whom emigrated to the Jabal al-Druze in Syria.[30]

This trend was accelerated between 1833 and 1841 when Lebanon and Syria were occupied by Muhammad Ali, the ruler of Egypt whose attempts to overthrow the sultan and seize control of all Ottoman domains were finally thwarted by great-power—especially British—intervention. During their eight-year occupation, the Egyptian forces attempted to impose forced conscription of Druze youths into their army. This led to armed resistance and a general uprising in both Mount Lebanon and the Jabal al-Druze. Many Druze fled from Lebanon to their refuge in Syria, where Muhammad Ali's son, Ibrahim Pasha, was unable to impose his authority, leading to an even greater decline in the Druze population of Mount Lebanon. Smaller numbers of Druze converted to Christianity, especially to the Protestant variety offered by the recently established American missionaries who had begun to set up schools in the Druze region shortly before the Egyptian invasion.

In general, however, the American mission to the Druze was unsuccessful in its goal of large-scale conversion. A. L. Tibawi quotes missionary sources as knowing "the Druze to be 'a deceitful and truculent race' who, under changed conditions 'professed themselves Muslims with the readiness that they declared themselves Protestant.'" Anglican missionaries envisioned large-scale Druze conversions to Protestant Christianity as an outgrowth of a Druze-British alliance against the French-backed Maronites. A Reverend Nicholayson, missionary at Jerusalem, after an interview with Druze princes

28. *Ibid.*, p. 212.

29. Churchill, *Druzes and Maronites*, vol. 3, p. 298. Having seen both palaces more than a century after Churchill, I would be inclined to disagree.

30. Abu-Izzeddin, *Druzes*, p. 215.

of Lebanon, sent a letter in August 1841 to the bishop of London encouraging an Anglican mission to the Druze, and, according to the American Methodist academic John Durbin, "incipient steps were taken to accomplish the momentous project. Yet it seems to have been suddenly abandoned, both by the government and the Church but wherefore does not clearly appear."[31]

By 1841 when Ottoman power was restored, the Druze who had once been the feudal lords of southern Lebanon were now more often than not the serfs, forced to work their former lands owned by the parvenu Christians. And the Maronites, assisted by their French benefactors, continued to make inroads, even though a Druze governor (*qa'im maqam*) now ruled Lebanon south of the Beirut-Damascus road under the new Ottoman arrangement (despite the Druze having become a minority even in this, their previous heartland). The British took on the Junbalati chief, Saʿid, grandson of Bashir, as their protégé and foil to the French-supported Maronites, but the Druze were by this time a clearly declining force politically and numerically—though not militarily, as the subsequent events of 1860 were to prove.

The weakening of Druze power following the collapse of the Shihabi *imara* was accompanied by another far-reaching consequence: the internationalization of the Lebanese question. As Iliya Harik has noted, "henceforth Lebanon became an object of concern for the European powers who were squabbling for the spoils of the sick man of Europe."[32] In retrospect it was inevitable that the hostilities would persist between the ascendant Maronites with their powerful French and Vatican backing, and the recently dispossessed Druze, hopeful of British and Ottoman support to regain their former position. An untenable truce was maintained for nearly twenty years, however, before it was irrevocably shattered by the massacres during the spring and summer of 1860 (*madhabih al-sittin*). A full-scale confrontation quickly developed out of a minor incident between Druze and Maronite peasants at Dayr al-Qamar, formerly a Druze town but now a Maronite stronghold clinging to a picturesque ridge in the central Shuf. The Druze, smaller in number but militarily stronger and better organized, inflicted savage losses on the local Christian population.

More than twelve thousand Christians were killed, and thousands more fled their homes to the safety of the Maronite districts to the north. A separate but related massacre of Christians in Damascus by the Sunni pop-

31. A. L. Tibawi, *American Interests in Syria, 1800–1901* (Oxford: At the Clarendon Press, 1966), pp. 97–98; Durbin, *Observations in the East,* vol. 2, p. 94. Ann Pottinger Saab in her article on the Druze-Maronite fighting in Mount Lebanon in 1860 notes that "after the campaign which restored Syria to the Porte, Lord Palmerston [then British prime minister] had played with the idea of a 'special relationship' with the Druse, a vision made the more attractive by missionary dreams of converting the Druse to Protestantism and using them as the basis for religious influence parallel to French influence over Roman Catholics and Maronites" ("English and Irish Reaction to the Massacres in Lebanon and Syria, 1860," *Muslim World* [Jan. 1984]: 20–21).

32. Harik, *Politics and Change,* p. 35.

ulation there (encouraged, like the Druze, by the Ottoman government), further exacerbated the situation. The leader of the Lebanon Druze, Saᶜid Junbalat, was aided by a contingent from the Syrian mountain led by Ismaᶜil al-Atrash, who successfully attacked Christian positions in the predominantly Druze towns of Hasbayya and Rashayya on the western slopes of Mount Hermon.[33] An appeal by the Maronite patriarch to the emperor Napoleon III resulted in the landing of seven thousand French troops in Beirut within weeks by mid-August, under the command of the marquis Charles de Beaufort d'Hautpoul, for the ostensible purpose of restoring order and protecting Christian, largely Catholic, lives.[34] Bonaparte clearly saw this as an opportunity for reviving the French claim to the Holy Land that dated back to the Crusades, and the British were highly suspicious of French territorial designs here or anywhere else. But the emperor had very properly and cleverly consulted the signatories to the Treaty of Paris of 1856 that had concluded the Crimean conflict, in order that there could be no overt opposition. The British, along with the Prussians, Austrians, and Russians concurred in two protocols concluded with the Ottoman government of August 3, 1860, which placed the French expeditionary force under "international auspices with a time limit of six months."[35]

In actual fact, the landing of French forces in Lebanon brought that troubled land under the sphere of France for over three-quarters of a century, with only brief interruptions. The arrival of d'Hautpoul meant that Ottoman authority in the Lebanon ceased, except in theory. In 1861 the great powers signed a *reglèment organique* establishing the autonomous governate (*mutasarrifiya*) of Mount Lebanon, largely Maronite with a Druze minority,[36] to be

33. John P. Spagnolo, *France and Ottoman Lebanon, 1861–1914* (London: Ithaca Press, 1977), p. 29.

34. Saab, "English and Irish Reaction," p. 19. She notes rather wryly that efforts in Ireland to raise funds to help the Christian survivors of the 1860 massacres caused concern among the Protestant minority that the funds raised would go entirely to Catholic refugees, and a confessional breakdown of the aid recipients was requested. "Apparently it was reassuring to learn that although the refugees were seven-eighths Catholic [Maronite], one-sixteenth Greek Orthodox and one-sixteenth Greek Catholic, an estimated 120 Protestants were at risk. Thus reassured, the Irish Protestant community was forthcoming with aid monies."

35. Spagnolo, *France and Ottoman Lebanon,* p. 34.

36. *Ibid.,* p. 24. Figures dated Dec. 25, 1865, put the total population for the autonomous governate of Mount Lebanon at 266,487, of which 171,800 (64.47 percent) were Maronites and only 28,560 (10.72 percent) Druze. The rest were Greek Orthodox (29,326, or 11.00 percent), Greek Catholics (19,370, or 7.27 percent), Shia (9,820, or 3.68 percent), and Sunni Muslims (7,611, or 2.86 percent). Thirty years later, figures quoted by the same author showed an overall population increase of 50 percent to 399,530, but the Maronite percentage had slipped to 57.49 percent, due principally to emigration. The Druze share had almost doubled, to 49,812 (12.47 percent), a rise that can be explained not only by the peaceful and prosperous conditions prevailing under the *mutasarrifiya* but also to the Druze returning from Syria, where they had fled after the European intervention in 1860–1861. The figures for the four other communities of Mount Lebanon were: Greek Orthodox (54,208, or 13.57 percent), Greek Catholic (34,472, or 8.63 percent), Shia (16,846, or 4.22 percent), and Sunni Muslim (13,576, or 3.40 percent).

ruled by a Christian (but not Maronite) governor appointed from Constantinople. The first governor, Dawud Pasha, was an Armenian Catholic. He was advised on matters of policy by a central council of twelve members elected by the people and representing the communities living in the mountain: four Maronite, three Druze, and five others (for the Greek Orthodox, Greek Catholic, Sunni, and Shia Muslim communities). By this stroke the ancient feudal system (*iqta*ᶜ) of the Druze-controlled *imara* was abolished.[37] The Druze leader, Saᶜid Junbalat, abandoned by his lukewarm British supporters, was arrested by the Ottomans as a scapegoat for the Christian massacres that the Turks themselves had encouraged in order to subdue the aggressively ambitious Maronites, and he died shortly afterward in prison. The Maronites came to enjoy absolute hegemony in the land of their former Druze masters, and the Druze themselves withdrew from their traditional role as ruling princes to that of a peaceful rural mountain community, quietly distrustful of the Christian-dominated government and loyal to their tribal leaders, the Arslans of ᶜAlayh and the Junbalats of al-Mukhtara.

In Syria the Druze enjoyed greater autonomy, owing to their isolation and the absence of aggressive neighbors. The land of the Jabal al-Druze, home to the vast majority of Syrian Druze, was of marginal agricultural value and barely supported its population. It did not attract the Sunnis of the fertile Hawran plain, who were content to leave the warlike settlers from Lebanon alone. Eventually a few Christians, mostly Greek Orthodox, established their presence in a handful of villages, but their total numbers never amounted to more than 10 percent.[38] The other Syrian Druze concentration was in the Jabal al-Aᶜla, an area of barren, rocky hillsides overlooking the fertile plain of Antioch some fifty kilometers west of Aleppo. Here were found a dozen Druze villages built among the impressive ruins of the so-called Dead Cities of northern Syria, which before the Arab conquest had been major centers of Byzantine Christianity.[39] Like the Druze of the Wadi

37. Harik, *Politics and Change,* p. 36.

38. In 1927, French statistics cited by Bouron (*Les Druzes,* p. 413) counted 4,699 Christians in the Jabal al-Druze *muhafaza* (governate) out of a total population of 49,674, or 9.46 percent. The Druze numbered 44,216 (89.01 percent), Sunnis 744, and others 15. In 1943, Syrian government figures put Christians at 8,314, or 10.38 percent of the total. The Druze now numbered 70,185, or 87.59 percent, the Sunnis 1,468, and others 161. Christians were divided principally between Greek Orthodox (4,560) and Greek Catholic (2,735), with 1,019 belonging to six other communities, notably the Syrian Protestant church (389) and the Armenian Orthodox (354). The 1956 Syrian statistical abstract reflected an unchanged confessional ratio. Of the total population of the Suwaydaʾ district (115,687), the Druze numbered 102,017, or 88.18 percent, Christians 11,383 (9.95 percent), and Sunnis 2,134. The rather suspect 1960 census conducted during the Syrian-Egyptian union of 1958–1961 counted only 5,109 Christians out of a total population of 92,011, or just 5.55 percent. No distinction was made between Druze and Muslim, as President Nasser (like Muhammad Ali before him) refused to accept the Druze (or Alawis or Yazidis) as anything but vaguely lapsed members of the Muslim *umma* (nation).

39. The total Druze population of Syria in 1943 was 87,184, all but four of whom

al-Taym, the inhabitants of the Jabal al-Aʿla had been among the original recipients of the Divine Call,[40] and in their extreme isolation they were able to preserve the Druze faith and way of life they still follow today. Like their coreligionists to the south they practiced subsistence farming on bits of soil reclaimed from the rocky terrain, devoted in recent years to tobacco and the keeping of livestock.

Until the civil disturbances that began in 1975 started to undermine the Lebanese state and economy, the Syrian Druze were noticeably poorer than their Lebanese cousins, and they were regarded with mild contempt by the descendants of the lords of the Shuf as *Hawranis* (people from the Hawran district), a term that can be roughly translated as "hillbilly" or "country bumpkin." They were also traditionally more tribal and warlike. Travelers frequently commented on the difference between the Druze of Mount Lebanon and Palestine and their wilder cousins who inhabited the fringe of the Syrian desert. On visiting the Jabal al-Druze stronghold of Salkhad in the 1880s, Gray Hill observed that its Druze inhabitants were "quite wanting in that grace of bearing and courtesy displayed by the Druses of Mount Carmel."[41] Under the leadership of the Atrash family, which dominated the political affairs of the region (the southern half in particular), the Druze inhabitants of this southern-Syrian enclave jealously and militantly guarded their autonomy. Feared as a fierce and warlike nation, they were no more subject to the governor of Damascus a hundred miles to the north than were the inhabitants of southern Arabia subject to the sultan in Constantinople. Although they were separated from the Druze of the Wadi al-Taym and Mount Lebanon by the farming district of Hawran with its predominantly Sunni Muslim population (intermingled with a substantial scattering of mainly Greek Catholic Christians), there was nevertheless regular contact between the two major Druze concentrations, and often one area served as a place of refuge for inhabitants of the other in times of trouble.

Distrustful of the Ottomans since the time of Fakhr al-Din, the Druze were in frequent revolt against the authority of the Turk—or of anyone else

---

were found in the Jabal al-Druze and the neighboring Damascus governate (70,185 and 15,194 respectively), the latter including a number of Druze villages on the Syrian slope of Mount Hermon, and in the Aleppo governate (1,601), which included the Jabal al-Aʿla. This last figure seems quite small in view of the thirty thousand to forty thousand living there today. The Druze community of Aleppo city had long since ceased to exist, but the family name of Halabi (someone from Aleppo, in Arabic, *Halab*) was still common among the Druze of Galilee and the northernmost villages of the Jabal al-Druze.

40. Abu-Izzeddin notes that "the faithfulness of the community in the Jabal al-Aʿlā is also reflected in the epithet Bahāʾ al-Dīn applies to the mountain which he calls the *Jabal al-Anwār,* the Mountain of Brilliant Light" (*Druzes,* p. 107). The area was also known as the *Jabal al-Summaq,* a name still applied to it by the local Druze. *Summaq* is the Arabic version of sumac, a very acid and bitter seed used in Arab—particularly Aleppo—cooking. The name could also come from the Arabic root *SMQ* meaning to be high, lofty, towering.

41. Hill, *Beduins,* p. 267.

who tried to impose his will on them, as Ibrahim Pasha discovered during the Egyptian occupation of Syria during 1833–1841. In 1896, thirty thousand Turkish soldiers invested the Jabal al-Druze to try to enforce military conscription. Some two hundred Druze notables were exiled to Anatolia, and whole villages were abandoned as most of the mountain's inhabitants filtered away into the desert. Foiled at every turn, the Turks eventually released their captives and abandoned their plans to draft young Druze into the army.

Within three years things were back to normal. But not for long. During 1909–1910 rebellion broke out once again, and after months of vicious warfare the Druze leaders were lured to Damascus by the Turks on the pretext of treating for peace. And once again, according to Bouron, "l'ineffable crédulité des Druzes . . . les jette désarmés sous le couteau de leurs ennemis," resulting in the execution of their leadership, among them the father of the Syrian nationalist figure, Sultan al-Atrash.[42] His dying words to his onlookers, as related by one source, were: "Tell my people never to trust a Turk."[43] It is probably safe to say that to this day they do not. Nor the Turks them, for the term *derzi* is still in common use in Turkish as a synonym for a liar or worse. The Sunni Muslim establishment likewise has traditionally distrusted the Druze not only for their insistence on maintaining their distance from orthodox Islam, which is always eager to embrace them, but also because devotion to their community above all else makes them unreliable in any intercommunal dealings. As a member of one of Jerusalem's two highest-ranking Sunni families confided to me, the Druze are "a detestable [*laᶜin*] people."

There were of course exceptions to the Druze pattern of separation from the Ottoman Muslim establishment, the most prominent being Prince Shakib Arslan, the father of May Junbalat, wife of Kamal and mother of Walid. Throughout his long and illustrious life (1869–1946) he was a champion of the pan-Islamic ideal and, after the irrevocable collapse of the Ottoman Empire, Muslim Arab nationalism.[44] Mistrustful suspicion of the

42. Bouron, *Les Druzes,* p. 218. According to Dr. (later Ambassador) Jabir al-Atrash, the insurrection of 1910, known as the War of Sami Pasha (after the Turkish general in charge of its suppression), was the most terrible of all the Druze-Turkish confrontations, resulting in the burning of 150 villages and the execution of thirty Druze leaders by hanging (Atrash, "Législation Coutoumière chez les Druzes du Hauran," unpublished Doctorate of Law thesis, University of Saint-Joseph, Beirut, Lebanon, 1946, p. 25).

43. Seabrook, *Adventures in Arabia,* p. 169. A year earlier, in 1909, a young Druze deputy to the revived Ottoman Parliament of the Young Turks, the *amir* Muhammad Arslan, was murdered in the chamber itself during the abortive countercoup led by the forces of Sultan Abdulhamit (Francis Yeats-Brown, *Golden Horn,* London: Victor Gollancz, 1932, p. 52).

44. Cleveland, *Islam,* pp. xvi, xvii. As an example of *taqiya* in recent times, his paternal uncle, Mustafa Arslan, the *qaʾim maqam* of al-Shuf district and leading figure of the Arslan family, was given Sunni, not Druze, funeral rites on his death in 1910 (*ibid.,* p. 4, citing Hitti, *Origins of the Druze,* p. 48). Despite his Druze birth and strong Sunni Muslim association throughout his life, however, Shakib and his brothers, like most prominent Druze to this day, were educated in French Maronite schools (*ibid.,* p. xvii).

majority, however, helped keep the Druze isolated from their neighbors and fiercely loyal to their own group. It also made them an ideal target for the French, British, and later Israeli occupying forces seeking to undermine Arab nationalism and its quest for Arab unity in the wake of the Ottoman collapse after World War I.

6

The Druze under British and French Mandate and the Independent States of Lebanon, Syria, and Israel

Following the fall of the Ottoman Empire on October 30, 1918, the Druze passed from the hands of a weak but traditionally Islamic authoritarian ruler to those of nominally Christian European industrial powers, who governed in the name of the recently established international political arbiter, the League of Nations. The people of Greater Syria were generally less than pleased with this transfer. The Sunni Muslim majority had hoped for the establishment of an independent Arab state in which they would have been included, but the serious contender for the achievement of this task, the sharif Husayn of Mecca, had been outmaneuvered by his erstwhile British allies at the Versailles and San Remo peace conferences (1918–1920), and he eventually lost even his own base of power in the Hijaz (1924) to Bedouin *Wahhabi* upstarts from the interior of the Arabian peninsula.

Husayn had tried in vain to dislodge the

French, who had forcibly imposed themselves on Syria, fired by a centuries-old ambition to reestablish their presence in the Holy Land and encouraged by appeals for protection from local Christians, especially the fanatically Francophile Maronites. At a decisive confrontation at Maysalun on the Damascus-Beirut road, the French defeated Husayn's pan-Arab forces on July 24, 1920. It was a severe blow for the Arab nationalist movement, which had grown out of the revival of Arabic as a language of instruction in the nineteenth century (partly, though by no means entirely, as the result of the establishment of American Protestant Mission schools). Those idealists who had envisioned a unified Arab state saw instead the Arabic-speaking territories of the sultan's domains divided into British and French spheres of influence.

The Druze, unlike the Arab Christians (especially the Greek Orthodox), had not been active in the Nationalist movement. The Druze and the Christians of Mount Lebanon had benefited from the schools established by foreign mission groups, particularly those set up by the American Protestants in a number of Druze towns and villages to the south and east, notably ʿAlayh, ʿUbayh, Shuwayfat, and Baʿqlin. Few of the Druze had any sympathy for those pan-Arab aims of Sharif Husayn so enthusiastically championed by their Sunni and Greek Orthodox neighbors. But what they genuinely feared was the imposition of French authority, not because of any particular dislike of the French themselves but because of France's traditional alliance with the Maronites, whom the Druze suspected would use French support to push even deeper into those districts remaining to them after 1860. What they hoped for more than anything else was inclusion within the sphere of influence of their sometime ally of the previous century, the British. This decision was, of course, not theirs to make. The final definition of the lines dividing the Fertile Crescent between France and Britain, which had first been discussed by Sykes and Picot in 1915,[1] gave all but a handful of Druze villages over to the French Mandate of Syria in 1920. Only the sixteen Druze settlements in Galilee, their two villages on Mount Carmel, and the half-Druze oasis of al-Azraq in the Syrian desert passed under the preferred British Mandates of Palestine and Transjordan.

The Druze in Lebanon and Syria, 1920–1975

The Druze of Syria, who had no Maronites in their vicinity to concern them, were at first more easily dealt with than the Druze of Mount Lebanon. No territory lent itself more readily to the principle of divide and rule than did

1. Mark Sykes and Georges Picot were the British and French plenipotentiaries respectively who drew up a secret agreement in 1916 by which the Ottoman Empire was to be divided into various Allied spheres of influence after World War I. See George Antonius, *The Arab Awakening* (London: Hamish Hamilton, 1939), pp. 248ff.

Syria in 1920. Most of the Sunni Arab majority was neatly confined to a narrow corridor stretching from Dirʿa (Deraa) in the south, north through Damascus, Hims (Homs), and Hama to Aleppo. The territory conveniently included large numbers of Christians, who, if not entirely resigned as in the case of the Orthodox to the inevitability of French rule, were in large part sympathetic to it. The other regions of the mandate had dominant minorities who were quite willing to accept French control in return for autonomy. The Alawis of the Jabal al-ʿAnsariya were given their own *Pays des Alaouites,* where they greatly outnumbered the Sunnis of the coastal towns and the Orthodox Christians of the southern hills (the Valley of the Christians—*Wadi al-Nasara*—in the shadow of the Krak des Chevaliers, the greatest of all Crusader bastions) and the minority presence of the Orthodox Christians among the Sunnis in Latakia and Tartus (Tortosa of Crusader times).

The Maronites of Lebanon, as a reward for their faithful subservience to French interests, were given the loaded prize of an enlarged *mutasarrifiya,* the *Grand Liban* (Greater Lebanon) that became an independent republic two decades later and that included within its expanded boundaries an increased number of other sects and a bare majority of Christians, which was soon to evaporate. It was into this explosive melting pot that the Druze of Mount Lebanon were poured.

The various Christian refugees from Turkish massacres in Anatolia—Armenians, Syrian Orthodox, and Chaldean Catholics—who had been resettled in the sparsely populated region of the Jazira between the Tigris and Euphrates rivers, were allowed to dominate the more numerous but largely nomadic Kurds and Arabs who roamed the marginal grasslands between the two ancient river valleys. The fertile district of Antioch and Alexandretta, like Lebanon an odd mixture of many sects (Sunni Arabs, Kurds, Turks and Turcomans, Alawis, Armenian and Greek Orthodox Christians), was likewise given autonomous status, a condition that facilitated its annexation by Turkey on the eve of World War II.

Finally, the Jabal al-Druze with its 90 percent Druze majority was granted similar autonomy, in which the French recognized the tribal authority of the dominant al-Atrash family. A semi-independent state was quite acceptable to the Druze of southern Syria, though they would have preferred a similar arrangement under the British. Where the agreement came adrift, however, was over the actual extent of Druze independence, the internal authority of the Atrash, and the overriding power of the French Mandate government, as the events of the 1925 uprising were to demonstrate.

The so-called Druze Rebellion of 1925–1927 grew out of a series of classic colonial blunders by the French Mandate administration. Much of the fault can be directly laid at the door of the French high commissioner, General Maurice Sarrail, appointed in December 1924. Stephen Longrigg describes him as "ageing, authoritarian, and impatient," and considers his selection as "almost the most unhappy imaginable."[2] The internal political situation of the French mandated territories, while ultimately untenable, was not yet on the verge of crisis. But already in the Jabal al-Druze there were signs of discontent. The Franco-Druze Agreement of 1921 had specified that the governor of the autonomous district should be a Druze. But since July 1923 a French army officer, Captain Carbillet, had held the office, temporarily at first with Druze approval, then permanently—over continued objections—as from October 1924. Determined to impose the benefits of modern French society on a population puzzled by the sudden flurry of road building and village cleanups, upset by the establishment of secular schools and courts, and outraged by successful tax collection, Carbillet soon found himself circumvented by deputations of Druze complaining directly to Damascus and Beirut.

This was not the first time the Druze had voiced strong protest over French rule. The most celebrated incident had occurred three years earlier in July 1922, when a Lebanese Shia nationalist, Adham Khanjar, suspected of involvement in the unsuccessful assassination attempt on the French high commissioner, General Henri Gouraud, as he motored from Zahlah to Damascus on June 23, 1921, was arrested near Sultan al-Atrash's home at al-Qurayyah. A number of Druze had heard Khanjar declare that he was a guest of Sultan al-Atrash, and although he never reached his intended sanctuary it was enough for them that this was his goal. The French, unaware or uncaring of what it meant to be the guest of a tribal ruler in Arabia, threw him into prison in al-Suwayda'. When Atrash heard of the incident he hastily organized a party of followers who ambushed the French convoy, killing a lieutenant and injuring others. It took the better part of a year for the governor, Salim al-Atrash, to restore order, and it was not until Druze Independence Day of the following year (April 5, 1923) that Sultan was granted amnesty. But the unrest that the unfortunate incident had provoked remained perilously near the surface.[3]

2. Stephen Hemsley Longrigg, *Syria and Lebanon under French Mandate* (London: Oxford University Press, 1958), p. 148.

3. Bouron, *Les Druzes,* pp. 229–30, and *Oriente Moderno* 2 (1922): 223–24. Also, George Haddad, *Fifty Years of Modern Syria and Lebanon* (Beirut: Dar al-Hayat, 1950), p. 73. Seabrook, *Adventures in Arabia,* writing closer to the events, gives a very colorful account, relating that when Sultan al-Atrash heard of the arrest of his intended guest, "he burst into tears and sang the Druze war song:

> We are the Children of Maruf!
> Among our rocks is sanctuary.
> When our spears grow rusty we make them bright
> With the blood of our enemies.

When he had finished singing he prayed, and sent a letter to the French governor at Suwayda saying, 'This man, though he had not set foot in my house, was coming as my guest,

General Sarrail, deeply anticlerical and as unimpressed by the protestations of Druze *shaykhs* as he was by those of Maronite bishops, arrested three prominent Druze leaders on July 11, 1925, and banished them to Palmyra. Sultan al-Atrash and his followers immediately responded with open rebellion. A French column of some two hundred men camped at Basra al-Sham (Bosra), where it was helping a French archaeological expedition clear the site of the splendid Roman theater there, was dispatched to rescue several stranded airmen shot down by Atrash forces on July 18 at Salkhad.[4] The column was totally annihilated on July 21 at the village of Kafar, a few miles to the southeast of al-Suwayda'. A major army was hastily organized, and it set out from the French garrison at the Christian town of Izra' on the Hijaz railway north of Dir'a in the Hawran on August 2. Composed of some one thousand French soldiers and two thousand poorly trained Syrians and troops from the French African colonies, this hapless force was fallen upon at night by Druze fighters as it entered the autonomous Druze territory at Mazra'a, seven miles west of al-Suwayda'. The entire convoy was captured; more than eight hundred officers and men were lost to death, wounds, capture, or desertion. The commander of the French colonials committed suicide on the battlefield, and the French general, Michaud, was recalled to France. The French garrison at al-Suwayda' bravely held out for two months but elsewhere in the Jabal al-Druze Mandate authority ceased to exist.

Emboldened by the unexpected scale of his victory, and armed with "two thousand rifles, a battery of artillery, and a large quantity of ammunition and supplies,"[5] Sultan al-Atrash found himself a hero not only to his own people but also to Syrian nationalists throughout the country, who had previously regarded the separatist Druze as the least likely source of a call to arms against French rule. The nationalist leaders in Damascus, notably 'Abd al-Rahman Shahbandar, founder of the *Hizb al-Sha'b* (the People's party), suddenly adopted the Druze forces as the vanguard of an independent Arab Syria, while Sultan al-Atrash was hailed as a fighter for the nationalist cause. It was a role that Sultan was willing to accept at the time, but not all the Syrian Druze shared his view. The Atrash clan had its rivals and enemies within the community, and many of the Jabal amirs (whom Longrigg describes as representing "very varying stages of evolution from the fully Europeanized to the primitive")[6] were highly suspicious of any involvement in affairs outside the world of peculiarly Druze interests. Nor was the Lebanese

---

and I beg you by our Sacred Laws of hospitality to free him on my word until his cause may be heard'" (p. 171). When the French ignored his plea, al-Atrash was obliged by honor to take action.

4. Maurice Dunand, *Mission archéologique au Djebel Druze* (Paris: Librairie Orientantaliste, 1934), p. 4.

5. Longrigg, *Syria and Lebanon,* p. 154. See also Bouron, *Les Druzes,* pp. 242–43.

6. *Ibid.,* p. 245. For an account of the rivalry between the al-Atrash and al-Sha'bi clans, see Arberry, *Religion,* vol. 2, p. 347.

Druze community more than marginally supportive. While the rebellion spread to a number of towns and cities in Syria, notably the conservative Sunni bastion of Hama, only the predominantly Druze town of Rashayya in southeastern Lebanon felt the brunt of actual fighting, and in late November the siege, led by Zayd al-Atrash, younger brother of Sultan, was relieved. In the meantime, retaliation by French forces had resulted in the burning and pillaging of a number of Druze villages.[7]

By late April 1926 the French had suppressed the uprising throughout Syria and restored their authority in much of the Jabal al-Druze after ten months of anarchy. Sultan al-Atrash withdrew to al-Azraq just across the border in Transjordan. He returned briefly but, following an agreement between the British and French at the Foreign Ministry level, was forced to seek refuge among the Wahhabis in the Najd (what is today central Saudi Arabia) during the summer of 1927. A number of Sultan's supporters, however, were allowed to remain at al-Azraq in Transjordan, and he retained the status of a heroic leader among many of his own people—as well as a considerable number of Syrian nationalists.

A French governor was once again in command from al-Suwayda', but a historic rapprochement had been effected between the Sunni-Greek Orthodox nationalist clique of Damascus and the leading family of the Syrian Druze establishment, previously shunned as a counterrevolutionary element in the pan-Arab movement. The Druze were to be increasingly accepted as participants in the fight for independence from European domination, and as a result they were steadily drawn out of the cocoon of their self-imposed isolation into ever-increasing contact with the highly politicized society around them.

But the immediate impact of the Druze Rebellion was clearly negative in terms of Syrian nationalist goals. On May 24, 1926, a month after French authority in the Jabal al-Druze had been restored, the French proclaimed a constitutional republic of Greater Lebanon. Twelve senators were appointed by the French high commissioner, who with the Chamber of Deputies elected Charles Dabbas, a Greek Orthodox lawyer, as president. The intent of the new high commissioner, Henri de Jouvenel, was twofold: to reassure the Christians of Lebanon who had felt threatened by the 1925 uprising (especially the incursion into their territory at Rashayya) and to send a message to the Syrian nationalists that armed revolt was counterproductive to their unionist aims.

7. One example of this occurred on October 15, 1925, when Circassian soldiers destroyed the Druze village of Jarmana in the Ghuta near Damascus. "Two days later, the corpses of 12 Circassians still dressed in their French uniforms were discovered lying outside Bab al-Sharqi [east entrance to the Christian quarter of Damascus]." Philip S. Khoury, *Syria and the French Mandate: The Politics of Arab Nationalism, 1920–1945* (Princeton: Princeton University Press, 1987), p. 175.

The long-term result of these moves was not, however, what the French had intended. Because of its unrealistic borders, the Lebanese state, created to assuage Christian fears, has become a Levantine powder keg that sixty years later threatens international order. The Syrian nationalist movement, meanwhile, continued to grow in popular support and political success. In 1932 the Syrian Nationalist party (the *Parti Populaire Syrien,* or the PPS) was formed as a secret society at the American University of Beirut by Antun Saʿada, a Greek Orthodox Lebanese demagogue brought up in Brazil by his emigrant parents and partly educated in Germany. In 1935 it became an open political party whose force is still strongly felt in the area today. In some respects the Baʿth party of Syria today is an outgrowth of the PPS movement, and President Hafiz al-Asad is very much the product of its primary message of a Greater Syrian secular society.[8] In 1936 the French were forced to come to terms with the realities of Syria a decade and a half after the mandate had been established, just as the British had been coerced into doing four years earlier in Iraq. Two treaties were signed by France that recognized both Lebanon and Syria as independent states and sovereign members of the League of Nations.[9] A French military presence, however, remained in both states until the end of the Second World War.

An integral part of the Franco-Syrian agreement of 1936 was the restoration of the Jabal al-Druze, the *Pays des Alaouites* (Latakia), and the Jazira autonomous regions to central nationalist control from Damascus.[10] All three resisted this centrifugal development, but the Druze Mountain was the least problematic. With the absence of any significant minority (other than the very docile and cooperative 10 percent who were Christians), it was only a matter of Damascus establishing once again the traditionally accepted role of local tribal leadership, notably the Atrash family. The problems that arose between 1936 and the outbreak of World War II were largely ones of internal Druze bickering over which member of the Atrash family would have control. The Suwaydaʾ *muhafaza* was given five seats in the Syrian Parliament of 1937, three of which were allotted to Druze and one each to Greek Orthodox and Bedouin Arab representatives.[11]

8. Although very much a representative of Syria's Alawite minority, particularly those from his region of the northern Latakia district, al-Asad's aims are clearly nationalistic and deeply opposed to Sunni Muslim fundamentalist revival. Both the Baʿth and the PPS in their original manifestos called for a Syrian Arab society free from religious prejudice and established confessional privilege.

9. Lebanon on Nov. 17, 1936, and Syria on Dec. 27, 1936.

10. Only the autonomous *sanjaq* of Alexandretta was allowed to retain its separate status, and in 1939 it was permitted to join the Republic of Turkey, even though its population was at most 40 percent Turkish and Turcoman, as a final lesson to Syrian nationalist intransigence and a sop to Turkey in order to encourage its neutrality as war clouds once again enveloped Europe.

11. Longrigg, *Syria and Lebanon,* p. 246. The leading figure in this confrontation was

The Druze of Lebanon enjoyed no comparable autonomy during the French Mandate period. Although they represented a larger share of the total population (nearly 7 percent according to official statistics, as opposed to barely 3 percent in Syria), they were not in one homogeneous concentration but intermixed with larger numbers of other religious communities, especially Maronite Christians. Although they lived in close proximity to each other in villages that were entirely or predominantly Druze, the boundaries of the country's districts (*muhafazat*) and subdistricts (*aqdiya*ʾ) were such that the Druze were never a majority. Only in the subdistrict (*qada*ʾ) of ʿAlayh (Aley) did they approach half the population—46.7 percent according to the French-conducted census of 1932, the last to be taken in this century. In three other subdistricts—al-Shuf, Rashayya, and Hasbayya—they were roughly one-third of the population. In Bʿabda they numbered less than one-fifth of the total, and in the remaining subdistricts their presence was minimal (as in al-Matn and the district of Beirut) or nonexistent.

Since the Lebanese Druze had no secure geographical base from which to lobby for any kind of autonomous regional authority and too small to demand any kind of powerful role in national affairs, which were dominated by the two largest sects (the Maronite Christians and the Sunni Muslims), they had to be content with the one privilege granted to them by the French that they had not enjoyed under the Ottomans—the right officially to administer their own civil affairs according to the laws and customs of their own community.[12] The Maronites and most other Christians would have been quite happy to have continued living under French protection indefinitely, but the rising tide of Arab nationalism among the Sunni Muslim and the collapse of France following Germany's invasion of 1940 brought the issue of independence to a head rather sooner than anyone had anticipated.

On the last day of December 1943, a fully independent Syria and Lebanon were proclaimed under the watchful eye of the Free French forces occupying the former mandates. Agreements had previously been reached between the leaders of the various communities guaranteeing the security and political representation of minority groups, and in Lebanon this took the form of the so-called National Covenant (*al-mithaq al-watani*)—an unwritten constitutional agreement between the leading Maronite and Sunni

---

a cousin of Sultan, Hasan al-Atrash, whom the Damascus government appointed governor of the Suwaydaʾ district in 1938 after it withdrew its earlier candidate, a Muslim (see Albert Hourani, *Syria and Lebanon: A Political Essay* (London: Oxford University Press, 1946), p. 214.

12. Article 9 of the constitution of Lebanon of 1926 states: "Liberty of conscience is absolute. In rendering homage to the Most High, the State respects all confessions and guarantees and protects the free exercise of them. . . . It also guarantees their personal status and their religious interests." (My translation from the French; for a complete English translation of the 1926 constitution see Helen Miller Davis, *Constitutions, Electoral Laws, Treaties of States in the Near and Middle East*, Durham: Duke University Press, 1947, pp. 170–185.)

political figures[13]—that established a system whereby the principal powers of government would be shared by these two major groups (28.72 percent and 22.45 percent of the total resident population respectively according to the 1932 census). All the religious communities were to be given a proportional share of seats in the unicameral Parliament based on that census. A ratio of six Christians for every five Muslim and Druze deputies was agreed upon, so that the total parliamentary membership had to be a multiple of eleven (the smallest ever to be elected in Lebanon's history was forty-four, the largest, ninety-nine).

Deputies were to be elected from each subdistrict from lists including candidates for all the confessionally allotted seats. Each candidate faced all the voters, thus discouraging fanatics of either side: Sunnis or Druze would be as unlikely to vote for a narrowly nationalistic Maronite as the Maronites for a Muslim fundamentalist. The cabinet, drawn from the elected deputies by the Sunni prime minister with the approval of the Maronite president (who was elected by Parliament and in turn selected his prime minister), was also to reflect Lebanon's confessional makeup. Since independence, therefore, there has been a Druze minister in every government except one;[14] occasionally there have been two, so as to satisfy both the Junbalati and Yazbaki factions. Deputy ministers, district governors, the diplomatic and civil services, as well as the officer corps of the national armed forces were likewise subject to confessional considerations, though the mathematical ratios were not so strictly imposed and usually worked in favor of the Christians.[15]

In Syria the Druze were at first reluctant to join an independent state

13. Riyad al-Sulh (assassinated in 1951 by a PPS extremist) and Bishara al-Khuri, who became Lebanon's first president, 1946–1952.

14. The exception occurred in 1975 following the outbreak of the hostilities that heralded the beginning of Lebanon's civil war. President al-Faranjiya appointed an unknown Sunni retired army officer, Nur al-Din al-Rifaʿi, as prime minister in an attempt to impose military rule. His brief cabinet was divided among the four major sects only: Maronites, Sunnis, Shias, and Greek Orthodox.

15. An example is the Lebanese diplomatic service. Ralph Crow, "Religious Sectarianism in Lebanese Politics," *Journal of Politics* 24 (Aug. 1962): 489–520, points out that between 1955 and 1961 Christians held 60 percent of Lebanese diplomatic posts abroad (the Maronites alone holding 40 percent, though officially only 29 percent of the population); of the remaining 40 percent, 27 percent were held by the Sunnis (officially 22 percent of the population). The Druze were slightly overrepresented, holding 7.25 percent of the posts compared with their official share of 6.7 percent of the population (*ibid.*, p. 518). Some Druze even rose to the rank of ambassador, among them ʿAbdallah al-Najjar, author of *The Druze*. The first twenty-six governments of the Republic of Lebanon, 1943–1961, were served by 208 cabinet ministers: 106 Christian and 102 Muslim and Druze. Within the latter category, the Druze, though only one-third as numerous as the Shia, were given nearly twice as many cabinet posts. This imbalance, however, has not been reflected in most governments since then. Yet underrepresentation of the Shia has been a fairly consistent feature of the overall power structure of Lebanon since independence, and their current dissatisfaction should come as no great surprise. Though they form about 30 percent of the population, they hold few diplomatic positions.

dominated by the Sunni establishment that they generally distrusted. After the withdrawal of the last French forces in 1946, serious unrest erupted over the issue of the representation of the Druze community in the Syrian Chamber of Deputies. Two factions, the Turshan (plural of Atrash) and the Abu Asali, disputed control of the choice of parliamentary delegates for nearly two years. By 1947 Sultan al-Atrash and his followers had triumphed, and their defeated opponents fled in large numbers to Jordan, augmenting the already considerable Druze community at al-Zarqaʾ.[16] The new government, moreover, favored the abolition of Druze representation at the ministerial level, and Sultan al-Atrash took serious exception to this. There were other complaints, too, such as the neglect of the Jabal al-Druze district in education and transportation. Many Syrian Druze, including the Anglophile al-Atrash, favored union with Transjordan, where he and his followers felt they would be granted greater autonomy. Neither the Druze nor the Jordanians were sufficiently strong (or in the Jordanian case sufficiently interested) to carry out such a territorial transfer, but there is no doubt that the Druze failed to thrive under early Syrian administrations. Although granted representation in Parliament and given a cabinet post in the short-lived Husni Zaʿim government of 1949,[17] the Druze were viewed with distrust in Damascus, particularly after the first Arab-Israeli war of 1948–1949, in which the Druze were seen by the Sunnis as having cooperated with the Israelis, at least tacitly, in the successful establishment of the Zionist state.

Suspicions as to their loyalty became even more pronounced when Druze from the villages of Galilee, now part of Israel, began serving in the Israeli armed forces. During the regime of Adib al-Shishakli (1950–1954), Druze rights in Syria were seriously curtailed. Many Syrian Druze sought refuge in Lebanon, and others were jailed or murdered outright when the army opened fire on Druze demonstrators in Sultan al-Atrash's home village of al-Qurayyah in the summer of 1953. Druze leadership was active in the events that led to Shishakli's overthrow (precipitated largely by the imprisonment of the Druze leader, Hasan al-Atrash), and full revenge was taken in 1964 when Shishakli, by this time in exile in Brazil, was assassinated by a Druze, Nawas al-Ghazali, at his farm at Ceres in the state of Goias, where he had been living since 1960.[18]

16. Moshe Zeltzer, *Aspects of Near East Society* (New York: Bookman Associates, 1962), p. 32, and Laurent and Annie Chabry, *Politique et minorités au Proche-Orient* (Paris: Editions Maisonneuve and Larose, 1984), p. 209.

17. Of 135 seats in the Syrian Parliament, three were allotted to the Druze, all from the Suwaydaʾ district. A fourth deputy from this district was a Greek Orthodox Christian (Haddad, *Modern Syria and Lebanon*, pp. 111–12). ʿAdil Arslan served as deputy prime minister and foreign minister during the short-lived government of Husni Zaʿim (Mar. 30–Aug. 14, 1949). He had been a cofounder of the pan-Arab *Istiqlal* (Independence) party in the 1920s.

18. Patrick Seale, *The Struggle for Syria: A Study of Post-War Arab Politics, 1945–1958* (London: Oxford University Press, 1965), p. 147. Also Gordon H. Torrey, *Syrian Politics and the Military, 1945–1958* (Columbus: Ohio State University Press, 1959), pp. 233–35.

Sultan al-Atrash continued to be a towering influence in the local affairs of the Jabal al-Druze (which the Sunni-dominated nationalist government had officially renamed the Jabal al-ʿArab, or Mountain of the Arabs)[19] until his death in 1982 at age 95 (the Israelis opened the border from the Golan to allow Syrian Druze, unilaterally annexed to Israel four months earlier, to attend the funeral). But it was his son Mansur, a political ally of Michel ʿAflaq (the Christian cofounder of the presently ruling Baʿth party), who took the active role in Syrian politics, serving as a cabinet minister in several Syrian governments.

The real path to power for minorities in Syria, however, proved to be via the armed forces. The Alawites of the Latakia district, the country's poorest and politically least powerful community, were especially drawn to the army as a career, although many Druze and some Christians were likewise attracted. In the secular atmosphere of the military, a person's religious background was less of a factor in his advancement than it was in the more public political sphere. While most of the very senior officers were taken from the Sunni Muslim majority, many Alawis, Druze, and even Christians reached positions of importance in the army and air force.[20] During Syria's 1958–1961 union with Egypt, the communal system in the political structure of Syria was abolished. Following the coup that brought the Baʿth (Renaissance) party to power in 1963, the government ceased to recognize any specific representational rights of minorities. The Sunni Muslims as the majority community were given a token of special recognition in the provisional constitution of April 25, 1964, which specified Islam as a qualification for the office of president and recognized Islamic law as "a major source" of legislation. But the Baʿthi government, reflecting the intensely secular bias of its ideology, actively tried to downplay the role of religion in government.

The Baʿth had attracted a disproportionately large minority membership ever since its formation in 1940 by two Damascene political theorists, the Greek Orthodox Christian Michal ʿAflaq and the Sunni Muslim Salah al-Din al-Bitar. With the coming of the Baʿth to power in 1963, the Druze found themselves if anything proportionally overrepresented in the new military government. The forces that spearheaded the Baʿthi coup of March 8, 1963, had been led by a Druze officer from al-Suwaydaʾ, Captain Salim Hatum,

19. A similar example of the erasure of a regional name with confessional connotations was the change of name for the Wadi al-Nasara (Valley of the Christians), a large area of southern Latakia province that is almost entirely Greek Orthodox, now called in government publications the Wadi al-Nadara (Valley of the Flowers). As in the case of the Jabal al-Druze, however, popular usage overwhelmingly favors the traditional name.

20. One Druze officer by the name of Zahr al-Din reached the rank of general before the Baʿthi era, and in September 1961 was chosen to be the nominal head of the Syrian Army, "since as a respectable but powerless senior officer he was considered a convenient and harmless choice." Itamar Rabinovich, *Syria under the Baʿth, 1963–1966* (Jerusalem: Israel Universities Press, 1972), p. 32.

though the officers who quickly emerged from obscurity as the new government was formed were the Alawis Lieutenant Colonel Salah al-Jadid and Captain Hafiz al-Asad. The Druze-Alawi factions were very soon in conflict.

During the period 1963–1966 the Baʿth government presented a public picture of nonsectarianism. But beneath the surface the deep rivalry between the older Sunni officers and the rising Alawi element brought in with the new government led to an attempt in late 1965 by the leading Sunni figure, Amin al-Hafiz, to overpower the growing strength of the Latakia upstarts. Until this point the Druze element in the army and the party had not been closely associated with al-Jadid or other Alawis, and there was certainly no traditional alliance between the two groups (who had little in common other than a very distant Shia connection in their early development and secrecy in their religious rites). The leading figure of the extreme Left within the party had been a Druze, Hamud al-Shufi, who served briefly as the elected secretary-general of the Syrian Regional Command (made up of five civilians and three military officers). But at the Sixth National Congress of the Syrian Baʿth party held in 1964, al-Shufi and his extremist faction were outvoted and replaced in the Regional Command by a more moderate group.[21]

Whether or not al-Shufi's ideological persuasion cast suspicion on other Druze in the eyes of the Sunni leaders cannot definitely be ascertained, but when it became clear that the latter were out to purge the army and party of al-Jadid, al-Asad, and the Alawis in general as a major force within both the army and the government, four important members of the power structure and previous supporters of Amin al-Hafiz transferred their loyalty to al-Jadid. Three of the four were Druze: General Hamad ʿUbayd, the new minister of defense, Jamil al-Shayyaʿ, a member of the Regional Command, and the former Captain now Major Salim Hatum.[22] This defection gave al-Jadid the power he needed, and on February 23, 1966, he staged a successful coup that overthrew al-Hafiz and brought his fellow Alawis into the position of power they have held ever since.

The coup was followed almost immediately by an Extraordinary Regional Congress of the Baʿth party, at which it was made strikingly clear that, despite their support, the Druze were not to be a significant part of the new government. Only al-Shayyaʿ was reelected to the Regional Command. General ʿUbayd was purged from the party and army and replaced as minister of defense by none other than Hafiz al-Asad, who within four years swept aside his former colleague al-Jadid and established himself as Syria's absolute, if intermittently benevolent, dictator.[23]

21. *Ibid.*, pp. 180, 192.

22. *Ibid.*, p. 181. The fourth defector was Mustafa Talas, a Sunni, who survives to the present day as deputy prime minister and minister of defense, one of the key Muslims in an otherwise tightly Alawi-controlled government.

23. Nikolaos van Dam, *The Struggle for Power in Syria: Sectarianism, Regionalism and Tribalism in Politics, 1961–1978* (London: Croom Helm, 1979), pp. 69–70.

Major Hatum was particularly bitter about his having been passed over after contributing "a lion's share in the execution of the February 23rd, 1966 *coup*."[24] Feeling that he had been betrayed by al-Jadid, Hatum began to build up his own military organization, drawn mostly from junior Druze officers, and a civilian network of members and supporters of the al-Shufi group, also mostly Druze. Anticipating Hatum's move, al-Jadid issued warrants in late August 1966 for the arrest of leading Druze in the army, including Fahd al-Shaʿir, the highest-ranking Druze officer.[25] Fearing—with good reason—that he had been discovered, Hatum quickly staged an abortive coup on September 8, fleeing to Jordan with his key supporters once it became clear that he had failed. In the wake of his fiasco many Druze were arrested, and most of those still in the army and party were purged and replaced by Alawis. The persecution of the Druze continued unabated for six months and began to ease only after Sultan al-Atrash sent an open telegram to the Syrian General Staff in December 1966 complaining of Druze sufferings.[26] Still, the situation remained tense, and it was many years before the Druze once again had confidence in the Damascus government. In the meantime many Syrian Druze quietly emigrated to Lebanon and abroad to await better days at home.

In contrast to the upheavals in Syria, Lebanon was enjoying golden years of peace, prosperity, and political calm. Unlike Syria, it had no national civil law. Legally the newly independent republic was a collection of a dozen totally autonomous communities based on the old Ottoman *millet* system, all loyal to the greater Lebanese entity but beholden to the laws of their own religious sect in matters of marriage, divorce, and inheritance, many of which predated the Islamic conquest. The Druze in Lebanon, however, were subject to the very recently drafted Law of Personal Status of the Druze Community, drawn up by a committee of judges (*qudah*), jurists, and members of Parliament, themselves all Druze, promulgated on February 24, 1948, and described by the leading authority on Druze legal affairs as "the most impressive modern family law so far enacted in any Middle Eastern Arab State."[27] Drawing on a wide variety of sources, it provided interesting insights into the origins of Druze thinking and belief with its synthesis of Sunni jurisprudence of the Hanafi school, Twelver (*Ithnʿashari*) Shia doctrine, Ottoman family-rights law, modern Egyptian matrimonial and succession legislation, and Lebanese legal provisions based on French civil law.[28]

> But there can be no doubt that one of the most important sources of inspiration of the Lebanese Druze Law, one which left a distinctive

24. *Ibid.*, p. 70.
25. *Ibid.*, p. 72.
26. *Ibid.*, p. 77.
27. Layish, *Marriage*, p. 10.
28. *Ibid.*

> mark on it, is ancient Druze religious law, which was probably in turn inspired by the Fātimid Ismāʿiliyya. From this source, the Lebanese Druze Law derived provisions appropriate to the modern nuclear family and to a definitely advanced status of women . . . for the most part attributed to al-Amīr al Sayyid ʿAbd-Allah al-Tanūkhī, last of the greater commentators on Druze religious law (d. 885 / 1480). . . .[29]

For the first time in their modern history the Druze, or at least a major grouping of them, enjoyed the protection of the laws of their own religious community fully recognized by the political administration of the state.

From the earliest days of Lebanon's independence Druze political interests at the national level were dominated by the figure of Kamal Junbalat. First elected to the Lebanese Parliament from the Shuf district in 1947 as an ally of the Maronite power structure, he soon fell out with President Bishara al-Khuri, a Maronite also from the Shuf, and founded his own party, the Progressive Socialist party (*al-Hizb al-Ishtiraki al-Taqaddumi*) in 1949, which called for far-reaching reform. Like all other so-called political parties in Lebanon, Junbalat's Socialist party never attracted a significant following outside his own Junbalati Druze loyalists, but as its president Junbalat was able to address a wide variety of social, political, and other secular issues, which he could not have done so readily in his more traditional role as the tribal chief of al-Mukhtara.

Throughout his career spanning three eventful decades during which he became recognized as one of the most influential politicians in Lebanon, Junbalat played with aplomb the roles both of feudal leader of a religious community and internationally recognized socialist theorist advocating major reform for his country. On the one hand he was very loyal to Druze traditions (he strongly disapproved, for example, of Druze women appearing in his presence without the traditional *mandil*, or white silk head covering); on the other hand he espoused a variety of radical causes and ideas including Marxism, Buddhist mysticism, and the dream of Palestinian liberation, with which the Druze in actual fact had little in the way of common aim.

More than most Lebanese politicians, Junbalat had reason to fear a violent end,[30] yet he nevertheless undertook a life of political activism and

29. *Ibid.*, p. 11.

30. Very few of the Junbalats followed the pattern set by their eighteenth-century ancestor Shaykh ʿAli Junbalat, who led a full and peaceful life and died in bed at an old age. Kamal's father, Fuʾad, was murdered in 1922 by a disgruntled member of the community, presumably over a land dispute but in fact, according to some sources, at Syrian instigation (Walid Junbalat is said to hold this belief). Kamal's only sister was murdered in 1976 by unknown assailants at her home in the Christian sector of Ashrafiya (East Beirut). Kamal was assassinated outside Baʿqlin in the Shuf in March 1977 (by unknown hands, widely held to be in the pay of President Hafiz al-Asad of Syria), and his son Walid has had several attempts made on his life since he assumed his father's mantle.

personal ambition that very likely encouraged the demise he finally met in 1977. He angered many of his own conservative Druze landowning families when at the outset of his Socialist party leadership he distributed some of his own hereditary feudal lands in the Shuf to local Druze constituents. When his rival, President Bishara al-Khuri, attempted to prolong the single six-year term allotted to him under the National Covenant in 1952, Junbalat joined forces with al-Khuri's opponent, Kamil Shamʿun (Camille Chamoun), another Maronite deputy from the Shuf (representing the Maronite town of Dayr al-Qamar), to bring about al-Khuri's resignation. Six years later Shamʿun tried the same ploy as his predecessor, this time precipitating the 1958 civil war that ultimately prompted American military intervention. Shamʿun claimed that the union of Syria and Egypt earlier that year threatened Lebanese independence in that President Nasser made no secret of his desire to bring Christian Lebanon into the political mainstream of his openly Islamic Arab socialist state. Although Junbalat was by no means a Nasserist and his own Druze community in Lebanon was no more enthusiastic than most Christians to join the United Arab Republic, he nevertheless had a major grievance against Shamʿun that he was determined to redress. In the previous year Shamʿun had redrawn the parliamentary districts of Lebanon and introduced the single-list constituency[31] system which resulted in Junbalat's defeat in the parliamentary elections of 1957. Junbalat therefore sided openly with the pro-Nasser forces, largely Sunni Muslim, and successfully controlled the Shuf district during the 1958 civil war, emerging as the leading politician of the Left when it ended.

There is little doubt that Junbalat's intransigence and cooperation with Rashid Karami and other Muslim politicians forced Shamʿun to give up his designs on a second term as president, something that Shamʿun himself never forgot nor forgave. During the presidency of Shamʿun's successor, Fu'ad Shihab (1958–1964), Junbalat remained outside the government but returned to Parliament in 1964, defeating Shamʿun's rival candidate in al-Shuf. He remained a pivotal figure of commanding influence until his death, serving as the head of various ministries (though none of them was vital).

Up to the 1967 Arab-Israeli war, the Druze had in fact often held the crucial Ministry of Defense, but Junbalat himself was never trusted with this portfolio by the suspicious Maronite leadership. Instead, this plum went to his political rival, Prince Majid Arslan, leader of the Yazbaki faction, though he was too ineffective and unimaginative to utilize his position to Druze advantage. A very traditional figure who was the butt of many jokes because of his old-fashioned mustaches and outmoded *tarbush*,[32] Arslan was content

31. For an explanation of the complicated Lebanese electoral system, see Robert Brenton Betts, *Christians*, pp. 181ff., and Michael C. Hudson, *Lebanon: The Precarious Republic* (New York: Random House, 1968), pp. 108ff.

32. The red tassled fez worn by the older generation of Syrian and Lebanese gentlemen

to play the role expected of him by his conservative Yazbaki constituency and the Maronite-Sunni power brokers to whom he was closely allied. With the arrival of armed Palestinian forces in Beirut and southern Lebanon after their forced exodus from Jordan in September 1970, the entire political picture in Lebanon began to change. The Maronites withheld the Ministry of Defense as exclusively theirs, increasingly dominated as they were in their internal politics by the radical forces of Pierre Jumayyil's *Kataʾib* (*Phalanges Libanaises*) party, which advocated a hard line on maintaining Maronite political supremacy.

For Junbalat, the ascendancy of the *Kataʾib* meant that he and the Druze community faced a future of being increasingly denied access to the corridors of power, a trend he saw as violating the traditional role of leadership that belonged to the Druze by historical right. In his book *I Speak for Lebanon,* completed just before his assassination, Junbalat put forward the argument that the Druze are the best—and perhaps the only—qualified defenders and leaders of Lebanon.[33] There is little doubt that in his own mind he believed himself the man most qualified to be president of the republic. He considered it a serious injustice that he as a leader of the sect whose ancestors had been the first to champion the autonomy of the Lebanese Mountain and its peoples was denied the opportunity to serve his country as president solely because of his religious affiliation. For the Maronites, however, he was simply a spoiler who refused to play the game by its rules, "the *enfant terrible* of the establishment"[34] whose personal ambitions had gained the upper hand over his primary goal and that of his party—which was to work for the betterment and well-being of all Lebanese.

Many Druze tended to agree, though not often publicly. Of particular concern to them was the increasing militancy of Junbalat's pro-Palestinian stance. Although clearly aimed at establishing himself and his party among the forefront of progressive Arab leadership (and satisfying the Baʿth party ideologues in Syria while at the same time baiting his Maronite enemies), it did not reflect the immediate or long-term interests of the Lebanese Druze, who had no deeply held sympathy for Palestinian nationalist goals and who

---

(of all religions) for many years, but decidedly out of fashion by the 1950s. Unlike his rival, Kamal Junbalat, Prince Majid succeeded in living to a ripe old age. He died peacefully at ʿAlayh on Sept. 5, 1983, at age 79. His son, Prince Faysal Arslan, has followed his father's policies and if anything has pushed the more conservative of the two Druze factions, the Yazbakis, even further to the right. He publicly welcomed the Israeli invasion of 1982 (see *International Herald Tribune,* Jul. 12, 1982, p. 2) and has a reputation of cooperating with the *Kataʾib*. In actual fact, since Prince Majid's death, his widow, Princess Khawla Arslan (born a Junbalat), has taken a more active political role than Faysal and is generally recognized as the most effective spokesman of the Yazbaki faction (see Washington *Post,* Mar. 2, 1984, p. A18).

33. Kamal Junbalat, *I Speak for Lebanon,* pp. 38–39.

34. David C. Gordon, *The Republic of Lebanon: Nation in Jeopardy* (Boulder, Col.: Westview Press, 1983), p. 85.

were, moreover, directly linked by communal and often family ties to the Druze of Israel, who had (with rare exceptions) become strong supporters of the Jewish state.

The Druze in Palestine and Israel, 1920–1986

The Palestinian Druze community, which numbered only a few thousand at the outset of the British Mandate in 1920, had prospered quietly despite the turbulent political situation swirling about them. Living as they did largely apart from the other Arab communities, they were indifferent to and for the most part ignored by the early Zionist settlers. When hostilities broke out in 1948 between Jew and Arab, the Druze looked principally to the protection of their homes and villages. Having long chafed under the rule of the overwhelming Sunni majority during Ottoman times, and even during the British Mandate (it being standard empire policy to curry favor with the ruling native elite), the Druze did not view their new Zionist rulers as any less preferable. When the various Arab forces (to which the Palestinian Druze had not contributed)[35] withdrew in 1949, no Druze exodus took place. Makarem explains this as due "to the fact that the Druzes have always been so attached to their land that it is traditional for them to die on their land rather than to leave it."[36] There is no doubt whatsoever that this devotion to their ancestral properties was the overriding concern of the Palestinian Druze, but Sunni Palestinians were likewise deeply attached to their native soil. The fact is that the Israelis encouraged or outright forced the majority of resident Muslims to leave, whereas all the Druze and most of the Christians were allowed to remain in the Galilee region that, according to the United Nations Partition Plan of 1947, was to have been included in the Arab Palestinian state. And there they continued to grow and prosper.

During the thirty-year period 1931–1961, the Druze population of Palestine/Israel nearly trebled, from 9,148 to 24,282.[37] In 1957 the Druze in Israel joined those in Lebanon in enjoying legal autonomy in their own civil affairs when they were recognized as a separate religious community on April 15 of that year through the Religious Communities Regulations, which were based on a 1926 ordinance of the British Mandate. The Druze were authorized to establish their own courts, which exercised exclusive jurisdic-

35. A small contingent of Lebanese forces, led by the veteran of the Druze uprising of 1925 in Syria, Fawzi al-Qawuqji, joined the Arab forces in 1948 but was quickly defeated and his men dispersed. See Ben-Dor, *Druzes in Israel,* p. 129, who asserts that pro-Israeli sentiments on the part of Palestinian Druze villagers dissuaded the volunteers from supporting the Arab armies.

36. Makarem, *Ismailis,* p. 3.

37. The British Mandate Census of Palestine, 1931, the Israeli Census of Population and Housing, 1961.

tion in matters of marriage and divorce for the Druze in the Jewish state.[38] In the same year, at their own request, the Druze became subject to the same compulsory military service required of Jewish citizens. After 1970 Druze affairs were no longer handled by the government departments in charge of Arab minority matters, thus separating the Israeli Druze even further from the larger communities of Palestinian Muslim and Christian Arabs sharing Israeli nationality.[39]

Such separation was very much encouraged by the Israeli government, which even went so far as officially to adopt the view the that Druze were not really Arabs at all but a separate ethnic entity that had somehow become Arabicized. Although tacitly accepted by many Israeli Druze in the early years of independence, this quaint distortion of history was discounted by many younger Druze, some of whom began to develop pro-Palestinian nationalist sentiments following the 1967 Arab-Israeli war. In 1975, Egon Mayer quoted a young Druze in a Galilee village as saying, "We are actually Arabs. Anyone who says otherwise is a liar. Some Druze intellectuals who work for the government have tried to prove that we are not really Arabs, but they are liars . . . we do not dislike the Jewish people; but the Israeli government is no good for us."[40] A sizable increment in the Druze population living in Israel that did not consider itself to be anything but Arab came with the forcible absorption into Israel of some twelve thousand Syrian Druze living in four villages[41] in the Golan (*Julan*) Heights, most of whom refused to accept Israeli nationality when the area was unilaterally annexed in July 1980.

38. At the end of 1962 (Dec. 25) Druze religious courts were established and given exclusive jurisdiction in matters of marriage and divorce; the old Muslim (Hanafi school) tradition gave way "almost overnight." See Layish, *Marriage,* pp. 5, 378.

39. The Ministry of Religious Affairs continued to exercise administrative jurisdiction over the appointment of religious officers and judges of the Druze Court. In February 1985, Shaykh Amin Tarif, religious head of the Israeli Druze community, appealed to the president of the Knesset to abolish this bureaucratic involvement. See *Report on the Palestinians Under Israeli Rule,* vol. 9, no. 142, Feb. 1985, p. 19.

40. Mayer, "Becoming Modern in Bayt al-Shabab," p. 293. One of the more blatantly unhistorical theories favored by the Israelis is that a daughter of the Druze prophet Shuʿayb (identified with the Old Testament figure of Jethro) was married to Moses, thereby establishing a blood link between the two communities. Other equally specious theories were suggested to convince the Druze that they were more Jewish than Arab, that they spoke Arabic only because they had lived among Arabs for centuries, and that, like the Maronites, they had become Arabicized. American Fundamentalist Christian groups, ever eager to discover modern links to the Old Testament, have likewise swallowed the Jethro fable. The Druze themselves point out that their *nabi* (prophet) Shuʿayb did not have any children, but as one prominent Israeli Druze remarked to me, "if the Jews want to claim us as in-laws [in spite of our belief to the contrary] then they are free to do so."

41. The Israeli Census of Population and Housing of 1983 (published in 1985) gives the following figures for the four Druze villages of the Golan: Majd al-Shams (5,639), Biqʿata (3,109), Masʿada (2,013), and ʿAyn Qiniya (1,152): of their combined population of 11,905, only 28 were non-Druze (18 Christian, 9 Muslim, and 1 Jew). A fifth Arab village in the Golan,

Passive resistance to the Israeli annexation has continued to the present day (villagers are periodically arrested for flying the Syrian flag in defiance of Israeli regulations), and it reached a peak on September 23, 1983, at a memorial service for Shaykh Kamal Kanj Abu-Salih, the spiritual head of the Golan Druze and a leader of the resistance movement who had been jailed by the Israelis a year earlier. An estimated twenty thousand Golan Druze and Israeli sympathizers massed on their side of the border and were joined by some fifteen thousand Druze villagers on the Syrian side. Lebanese Druze leader Walid Junbalat addressed the rally through loudspeakers from the Syrian side and praised the Golan villagers' resistance to Israeli annexation. By October 1984, only 250 of the Golan Druze had accepted Israeli identity cards. The seventy who voted in the July elections for the Knesset all received threatening letters from the pro-Syrian faction. In December they complained to the government that the pro-Syrian group had renewed a boycott against them and that they were not being given government help as had been promised. Israeli authorities continue to report a steady number of Golan Druze requesting Israeli citizenship, if for no other reason than to qualify for Israeli pension benefits. But Druze sources with whom I spoke in September 1985 confessed that the pro-Syrian faction had been successful, at least for the time being, and that all those who had taken out Israeli nationality had renounced it and were now classified as inhabitants, not citizens. On February 10, 1985, more than three hundred Golan Druze voted in the Syrian presidential elections by shouting their names to Syrian election officials across the border. Four days later a general strike and political demonstration were held at Majd al-Shams to protest the third anniversary of Israel's unilateral annexation of the Golan Heights.[42] Serious violence also occurred in February 1987 when thirteen Druze from the town of Majd al-

al-Ghajar, was listed as containing 938 Muslims and 3 Druze. But since all the Sunni Muslim (Arab and Circassian) and Christian inhabitants of the Golan Heights (some one hundred thousand in all) were forcibly expelled following the 1967 Israeli seizure, it is certain that the inhabitants of al-Ghajar are Alawi, not Muslim. In its July 1982 issue, *The Middle East* (p. 17) refers to an Alawite village in the Israeli occupied Golan, and Guérin describes the village of "Rhadjar" as containing 600 "Ansariés" (*Description de la Palestine,* vol. 2, p. 344). Interestingly, the word *ghajar* in Arabic means gypsy or those who curse and swear; in view of how the Alawis are looked upon by other Arabs it is not surprising that a settlement of theirs would be so named.

42. *Report on Palestinians Under Israeli Rule,* Oct. 1984, p. 25, Dec. 1984, p. 24, Feb. 1985, p. 22, Mar. 1985, p. 28. Scott MacLeod, writing in *Middle East International* of a visit to Majd al-Shams, relates how at a wedding celebration the young people ("in their jeans and print dresses," in contrast to the traditionally dressed elders) "shouted political songs" (including a paean of praise to the young Shia girl who had carried out a successful suicide car-bomb attack on Israeli forces in southern Lebanon some weeks earlier—and whose victims included several Druze). See "Letter from Majd ash-Shams," *Middle East International,* July 26, 1985, back page. See also R. Scott Kennedy, "The Druze of the Golan: A Case of Non-Violent Resistance," *Journal of Palestine Studies* 50 (Winter 1984): 48–64.

Shams were arrested following clashes with Israeli police during demonstrations marking the fifth anniversary of the imposition of Israeli law on the villagers, who insist that they remain Syrians despite Zionist occupation since 1967.

Following the establishment of the PLO forces in Beirut and southern Lebanon after 1969, Druze disaffection with Israel became more widespread. In May 1973 Israeli police uncovered a forty-man Druze spy ring working on behalf of the PLO inside Israel itself. The following year, in March 1974, there were further arrests of Druze accused of working on behalf of Syria in the Golan area. At the same time there were incidents of Druze border guards (who make up between one-quarter and one-third of this vital Israeli security force) being attacked by Jewish villagers for allegedly assisting PLO commandos in carrying out their attacks on the town of Qiryat Shimonah. More recently a Druze from Majd al-Shams, Rafiq Qalani, aged 20, was detained in April 1985 for illegal infiltration into Syria, and on October 16 of that year he was convicted by a Nazareth court of spying and sentenced to four and a half years in prison. On May 20, 1986, five more Druze residents of the same town were sentenced to twenty-seven years' imprisonment by a military court in Lydda for attempting to kidnap an Israeli soldier and for "making contact with Syrian agents"; four other men, also from Majd al-Shams, were given lesser sentences ranging from seven to twelve years.[43]

Nonetheless, the majority of the Druze community remained loyal to the Israeli state, if simply for reasons of political and economic security. By serving in the army the Druze have been able to profit from the many financial benefits available to Israeli Defense Force veterans. For the most part their villages were spared the wholesale confiscation of "unregistered" land by the state for use by new Jewish settlers or the military.[44] In September 1986 the predominantly Druze village of Hurfaysh in northern Galilee on the Lebanese border (population in 1983: Druze 2,649; Christian 129; Muslim 43) was designated a "confrontation settlement," enabling it to apply for special aid for development projects. It is the only non-Jewish settlement in Galilee (and, to my knowledge, in all of Israel) to have been granted this special status. In the early years of Israeli independence the Druze loyally supported the largest political party, Labor, which formed all Israeli governments until the LIKUD upset in 1977. Members of leading Druze families were given jobs in the party, the *Histradut* (the Trade Union Federation), and

43. *Report on Palestinians Under Israeli Rule,* vol. 9, no. 149, Sept. 1985, p. 20; *ibid.*, no. 150, Oct. 1985, p. 19; *ibid.*, vol. 10, no. 157, May 1986, pp. 18–19, 22–23.

44. Since 1948, half of the land of the large Druze village of Daliyat al-Karmil has been forcibly sold or confiscated, and other villages such as Bayt Jann have likewise lost thousands of *dunums* to the military *The Middle East* (July 1982): 18–19. On Mar. 8, 1984, the villagers rioted over what they claimed were Israeli authorities' attempts to seize twenty thousand *dunums* of village land on Mount Meron (*Report on Palestinians Under Israeli Rule,* vol. 6, no.131, Mar. 1984, p. 14).

government service, especially in education. The Druze candidates to the Knesset (Parliament) regularly stood for election on the "minorities list" affiliated with the Labor party.[45]

As the political climate began to change in the early 1970s and more and more Druze began to question subservience to the state, other political parties started making inroads among Druze voters, notably the religious bloc on the Right and the Communist party (RAKAH) on the Left. By 1973 the Druze deputy from Galilee, Shaykh Jabir Muʿaddi, the deputy minister of communications and a candidate for the grouping aligned to the Labor party, was in danger of losing his seat by more than one thousand votes until the Bedouin deputy from Biʾr Sabʿa (Beersheba) gave the endangered Druze fifteen hundred surplus votes of his own, a practice allowable under Israel's complicated election laws.[46]

In 1972 a group of radical Druze (including a few more traditional politicians) set up the Druze Action Committee (*Lajnat al-Mubadarat al-Durziya*) to work on behalf of those of their community opposed to the Israeli government because of unpopular policies, including those of military age who did not wish to serve in the Israeli Army.[47] Despite more than a decade of active opposition to the military draft by this committee, however, more than three-quarters of young Druze men of military age serve willingly (thirty-seven Druze were killed in Israel's occupation of Lebanon during 1982–1985, or almost 7 percent of the total number of Israeli soldiers who died, though Druze comprise only a little over 1 percent of the total population; more than 150 Druze have been killed in Israel's wars since 1948). Those Druze youths who refuse to serve face prison sentences. A small number have taken the extreme step of formal conversion to Islam in order to avoid the draft, but by and large the dissenters serve out their sentences.[48]

45. *Report on Palestinians,* vol. 6, no. 131, Mar. 1984, p. 14.

46. Betts, *Christians,* p. 267, *n.* 257.

47. The Druze Action Committee has three goals. The first two are in line with the group's Communist backing: the rights of the Palestinian people, of whom the Druze are viewed as an integral part, and the right of Druze to refuse conscription into the IDF. The third is the right of the Druze to be given the end of *Ramadan* (*ʿid al-fitr*) holidays along with the Muslims, somewhat anomalous given that the Druze do not observe the Muslim fast and were allowed to take the Muslim holiday only when the state refused to recognize their separate status under Ottoman and British rule. To identify both with traditionally leftist goals and solidarity with the Sunni community, which virtually all Druze refuse to consider themselves a part of, guarantees that the Druze Action Committee will attract only an insignificant number of supporters.

48. Pat McConnell, writing in *The Middle East* (July 1982), cites Druze sources as estimating the number of apostates at two hundred. He does not state whether or not these defections were justifiable under *taqiya*. The prison terms for those refusing to serve in the IDF are usually a matter of a few months, but on Mar. 25, 1984, a Druze from Buqayʿa, Walid Nayif Salim, was sentenced to eighteen months (*Report on Palestinians Under Israeli Rule,* vol. 6, no. 31, Mar. 1984, p. 13). Interestingly, the Israeli government recently approved a small but significant number of Israeli Christians and Muslims who asked for permission to serve (*ibid.,*

Opposition reached a peak with the troubles following the Golan annexation in 1980, then declined with the invasion of Lebanon in June 1982, particularly when the Israeli forces were seen as assisting the Lebanese Druze against incursions into their territory by Christian forces of, or allied to, the *Kataʾib*.

An unknown but significant number of Druze in the IDF went on unauthorized leave during the struggle between the Lebanese Druze Militia and the Lebanese Army to assist their coreligionists in the north. The Israeli military authorities refused to grant them official leave, but on December 22, 1984, a large meeting in the Druze village of Yirka was attended by many local leaders, several of whom, including Knesset member Zaydan ʿAtsha, warned that even if the government did not give official permission to these soldiers to fight they would do so anyway.[49]

The spiritual leader of the Druze community, Shaykh Amin Tarif of Julis in western Galilee, has remained openly loyal to the Israeli government despite dissident elements within his community. He has repeatedly criticized those who support PLO activities and recently appealed to the Druze in Lebanon not to give aid to Palestinian nationalist activity there.[50] He has also tried to mediate between the small pro-Israeli and greatly larger pro-Syrian factions among the Golan Druze, coming out in strong opposition to the social boycott that the pro-Syrian group imposed after August 10, 1984, on those of their community who accepted Israeli nationality. He was embarrassed by contingents of the pro-Syrian group who shouted anti-Israeli slogans at a conference of Druze from Lebanon and Israel held at the *mazar* of al-Nabi Shuʿayb on March 7, 1984,[51] and has therefore sought all possible means to resolve this discord in order to maintain the security of his community in the face of recent Jewish suspicion as to its loyalty.

The Druze representatives in the Knesset have not toed the government line quite so readily, and the SHINUI deputy, Zaydan ʿAtsha of ʿIsifiya has been openly critical of many government policies (unlike the other Druze deputy, Amal Nasr al-Din of Daliyat Karmil, formerly a member of Labor but more recently of LIKUD). Though not as radical as three of the other five

---

Dec. 1984, p. 23). The small community of Circassian Muslims, descendants of refugees from the southern Caucasus displaced by Russian expansion in the late nineteenth century, also willingly contributed sons to the IDF (see the New York *Times* coverage of the shameful treatment given a Circassian Muslim officer in the IDF wrongly accused of treason and espionage, May 26, 1987, p. 1).

49. Ten days earlier ʿAtsha had appealed to Prime Minister Shimon Peres by letter to grant the permission. His appeal received a polite but negative reply from Peres, but ʿAtsha's expressed concern on behalf of his constituents did not go unnoticed. In return for continued Druze loyalty in Israel the area of al-Kharrub (the coastal region between Damur and Sidon) soon evacuated by the IDF was not given to the *Kataʾib*, and within months the Druze Militia had overrun it.

50. *Report on Palestinians Under Israeli Rule*, vol. 6, no. 131, Mar. 1984, p. 13.

51. *Ibid.*, p. 16.

non-Druze Arab deputies elected in 1984, two of whom are Communists and one from the Progressive List for Peace, which advocates an independent Palestinian State,[52] ʿAtsha has publicly stated his opposition to Israeli settlements on the West Bank and any future annexation of this overwhelmingly Muslim Arab territory, occupied by Israel since 1967.[53] He does, however, support the Israeli annexation of the Golan, explaining the continued opposition of the Druze there to inclusion in Israel as a response to a fear of reprisal from the Syrians against their relatives on the Syrian side—and as an insurance policy of sorts against the day they may be returned to Syria, when they would be able to say that "they resisted the law and didn't accept it with open arms."[54] ʿAtsha believes that most of the Golan Druze would like to become part of Israel, and despite the refusal of most to accept Israeli citizenship, there has been a considerable amount of social and professional interchange with the Druze of Galilee, including marriages between families of the two groups.[55]

There is no doubt that of all the Arab communities in Israel the Druze are the most loyal. In a study conducted by the head of the Arab department in Haifa University's Jewish-Arab Center, 85 percent of Israeli Druze acknowledge Israel's right to exist "without reservation," as opposed to 69 percent of Israeli Christians and 59 percent of the Muslim community.[56] There is no doubt that many Muslim and Christian Palestinians resent the extent of Druze cooperation, particularly those on the West Bank and in the Gaza (Ghazza) Strip, where the Druze members of the IDF are especially disliked. Acts of violence against Druze members of the IDF by other Palestinian Arabs are far from unknown, and extremist elements seem in fact to single them out for special treatment as collaborators. The most recent incidents occurred on April 17, 1985, and January 11, 1986: the former at a restaurant in Gaza where a masked gunman opened fire on two Druze sol-

52. Of the 120 members of the Knesset in 1981, only five were Arabs, although the 17 percent of the Israeli population that is Arab (not including the West Bank and the Gaza Strip) should be entitled to twenty seats if proportional representation were a reality. The 1984 elections returned seven Arabs—four Muslims, two Druze, and one Christian—from a wide spectrum of political leanings (two Communists, of which one is Christian and one Muslim); one LIKUD, a Druze; one Labor, a Muslim; one MAPAM, a Muslim; one SHINUI, a Druze; and one from the Progressive List for Peace, a Muslim.

53. ʿAtsha in an interview with the Los Angeles *Herald Examiner,* Apr. 15, 1982, pp. 2, 7. He was elected to the Knesset in 1977 and before that was the first non-Jewish Israeli to hold a diplomatic post abroad as an information officer at the consulate in New York, 1972–1977. He did not win re-election in 1981 when the party list on which he was originally elected, the Democratic Movement for Change, split, but won a seat again in the 1984 elections.

54. *Ibid.*

55. Although the Golan Druze have refused Israeli nationality they are in frequent contact with both the Druze religious and political leadership of Galilee and Mount Carmel, who act as their liaison with the government they refuse to recognize.

56. *Report on Palestinians Under Israeli Rule,* vol. 6, no. 131, Mar. 1984, p. 16.

diers, seriously injuring one before the other was able to shoot the assailant, and the other outside a clothing store on the main commercial street of Nablus, where a Druze member of the paramilitary border police was murdered while shopping with his wife and children.[57] Relations between the Druze of Galilee and Mount Carmel and their non-Druze Arab neighbors are peaceful, if not without the occasional disruption stemming from intercommunity (and intercommunal) rivalry.[58] In an area rife with instability their position in Israel is reasonably secure and prosperous, and the overwhelming majority of the Palestinian Druze is loath to risk any political stance that would permanently jeopardize it.

There remains, however, the unanswered question as to why the Druze in Israel have not been more generously rewarded by the Israeli state for their loyalty over the past four decades. Why are there no Druze generals or cabinet ministers? Why only two Druze members of the Israeli Diplomatic Service in the four decades of its existence? (Both appointments were at a very junior level: the first was Zaydan ʿAtsha, who served at the consulate in New York from 1972 to 1977 as an information officer, and the second is Asad Asad, a former IDF colonel, appointed on April 5, 1986, to the Israeli U.N. delegation attached to the Israeli Embassy in Washington as an information officer.) The Druze commitment to Israel is such that they have nothing to lose in the eyes of their Arab nationalist critics, who already thoroughly mistrust them. The refusal of the Israeli government to offer more tangible recognition for their service to the state remains somewhat of a mystery.

The Druze in Lebanon and Syria since 1975

The period from the outbreak of civil unrest in Lebanon in April 1975 up to the present has been of particular significance for the Druze in the Middle East, both in terms of immediate consequence and long-term prospects. For the first time in this century at least, the term *Druze* has been frequently

57. *Israel and Palestine,* May/June 1985, and the Washington *Post,* Jan. 12, 1986. Only four weeks before the Nablus slaying, the military governor of that heavily Muslim and militantly Palestinian nationalist Arab town, a Druze officer in the Israeli Army, had been replaced by the first civilian mayor since 1982 (see the Washington *Post,* Dec. 11, 1985), who within weeks of his appointment was assassinated by Syrian-backed gunmen.

58. In April 1981, hundreds of armed Druze from Julis in Galilee attacked neighboring Kafr Yasif (57 percent Christian, 40 percent Muslim, and 3 percent Druze), site of an important Druze *mazar,* or shrine, where they killed three persons, wounded eleven, and left much of the town in ruins. This was in apparent retaliation for the fatal stabbing of a young Druze man from Julis during a soccer match between the teams of the two villages three days earlier. The Druze villagers were armed with IDF weaponry, whereas the Christian and Muslim villagers were virtually unarmed—which caused considerable resentment among non-Druze Arabs (see *Israel and Palestine,* April 1981). I visited both villages in early September 1985 but saw no remaining evidence of the destruction reportedly caused by the incident.

found on the front pages of most American and European newspapers, often confused with Islamic groups and generally in a pejorative perspective, suggesting ruthless warriors savaging Christian women and babies—a grossly unfair view, particularly in that the Druze fighters as a matter of historical record have never touched women in combat, unlike Muslims and Christians, who have often made a point of doing so. G. Kheirallah cites Daniel Bliss, founder of the American University of Beirut, as recording how, during the upheavals of 1860, "it was possible for any woman to pass through the warring Druze armies in perfect safety." He also notes that during the First World War, scarcity of food drove many Christian women and their children from Lebanon into the Jabal al-Druze in Syria, "where they were given refuge, work and sustenance that enabled them to survive. At the end of the war," he continues, "the Druzes did not permit them to return to their homes until the Christian clergy came and investigated, certifying that none had been molested, dishonored or maltreated during their stay."[59]

Popular misconceptions of the Druze as a secretive band of savage warriors who showed no mercy ("the 'signature' of a Druze is to cut the throat of an enemy from ear to ear")[60] were nonetheless perpetuated in press accounts, with encouragement from the *Kataʾib* and other extremist Christian groups, and it has only been recently that a fairer, more balanced view reflecting of some well-intentioned research had begun to appear in the media. Some credit for this trend must go to the American Druze Public Affairs Committee (ADPAC), an outgrowth of the American Druze Society, whose chairman, Raymond Hamden, had undertaken an educational program of publications and meetings designed to familiarize Americans (including those of Druze extraction like Dr. Hamden, originally Hamdan) with Druze traditions and practices.[61] Nevertheless old myths die hard. As recently as February 8, 1987, Colin Smith writing in the London *Observer,* a weekly noted for its balanced reporting on the Middle East, made the statement that "Lebanon has long had a tradition of sectional strife in which hostage-taking is a fairly common practice, except, perhaps, for the Druse, who normally kill their prisoners" (p. 13). No accusation could be more inaccurate or more unfair.

59. G. Kheirallah, "The Druzes," *The Arab World* (Autumn 1944): 20.

60. Helen Cameron Gordon, *Syria As It Is* (London: Methuen and Co., Ltd., 1939), p. 84. In the early stages of the fighting at Suq al-Gharb the Western press made light of Junbalat and his leadership role, referring to him in such terms as "King of the Mountain" (Los Angeles *Times,* Aug. 23, 1984, pp. 1–8) and "Playboy Warlord" (the *Sunday Times,* London, Sept. 11, 1983, p. 20).

61. One of the principal targets was the ignorance of the American media as to who the Druze were and are. Much time and effort has been spent pointing out that they are neither Muslim, nor leftists in any recognizable sense outside the context of the Lebanese conflict, nor anti-American. What they are is a highly cohesive community determined to fight if necessary to protect what they consider to be their land and their traditions.

A second consequence of the war in Lebanon has been, also for the first time since the end of the mandate era, the bringing together at one stage or another of the Druze from all three of the countries in which they live in large numbers. Although the Syrian and Lebanese Druze have been in contact off and on ever since the defeated Yamani faction settled the *Lija*ʾ early in the eighteenth century, the effective occupation of Lebanon in late 1976 by the Syrian army brought large numbers of Syrian Druze soldiers and officers into daily contact with Lebanese Druze villagers, with the inevitable consequence of intermarriage. Similarly, the Israeli invasion of 1982 brought Israeli Druze soldiers into the Shuf mountains where, for the first time since 1948, Lebanese Druze were able to meet their coreligionists and relatives from Galilee and Mount Carmel. Again, familiarity bred family alliances, and many young women from the Shuf found themselves transplanted to Israel as brides of Druze soldiers.[62] The inclusion of the Syrian Druze of Golan within the borders of Israel likewise brought the Galilean Druze into direct contact with their more numerous cousins beyond the borders of Palestine.[63]

The Druze of Syria have increased and prospered admirably since the harassment that followed the Hatum affair after 1970, and their prosperity has made the Druze of the Golan even more unhappy about their post-1981 detachment from their country. The decade of war in Lebanon has made the peace and stability of the Jabal al-Druze a magnet of sorts for those who previously looked down on the region as backward and deprived. In the ten years between my first visit to the Syrian Jabal in the summer of 1975 and my most recent trip in June 1985, the growth and development there was impressive. The administrative center, al-Suwaydaʾ, which ten years ago was a small, sleepy town of perhaps thirty thousand residents, is now a flourishing city of anywhere from seventy-five thousand to 150,000 inhabitants, depending on whose estimate you accept. The dusty villages of the surrounding region have sprouted modern new homes and businesses that reflect the expanding economy of the region as well as the investment by returning émigrés from Africa and South America,[64] by others who have made smaller

62. The *Sunday Telegraph*, Oct. 23, 1983, p. 2, reported that "hundreds of Lebanese women trying to escape the war in Lebanon have been crossing the border into Northern Israel searching for husbands. Since the start of the war 17 months ago [sic] more than 500 have married Israeli Arabs and many are living without permits to stay in Israel." The Israeli Ministry of the Interior was said to be "alarmed" at the growing number of what are considered to be "marriages of convenience." An influx of Arab immigrants seeking Israeli nationality is certainly a prospect that the more militantly racist Zionists could only regard with considerable disapproval.

63. The Israeli government has been largely unsuccessful in its attempts to inhibit the Golan Druze from maintaining their contacts with the Druze of Syria, and thus acting as a bridge of communication between the Galilee and Mount Carmel communities and the major Druze center in the Suwaydaʾ district.

64. Many Druze emigrated to West Africa during the late colonial era, along with the

fortunes working in Saudi Arabia and the Gulf, and by wealthy Druze from Lebanon who have found Syria to be a safer prospect for present investment than their war-torn homeland.

President Hafiz al-Asad, firmly in control and basking in the comfort of a third seven-year term awarded him by more than 99 percent of his subjects on February 10, 1985, has allowed some Druze once again to rise to posts of importance in both the government and the military. The cabinet appointed in March 1985 included a Druze minister of higher education, Kamal Sharaf. The twenty-one-member Regional Command of the ruling Baʿth party also had its lone Druze, Tawfiq Salha. There are Druze in other areas of government also, but not in significant numbers or positions of influence where they could reasonably hope to threaten the dominance of the president's coterie of Alawis from his home village of Qardaha. In return for having accepted the *Pax Alawiya,* however, the Druze are effectively in control of their own affairs once more, though not sufficiently trusted as to have one of their own as governor of the Suwaydaʾ *muhafaza.* The present incumbent is a Syriac Christian from Aleppo. Still, there is much to be said for stability, peace, and relative prosperity. So long as one gives lip service to the fiction of a Baʿthi democracy and a socialist economy, one can happily profit from the capitalist reality that is Syria today—most Syrian Druze do.

The major casualty of the political events that have brought the Druze of Lebanon, Syria, and Israel into closer contact since 1975 has been their dominant political figure for three decades, Kamal Junbalat, the leading Druze force in Lebanese politics since independence. Although it might have been expected for the Druze to steer clear of a confrontation between the Maronite Phalangists and the militant Palestinians and their Sunni Lebanese allies, the fact that Junbalat had been so publicly verbal in recent years in defense of the Palestinian cause made total neutrality difficult. Most educated Druze in Lebanon were uncomfortable with their leader's position, among them the Lebanese *Shaykh al-ʿAql,* Muhammad Abu Shaqra, who constantly counseled caution; but loyalty to religion, clan, and godfather brought many Druze to Junbalat's support.

Junbalat was distrusted by too many in the Lebanese establishment to be included in the government assembled in the fatal summer of 1975 by the veteran Sunni prime minister, Rashid Karami of Tripoli, and the Maronite member of this so-called National Salvation Cabinet was none other than Junbalat's old nemesis, former president (1952–1958) Kamil Shamʿun.

---

other Lebanese, mainly Christians and Shia Muslims, where they made their fortunes in such areas as import-export and transportation ventures. Most have returned to the Middle East, although some still maintain their businesses, usually through local representatives. It is quite common to find *maté,* the strong tea of the Argentinian pampas, served in Druze villages in the Shuf, a custom brought back by returning émigrés from South America.

The Druze slot fell to Junbalat's rival, the jolly and ineffective Majid Arslan, already suffering from the first stages of his final illness. Many attempts were made by the various protagonists to draw the Druze into the growing conflagration, among them the assassination of the Druze governor of northern Lebanon in the city of Tripoli. But Junbalat bided his time until January of 1976, when he finally joined forces with the Palestinians in capturing the strategic Maronite coastal town of Damur at the northern entrance to the Shuf mountains, ten miles south of Beirut, massacring hundreds and sending thousands more north into exile.[65]

For the Palestinians it was revenge for the *Kata'ib* massacre at the Karantina refugee camp east of Beirut; for Junbalat it was a chance to remove a dangerous Phalangist base of operation on the edge of his home turf and at the same time to strike a blow at his enemy, Kamil Shamʿun, whose palatial retirement villa at al-Mashrif on a hill overlooking the prosperous banana groves and fruit orchards of Damur was totally destroyed in the fighting. By the end of the year the Maronite forces were clearly on the defensive, and it looked as if a major change in the Lebanese political picture was at hand. But just at the moment when it seemed that victory for the so-called Leftists was inevitable, and that Junbalat must surely have been savoring the prospect of humiliating his Maronite rivals and perhaps even achieving the Lebanese presidency to which he felt he was entitled but denied by the 1943 National Covenant, the Syrian government intervened on behalf of the Maronites and their allies. Junbalat, who had always taken Syrian counsel very seriously in the past, loudly opposed this latest move which so clearly acted against his own personal interests and goals.

It was probably Junbalat's steadfast refusal to accept a stalemate rather than outright victory that led to his brutal assassination in March 1977 as he drove with bodyguards from his feudal mansion in al-Mukhtara toward Beirut, carefully avoiding the Maronite stronghold of Dayr al-Qamar that straddled the main road and taking instead a side route through the Druze town of Baʿqlin, where he felt safer. As the road took a particularly circuitous series of downhill hairpin curves outside the small village of Mughamis, known for its *ʿaraq,* he was set upon by unknown assailants who successfully made their escape after murdering Junbalat and his party. It is generally accepted that it was the Syrians who engineered the assassination, though many at the time thought Shamʿun may have had a hand in the arrangements as revenge for the events at Damur a year earlier.

Whoever was responsible for the murder, they succeeded in removing the Opposition in Lebanon of its most effective spokesman, and the Druze community of a great personality and dedicated, if quixotic and egocentric, reformer. It is commonly acknowledged that Junbalat was the one politician

65. Kamal Salibi, *Crossroads to Civil War: Lebanon 1958–1976* (Delmar, New York: Caravan, 1976), p. 158.

who did not enrich himself outright during the fighting and who genuinely deplored its consequences for the Lebanese. He would doubtless have been grieved at the massacres of Christians in Shuf villages, particularly at Mazraʿat al-Shuf and Butma near al-Mukhtara, that took place within the first six hours after his death became known. Nevertheless, it is certainly arguable that had it not been for Junbalat's personal ambition and deeply felt political convictions the Druze might not have become involved in the fighting at all. Certainly once he was removed from the scene Druze involvement ceased, and the Shuf remained a haven of tranquillity throughout the ensuing hostilities until the Lebanese Army attempted to assert its authority in the Druze areas of the mountain following the Israeli troop withdrawal in 1983. These troubles were the direct result of an attempt by the Maronite *Kataʾib* leadership behind President Amin Gemayel to force its presence on a region that had in effect been a Druze canton since 1975.[66]

This move, so costly to all concerned, would not have been made had the Phalangists not believed they had the backing of the United States, a notion of which they were soon disabused. The United States had steadfastly adhered to an official policy of supporting the central government in Lebanon in its efforts to exercise its internal authority. But when it became clear that the Gemayel government was primarily acting on behalf of the *Kataʾib* efforts to advance Maronite territorial rights at the expense of existing Druze ones, American support for the Lebanese Army campaign in the northern Shuf evaporated. Unfortunately the American public had by this time been disserved by its news media, which made it appear that Druze resistance to Maronite expansionism (or, from the latter's point of view, irredentism) was somehow an expression of anti-American and pro-Communist sympathies by the Druze, a totally inaccurate and unjustifiable appraisal.

At the time of the outbreak of the troubles, Druze-Maronite relations had not yet reached an impasse. While other non-Christian groups had either been purposely excluded from the Lebanese Armed Forces or had left their positions to join their own communal militias, the Druze were highly placed in the army and had continued to hold important ranks throughout the previous ten years, even at the time of the bitterest fighting between Druze forces and the Lebanese Army in the late summer and early fall of 1983 around the crucial crossroads at Suq al-Gharb. The Druze, with their historical tradition of military excellence, have been a strong presence in the Lebanese Army since independence. Although never permitted to reach the positions of commanding importance reserved for Maronites, they did attain senior ranks, the only non-Christians for many years to do so. Throughout

66. When I visited the Shuf in 1980 for the first time since July 1975, my driver, the son of close Druze friends and a member of the Druze Militia, announced as we drove over the hill from Baʿqlin to al-Simqaniya, "Ahlan wa sahlan biʾl jumhuriya al-durziya!" ("Welcome to the Druze Republic!"). He was smiling but was not joking.

the 1960s and early 1970s the highest-ranking Druze was Colonel Yusuf Shumayt, army chief of staff from 1959, who was retired on the eve of the civil war as a general. He was replaced by Saʿid Nasrallah (a Druze loyal to the Maronite leader Kamil Shamʿun rather than Kamal Junbalat), who on February 9, 1975, was promoted to the rank of brigadier general (*ʿamid awwal*). In late August 1983, the Gemayel government named another Druze, Brigadier General Mahmud Abu Dargham (a native of the Shuf village of Kafarhim), as commander of the Lebanese force assigned to the central mountain region where fighting raged with the Druze Militia over control of Suq al-Gharb and Shimlan, Orthodox Christian villages in an otherwise predominantly Druze region south of ʿAlayh.

This did not prevent most Druze from supporting the Junbalat militiamen. On October 3, some six hundred Druze soldiers of the Lebanese Army barracked at Hammana in the Matn region were reported as having deserted to the Druze Militia, among them some thirty officers. In Beirut the Druze Army chief of staff "acknowledged there might have been some defections from the Army, but he thought the figure of 600 was wildly exaggerated." The leader of the defectors, Colonel Fuʾad Hasan, explained that "we can no longer go on being the tools of our country." The deserters reportedly cheered Walid Junbalat when he spoke to them, rather ironically, of his desire for "a unified army in Lebanon." Shortly before the soldiers staged their defection, the only Druze member of the cabinet, ʿAdil Hamiya, minister of finance, resigned in protest over the government's role in the Shuf fighting and was not replaced by Prime Minister Shafiq Wazzan, who tendered his own resignation five months later in February, 1984.

For those Druze remaining in the Lebanese Army the risk of reprisals (or random attacks, depending upon whom you speak to) has grown. On August 23, 1984, the highest-ranking Druze in the army, Major General Nadim Hakim, aged 55, was killed in a helicopter crash in the mountains of northern Lebanon. Although the *Kataʾib* radio station described the event as "a tragic accident," many Druze, including Walid Junbalat, publicly expressed suspicions of a Phalangist assassination. On December 14, 1984, a Druze officer, Lieutenant Colonel ʿAdil Abu Rabiʿa, was shot dead in West Beirut by four unknown assailants. He was a commander in the predominantly Shia Sixth Brigade.[67] Not surprisingly, therefore, the Druze were un-

67. *International Herald Tribune,* Aug. 26, 1983, p. 2; *Daily Telegraph,* Oct. 3, 1983, p. 32; Washington *Post,* Feb. 6, 1984, pp. A1, A18, and Aug. 24, 1984, p. A25. On Aug. 3, 1985, the operations manager for ABC Television in Lebanon, Shakib Humaydan, a Druze, was kidnapped while traveling through *Amal*-controlled territory on the way to Beirut Airport (*International Herald Tribune,* Aug. 5, 1985, p. 5). On Aug. 19 a car bomb exploded near the Druze community center in Musaytba, West Beirut, killing twenty-two and wounding seventy-seven in retaliation for a car bombing in Antilyas on the Christian side two days earlier, which had killed fifty-five and wounded 119. "Christian leaders" blamed the Druze Militia for that bombing (*International Herald Tribune,* Aug. 20, 1985, p. 5).

willing to trust the presence of predominantly Maronite forces in their heartland, and their intransigence was strengthened by the gruesome massacre of Druze villagers at Kafar Mata in the Shuf foothills near Damur by retreating Lebanese militiamen from the *Kata'ib* in September 1983 (which were not discovered until Druze Militia forces took over the area in February 1984).[68]

The heir to the Junbalat leadership, Kamal's only son, Walid (aged 29 at the time of his father's assassination), quickly shed his image of an apolitical Good-time Charlie and reluctantly took up the responsibilities of leadership, which he has since exercised with an aplomb that has surprised many. Though not the towering figure that his father was—and perhaps the Lebanese Druze who owe him loyalty are better off for it—he has shown himself capable of assuming the mantle of traditional leadership in extremely troubled times. Though more frequently based in Damascus, where he has to give serious attention to the advice of the man who probably gave the order for his father's death, or in Amman, the home of his wife's family,[69] Walid Junbalat keeps abreast of developments in Lebanon by frequent visits to his family seat in al-Mukhtara. He has sensibly avoided Beirut as much as possible since the almost successful attempt on his life there on December 1, 1982.[70]

What has very obviously emerged as policy during the last three years, despite what Junbalat or his chief spokesman, Marwan Hammadi, might say publicly, is the creation of a very clearly defined sphere of Druze influence—a Druze antipode to the Maronite canton farther north. Should it be possible for the Lebanon demarcated by the 1926 boundaries to function once again then Junbalat would at least be able to speak on behalf of an area whose parameters were clear in everyone's mind. In order to achieve this policy he has had to rely at times on various outside sources of support, such as the Soviets and the Libyans, and to enter into temporary alliances with virtually every political grouping in the area, including the Maronites, Israel, and even Nabih Birri's *Amal* party of Shia, regardless of the visceral animosity felt by most Druze toward this sectarian Islamic group as a whole.[71] The Druze do

68. *Wall Street Journal* (European Edition), Sept. 7, 1983, p. 2. The Kafar Mata massacre was in retaliation for an earlier killing of thirty-four Christian civilians by Druze Militia at Bimaryam near Bihamdun on the Beirut-Damascus highway a few days before.

69. A Jordanian citizen from a mixed Druze and Sunni Muslim family of Circassian extraction, like Walid's mother. They have two young sons.

70. Exactly one year later, on Dec. 1, 1983, the chief Druze legal authority, Shaykh Halim Taqi al-Din, was assassinated by a lone gunman at his home in West Beirut. In Damascus, Walid Junbalat blamed the killing, which occurred on the first anniversary of the unsuccessful attempt on his life, on "criminals belonging to the Fascist gangs of the Christian Phalange" (Washington *Post,* Dec. 2, 1983, p. A22), a pretty safe supposition, since he had signed the *thawabit al-Islamiya* of Sept. 21. See *n.* 80 below.

71. Such support on occasion has required a grudging return of favors, as when Jun-

share with the Shia a desire to keep the PLO from ever again establishing a military base of operation in southern Lebanon,[72] and like Nabih Birri, Walid Junbalat has expressed willingness to negotiate directly with the Israelis for the withdrawal of the IDF from its remaining positions in the south.[73] But ultimately Druze and Shia goals of territorial spheres of influence are incompatible.

Apart from their rival claims within West Beirut itself,[74] there exists the question of controlling the south. Any attempt by the Shia to link their lands in the south with the large Shia population in West and South Beirut or in the northern Biqaʿ Valley (now controlled by the Syrians) would of necessity require control of the narrow coastal strip between Sidon and al-Khaldah (Khaldé) now held by Druze forces. It is at al-Khaldah that Junbalat has ordered the construction of a new port to serve the Druze canton, just as the Phalangist-sponsored port at al-Juniya (Junieh), fifteen kilometers north of Beirut, services the Maronite enclave. Taxes on incoming goods are levied by Junbalat's Druze government of the region, and it is estimated that between the two illegal ports the Lebanese treasury is deprived of nearly three-quarters of the revenues that would otherwise be coming to it. These revenues, though less than anticipated, have given the Druze canton at least some of the income the community believes it was denied when the Lebanese government and economy was controlled by the Maronites.

This crucial coastal territory, acquired at considerable cost by the Druze Militia in confrontation with Christian groups, most recently in late April of 1985,[75] is therefore essential to the viability of the canton Junbalat

---

balat felt constrained to send a token force of Druze fighters to assist Qaddhafi in his war with Chad (August 1987). With regard to Druze animosity toward the Shia, it should be understood that the hatred between Druze and Maronite is a hatred of equals; mutual respect exists on both sides. The hatred between Druze and Shia is magnified in its intensity by Druze contempt for the Shia as inferiors.

72. Los Angeles *Times,* Sept. 3, 1984.

73. Washington *Post,* Aug. 28, 1984.

74. On March 22, 1984, Druze militiamen completely destroyed the Sunni Muslim paramilitary group known as *al-Murabitun* in three hours of predawn street fighting. This left predominantly Muslim West Beirut in the hands of the Druze and the Shia *Amal* militias. The Druze controlled the area behind the Bristol Hotel south of al-Hamra, where most Druze in Beirut live (in the vicinity of their community center), as well as the airport. During the TWA hostage crisis of June 14–30, 1985, however, Junbalat abdicated the role of negotiating their release to the *Amal* leader, Nabih Birri, appropriately enough the minister of justice. Once the highjacking crisis was over, serious rifts began to appear in the Druze-Shia alliance. The attempted assassination of Druze Militia Regional Commander ʿImad Nawfal in West Beirut, probably by Shia Amal forces on July 19, 1985, brought matters to a head, and by late August the two sides were shooting at each other.

75. Estimates of displaced Christians vary greatly, from twenty thousand to sixty thousand (the latter figure suggested by the Maronite archbishop of Sidon, quoted in *La revue du Liban* (May 11–18, 1985, p. 20). The expulsion included grim desecrations of the monasteries of Dayr al-Mashmushah (Maronite) near Jazzin and Dayr al-Mukhallis (the Greek Catholic

has effectively created. Although it is not entirely devoid of Christians—there remains the major Maronite stronghold of Dayr al-Qamar in the very heart of the Shuf,[76] as well as several large Sunni towns, notably Barja and Shihim, overlooking the coast road between Sidon and Damur—the Druze Militia is in control of the entire area stretching from Sidon east to (but not including) the Christian (Maronite and Greek Catholic) town of Jazzin, north along the ridge of Mount Lebanon to the Beirut-Damascus highway, and along the coast to al-Khaldah just south of Beirut International Airport. Here the border runs slightly inland to the edge of Bʿabda (so as to include the Druze town of Shuwayfat) and from there east to ʿAlayh and ʿAyn Zahalta. From just north of Jazzin an extension protrudes across the Mount Lebanon ridge to the southern Biqaʿ Valley in order to include much of the historic cradle of Druzism, the Wadi al-Taym, in particular the town of Rashayya (one-quarter Greek Orthodox, three-quarters Druze). The remainder of the southern Lebanon Druze, including their principal concentration at Hasbayya, live within the jurisdiction of Israel or its South Lebanon Army (SLA) vassals, largely Christian in makeup but inclusive of significant numbers of Shia and Druze soldiers.[77] A smaller number of Druze live within the territory still occupied by the Syrian Army, which controls the strategic Beirut-Damascus highway as it descends from the Dahrat al-Baydaʾ pass to below the Druze resort town of Sawfar (Sofar) on the western slope of Mount Lebanon.

Unlike much of Lebanon, the region controlled by Junbalat's forces has for the most part been spared prolonged fighting or widespread destruction. Many Druze from Beirut and abroad have returned to their mountain villages to build new homes and establish businesses. A whole new com-

---

convent of the Holy Saviour) outside Jun, the oldest Catholic monastic establishment in southern Lebanon, where, according to reliable diplomatic sources quoting Junbalat, Druze militiamen defiled the iconostatis in the principal chapel in the same fashion as had been done in the 1860 massacres. The Druze contended that the land for the monastery had been given in 1709 by the father-in-law of Shaykh Ali Junbalat, who extended the donation (Abu-Izzeddin, *Druzes,* p. 208), but not, it would appear, in perpetuity.

76. In the fall of 1983, Dayr al-Qamar was the refuge of more than twenty-five thousand Christians who had fled the Druze-Lebanese forces fighting around Suq al-Gharb to the north. After three months' entrapment by Druze militiamen surrounding the hilltop town, Junbalat lifted the siege on Dec. 4, but the message of isolation was driven home to the townspeople who remained (Washington *Post,* Dec. 5, 1983, p. A13). The Maronites remain in Dayr al-Qamar with free access through Druze-controlled territory to Beirut and the north. Neighboring Bayt al-Din, however, has become the administrative center of the new Druze canton and no longer has a Christian population.

77. In September 1984, Druze members of General Antoine Lahhad's South Lebanon Army (SLA) attacked the Shia village of Sahmur in the Lower Biqaʿ Valley near Lake Qaraʿun and massacred thirteen male villagers in revenge for the killing of three Druze SLA soldiers the night before in an ambush at Sahmur by unknown assailants, presumably local Shia villagers (*Sunday Times,* Sept. 23, 1984, p. 19).

mercial center has mushroomed at Biqᶜata midway between Baᶜqlin and al-Mukhtara, where ten years ago there were only a few houses. It is such evidence of Druze determination to persevere, even thrive, in their ancient settlements that gives Junbalat and his militia the strength and confidence successfully to challenge President Gemayel's efforts to reestablish a Lebanon that reflects the 1943 National Covenant and its inherent Maronite dominance. Although officially a member of the national cabinet (as minister of transportation and public works), Junbalat has hardly concerned himself with its duties since Prince Minister Karami stopped attending to his own post in the spring of 1985 (he finally resigned on May 3, 1987, a month prior to his assassination on June 1). Junbalat's responsibility as he sees it is to fulfill his duties to the people of the Druze canton that his forces have created in the wake of the Israeli withdrawal from most of Lebanon. His challenge is to deal as best he can with those Druze still loyal to the Arslans (who, since the Kafar Mata massacre of September, 1983, have been far less supportive of the Gemayel government),[78] to fend off whenever possible the pressures of the Syrians and Israelis, both of whom hold large numbers of Druze within their boundaries, and to make the most of his position in dealing with President Gemayel and the more radical Christian factions that Gemayel seeks to control in attempting a solution to the seemingly insoluble problem of Lebanon's political structure. Junbalat's most recent tactic, perhaps in anticipation of the 1988 presidential election in Parliament, has been to ally himself with the Sunni Lebanese and the Palestinians (nearly all Sunnis) in Lebanon to counterbalance the rising strength of the Shia in what has been termed "a Palestinian-Sunni-Druze axis."[79]

What has been very carefully avoided are attempts to bring the Druze into any kind of umbrella declaration of "Islamic unity." Both Junbalat and the *shaykh al-ᶜaql,* Muhammad Abu-Shaqra, despite their personal antipathies (Abu-Shaqra is of the Yazbaki faction and frequently at odds with Junbalat over the latter's reputed profligacy), declined to participate in or sign the *thawabit al-islamiyya* (Declaration of the Fundamentals of the Islamic Position) signed by both the political and religious heads of the Sunni and Shia communities on September 21, 1983. Two Druze notables, however, did sign the document, including the leading legal authority of the Druze, Shaykh Halim Taqi al-Din (regarded at the time as second in spiritual matters to the *shaykh al-ᶜaql*); he was assassinated ten weeks later by unknown assailants.[80]

78. Both Junbalat and Khawla Arslan roundly condemned Gemayel and his government following the discovery of one hundred or more massacred Druze villagers at Kafar Matta (Washington *Post,* Mar. 2, 1984, p. A18).

79. See Rashid Hassan, "The PLO's Return to the Lebanese Equation," *Middle East International* (Feb. 6, 1987): 17–19.

80. See Marius K. Deeb, "Lebanon: Prospects for National Reconciliation in the mid-1980's," *Middle East Journal* 38, no. 2 (Spring 1984): 276–78. See also *n.* 70 above.

The overriding question that doubtless haunts Junbalat and other Druze leaders is how permanent the structure is of the Druze canton that has existed openly since 1982 (and in fact since the beginning of the breakdown of Lebanese civil government in 1975). The very existence of an autonomous "Druzistan" is a paradox of sorts because the Druze themselves are the most loyal of the various peoples and sects of Lebanon to the republic as belonging to all its inhabitants. The devotion of the Druze of Lebanon to their country is beyond doubt, despite their being denied full participation in the nation's government by the Maronite establishment since independence. Even today, with the Republic of Lebanon a political fiction, the Druze people and their leadership would welcome the return of political order so long as they felt they were offered a significant role in its administration, either on a purely secular basis or a restructured confessional distribution of power that fairly reflected Druze strength. There are signs that a compromise may indeed be in the offing, but for the present the other aspect of Druze loyalty, that which they owe to their own faith and sectarian community, dominates their thinking.

The Druze of Lebanon are perhaps the most fortunate of all their diverse countrymen in that they possess a geographically unified and politically tenable base that they are sufficiently strong culturally and militarily to defend. Most observers would judge, however, that this canton is not viable in the long term. And while it does encompass the vast majority of Druze settlements and inhabitants of Lebanon it does not of course include the larger Druze population in Syria, Israel, and Jordan, nor is it likely ever to do so. The Syrian Druze might like to dream of the possibility of linking themselves with the Druze canton on the other side of Mount Hermon, but the political and geographical realities argue strongly against such a hope becoming fact. The Druze of Galilee in Israel are too few, too dispersed, and too indifferent even to consider the possibility of union with Junbalat's fiefdom to the north. The canton exists today for the same reason that small principalities existed at the time of the Crusades—the collapse of local authority and the rivalries of major powers in the area who found it in their interest to allow the status quo to continue undisturbed. The strongest argument in favor of the possible permanence of a Druze canton is of course its continued existence over a period of years, during which a political, economic, and administrative infrastructure would develop and become increasingly difficult to dismantle. Already the Junbalat administration is collecting taxes, maintaining an army, building roads and hospitals, and performing every other function of responsible government, as are the Maronite canton's rulers to the north. If it remains at the moment a rather loose, ad hoc structure (not unreminiscent of the two qaʾim maqamates that existed between 1841 and 1860), this is not to say that it will fail to become more and more formalized and institutionalized as the years pass.

All major powers involved in the area refuse to accept the formal partition or even informal cantonization of Lebanon, and like the United States they insist on the country's territorial integrity as nonnegotiable. Reality of course paints a radically different picture, and unless some sort of compromise is worked out by the leaders (*al-zuʿamaʾ*) of the various communities in Lebanon whereby a centralized administration with authority everywhere within its internationally recognized frontiers can be reestablished to the overall satisfaction of the parties involved, then a Druze canton will continue to exist and gradually begin to entrench itself. Israel will not interfere, as it has no complaint with the Druze and certainly will not champion the Maronite cause against them after the political disaster resulting from the Israelis' 1982 efforts to aid the *Kataʾib*. Syria is unlikely to confront the Druze for a variety of reasons, not least of which is the fear of a Druze uprising at home such as those that twice shook the foundations of power in Damascus this century (in 1925 and 1953). With Hafiz al-Asad ruling his nation over the silent objection of the Sunni majority, Druze unrest could lead to serious consequences for the Alawi power structure.

An overall settlement of the Arab-Israeli question, hackneyed as this refrain may sound, coupled with a determination by all the principal factions in Lebanon to reach a workable compromise, is required before the temporary expedient of a quasi-independent Druze statelet in central and southern Lebanon can safely be abandoned by its inhabitants. History has proven the Druze to be fiercely tenacious in preserving their community's freedom to carry on their affairs as they see fit. They are not likely to abandon this tradition—as all those who have challenged Druze power have learned to their own distress, and a Druze canton is bound to remain an important factor in the area's political equation until a major change in its overall composition occurs.

Appendix

TABLE 1.
Confessional Distribution of the Six Subdistricts of Lebanon with Substantial Druze Population, 1932 Census

Qada'	Total	Druze	Christian	Sunni and Shia Muslim	% Druze
al-Matn	39,626	751	38,191	344	1.90
Bᶜabda	42,268	7,392	27,089	7,682	17.49
ᶜAlayh	37,847	17,588	19,324	850	46.47
al-Shuf	53,025	17,049	23,188	12,948	32.15
Marjᶜuyun*	32,867	4,171	8,315	20,323	12.04
Rashayya	11,711	4,424	3,779	3,508	37.78

*This includes the area of Hasbayya, where all the Druze population was concentrated.

TABLE 2.
Confessional Distribution of the Six Subdistricts of Lebanon with Substantial Druze Population, 1956 Estimate

*Qada*ʾ	Total*	Druze	Christian	Sunni and Shia Muslim	% Druze
al-Matn	85,610	1,700	82,844	940	1.99
Bʿabda	79,345	12,828	51,851	14,662	16.17
ʿAlayh	67,579	29,466	36,378	1,618	43.60
al-Shuf	96,009	28,083	45,244	22,702	29.25
Marjʿuyun/Hasbayya**	55,051	6,630	18,907	29,514	12.04
Rashayya	18,914	6,617	7,057	5,240	34.90

*Figures taken from *al-Nahar,* April 28, 1956.
**Nearly all the Druze (6,206) were found in and around the town of Hasbayya, where they accounted for 29.23 percent of the total population of 21,233.

TABLE 3.
Lebanese Population Figures According to *al-Nahar* (1975) and the New York *Times* (1984).

Community	*al-Nahar*	New York *Times*
Shia	970,000	1,000,000
Sunni	690,000	600,000
Druze	348,000	350,000
(Non-Christian subtotal)	(2,008,000)	(1,950,000)
Maronite	496,000	580,000
Greek Orthodox	230,000	350,000
Armenian Orthodox	260,000	220,000
Greek and Other Catholic	213,000	250,000
Other Christian	50,000	———
(Christian subtotal)	(1,249,000)	(1,400,000)
TOTAL	3,257,000	3,350,000

TABLE 4.
The Druze Settlements in Galilee as Reported in M. V. Guérin, *Description . . . de la Palestine,* 2 vols. (Paris: L'Imprimerie Nationale, 1880)

Settlement (Guérin's spelling in parentheses)	Citation (volume and page)	Statistics*
Shafa ʿAmr (Chefa Aʾmer)	I:410	Cette grosse bourgade . . . compte 2,500 habitants qui se décomposent ainsi: 705 Grecs unis, 400 Musulmans, 300 Druses, 80 Juifs et quelques protestants.
Sajur (Sedjour)	I:453	. . . un petit village, habité par des Druses. . . .
al-Rama (Er-Rameh)	I:453–4	Ce village, composé de 800 habitants, moitié Druses et moitié Grecs schismatiques, et divisé, par consequent, en deux quartiers différents. . . .
Mughar (El-Merhar)	I:457	C'est un grand village de 1,200 habitants, et divisé en trois quartiers, celui des Druses, celui des Musulmans et celui des Chrétiens. Ces derniers sont des Grecs unis. . . .
Kafar Yasif (Kefr Yasif)	II:4	Kefr Yasif renferme 600 habitants, parmi lesquelles 100 tout au plus sont Musulmans; les autres appartiennent à la religion grecque schismatique.
Julis (Djoules)	II:8	Ce village se compose d'une quarantaine de maisons, habitées par des Druses.
Yirka (Yerka)	II:16	Il continent une population de 850 Druses.
Jathth (Djett)	II:18	Ce village, habité par 150 Druses. . . .
Yanuh (Yanouah)	II:18	Ce village, habité par des Druses. . . .
Abu Sinan (Abou Senan)	II:21	Il est composé de 400 habitants au moins, parmi lesquels 260 sont Druses et 140 Grecs schismatiques.
Hurfaysh (Harfich)	II:73–4	Ce village, situé sur une colline dont les pentes, cultivées en terrasses, sont plantées d'oliviers, de vignes, de figuiers et de tabac, renferme une population de 300 Druses et de 50 Grecs unis.
Kafar Sumayʿ (Kefr Semeiaʾ)	II:77	Les habitants de Semeiaʾ sont presque tous Druses; un petit nombre de familles seulement appartiennent à la religion grecque schismatique.
Kisra (Kesra)	II:77–8	Ce village, habité aujourd'hui seulement par une certaine de Druses. . . .
al-Buqayʿa (Bekeiaʾ)	II:78–9	Celle qui l'habite aujourd'hui se compose de 600 individus, Druses, Grecs unis et Grecs schismatiques, auxquels il faut ajouter quelques familles juives, qui prétendent descendre des anciens habitants du pays.

TABLE 4. (*continued*)
The Druze Settlements in Galilee as Reported in M. V. Guérin, *Description . . . de la Palestine,* 2 vols. (Paris: L'Imprimerie Nationale, 1880)

Settlement (Guérin's spelling in parentheses)	Citation (volume and page)	Statistics*
Bayt Jann (Beit Djenn)	II:82–3	Ce village ne renferme plus en ce moment que 200 habitants, tous Druses; il était, il y a quelques années encore, bien plus considérable, comme l'indiquent beaucoup de maisons abandonnées qui commencent à tomber en ruine. On me dit que ceux qui les occupaient ont émigré dans le Hauran, pour échapper à la conscription.

*From these statistics one can infer a population of approximately 4,500–5,000 Druze in Galilee at the beginning of the last quarter of the nineteenth century. ʿAyn al-Asad is not mentioned.

TABLE 5.
Population of Principal Druze Settlements in Israel, 1961 Census

Settlement	Druze	Christian	Muslim	Total	% Druze
Yanuh	754	—	—	754	100.00
Sajur	628	—	—	628	100.00
Kisra	671	1	2	674	99.55
Bayt Jann and ʿAyn al-Asad	2,812	1	23	2,836	99.15
Yirka	2,688	—	31	2,719	98.86
Julis	1,378	2	69	1,449	95.10
Daliyat Karmil	3,914	10	196	4,120	95.00
Jathth	364	1	20	385	94.55
Hurfaysh	1,092	81	47	1,220	89.51
ʿIsifiya	2,227	628	47	2,902	76.74
Kafar Sumayʿ	427	122	27	576	74.13
al-Buqayʿa	997	433	61	1,491	66.87
Mughar	2,185	1,305	515	4,005	54.56
Abu Sinan	793	594	193	1,580	50.19
al-Rama	760	1,989	237	2,986	25.45
Shafa ʿAmru	1,470	3,217	2,529	7,216	20.37
Kafar Yasif	90	1,747	1,138	2,975	3.33
Total	23,250	10,131	5,135	38,516	60.36

TABLE 6.
Population of Principal Druze Settlements in Israel, 1972 Census

Settlement	Druze	Christian	Muslim	Total	% Druze
Julis	2,178	—	—	2,178	100.00
Yanuh	1,167	—	—	1,167	100.00
Jathth	599	—	—	599	100.00
Sajur	1,031	1	—	1,032	99.90
Bayt Jann	3,801	—	5	3,806	99.87
Yirka	4,375	3	4	4,382	99.84
Kisra	1,094	—	11	1,105	99.00
Daliyat Karmil	5,949	4	187	6,140	96.89
ᶜAyn al-Asad	359	1	14	374	95.99
Hurfaysh	1,715	110	51	1,876	91.42
ᶜIsifiya	3,396	791	65	4,252	79.87
Kafar Sumayᶜ	696	180	30	906	76.82
al-Buqayᶜa	1,418	753	82	2,253	62.94
Mughar	3,746	1,884	847	6,477	57.84
Abu Sinan	1,162	942	1,482	3,586	32.41
al-Rama	1,081	2,421	420	3,922	27.56
Shafa ᶜAmru	2,046	4,558	5,012	11,616	17.61
Kafar Yasif	130	2,286	1,392	3,808	3.41
Total	35,943	13,934	9,547	59,474	60.43

TABLE 7.
Population of Druze Settlements in Israel, 1983 Census

Settlement	Druze	Christian	Muslim	Jew/Other	Total	% Druze
Kisra	1,900	—	2	1	1,903	99.842
Julis	3,036	1	2	2	3,041	99.836
Jathth	942	—	2	—	944	99.79
Yanuh	1,866	—	6	—	1,872	99.679
Bayt Jann	5,555	2	10	6	5,573	99.677
Sajur	1,768	—	9	—	1,777	99.49
Yirka	6,406	4	66	5	6,481	98.84
Daliyat Karmil	8,227	1	220	3	8,451	97.35
ᶜAyn al-Asad	440	—	22	1	463	95.03
Hurfaysh	2,649	129	43	2	2,823	93.84
Kafar Sumayᶜ	1,038	230	32	—	1,300	79.85
ᶜIsifiya	4,827	1,111	372	12	6,322	76.67
al-Buqayᶜa	2,060	810	77	4	2,951	69.81
Mughar	5,756	2,554	2,008	5	10,323	55.76
Abu Sinan	1,778	1,336	2,833	1	5,948	29.89
al-Rama	1,475	2,836	721	2	5,034	29.30
Shafa ᶜAmru	2,892	5,608	8,367	12	16,879	17.13
Kafar Yasif	174	2,932	2,055	2	5,163	3.37
Total	52,789	17,554	16,847	58	87,248	60.51

TABLE 8.
Population of Arab Settlements in the Golan District, 1983 Census

Settlement	Druze	Christian	Muslim	Jew/Other	Total	% Druze
Biqʿata	3,109	—	—	—	3,109	100.00
Majd al-Shams	5,639	7	2	—	5,648	99.84
Masʿada	2,005	—	7	1	2,013	99.60
ʿAyn Qiniya	1,152	11	—	—	1,163	99.05
al-Ghajar	3	—	938*	—	941	00.32
Total	11,908	18	947	1	12,881	92.97

*Alawi (see Chapter 6, footnote 41).

Glossary of Arabic and Islamic Terms, Persons, and Places

Abbasids—Dynasty of caliphs who ruled from Baghdad, 750–1254. Within a hundred years of its founding by Abū al-ʿAbbās (who overthrew the Umayyads of Damascus) the actual power exercised by his successors began to wane. By the time of the rise of Druzism in the early eleventh century A.D. they were largely figureheads, and their government's authority did not extend much beyond Baghdad and the surrounding region of Mesopotamia.

ʿAbdallah ibn Maymūn al-Qaddāḥ—Adopted son and spiritual heir of Muḥammad ibn Ismāʿīl, son of Ismāʿīl ibn Jaʿfar, who is considered by the Sevener (Ismāʿīlī) sect of Shīʿa Islām to be the true successor to the prophet Muḥammad. Al-Qaddāḥ is regarded as the "second founder" (Hitti, *History of the Arabs,* p. 617) of Isma'ili Shi'ism, and his descendants founded the Fatimid empire in Egypt and North Africa as well as the Qarmaṭian movement in Arabia and Mesopotamia. His teaching was of considerable influence on the founders of the Druze faith.

Abū-Nakad—Prominent Druze family of the Yamani faction, centered in the northern Shūf district of Lebanon.

Abū Shaqra—Prominent Druze family of Lebanon from the village of ʿAmaṭūr in the southern Shūf mountains. The present Shaykh al-ʿAql of the Lebanese Druze community is Muḥammad Abū Shaqra.

Abū Sinān—Village in western Galilee of mixed Muslim, Christian, and Druze population; of these the Druze were the largest until the early 1970s, when they were surpassed in numbers by the Muslims.

Acre—See *ʿAkkā.*

ā'ima—Plural of *imām,* q.v.

Ajāwīd—Literally, the "righteous" (singular *Jawād*). The highest rank of the religiously initiated Druze.

ʿAkkā (Acre)—Seaport in northern Israel (largely Jewish but with a substantial Arab, chiefly Muslim, minority); last stronghold of the Crusaders in Palestine, which fell to the Mamlūks in 1291. Many villages in the immediate hinterland are Druze.

ʿAlam al-Dīn—Prominent Lebanese Druze family, one of whose leading members, Najīb ʿAlam al-Dīn, was president of Middle East Airlines.

ʿAlawī (also Alawite and Nusairi)—A secretive quasi-Islamic sect, like the Druze an offshoot of extremist Ismāʿīli Shi'ism. Its adherents, who make up approximately 11 percent of Syria's population, are found principally in the district of Latakia. Syria's president, Ḥāfiẓ al-Asad, and much of the ruling elite are members of this sect.

ʿAlayh (Aley)—Resort town on the lower slope of Mount Lebanon, administrative seat of the *qaḍā'* (caza) of the same name. Largely Druze in population and traditional residence of the Arslāns, one of the two principal Druze ruling families of Lebanon.

ʿAlī—Kinsman of the prophet Muḥammad who married his only daughter, Fāṭima; ruled as the fourth caliph of Islām (656–661) from al-Kūfa in Iraq, where he was assassinated. His sons and heirs were the spiritual and political leaders of the Shia sect until the disappearance of the twelfth *imām,* al-Muntaẓar in the late ninth century. Al-Ḥākim, the founder of the Druze movement, like all Fatimid caliphs claimed ʿAlī and Fāṭima as his ancestors.

ʿAmaṭūr—Large Druze village in the southern Shūf mountains of Lebanon; home of the Abū Shaqra family (q.v.).

amīr (emir)—Literally, "prince." A title taken by leading Druze political figures of the Tanūkh, Arslān, Maʿn, and Shihāb families.

amīr al-Ḥajj—Title given to the leader of the annual pilgrimage (*ḥajj*) to Mecca; honor accorded the son of Fakhr al-Dīn II at the height of Druze power in Lebanon in the early seventeenth century, despite his dubious Islamic orthodoxy.

al-Amīr al-Sayyid al-Tanūkhī—A fifteenth-century Lebanese Druze leader and sage (1417–1479) who is deeply revered by the Druze community.

ʿāqil and *ʿāqila*—The masculine and feminine forms respectively of the title given to those who have been initiated into the secrets of the Druze religion. The plural is *ʿuqqāl* (feminine *ʿāqilāt*).

al-ʿAql—The title, meaning "Universal Intelligence," given to Ḥamza, the leading propagator of the Druze faith, as first among the five *ḥudūd,* or dignitaries, of the movement.

al-ʿAql al-Kullī—The Universal Intelligence of God that has manifested its presence in human form in such persons as Shuʿayb (Jethro) in Old Testament times, Salmān al-Fārisī, contemporary with the life of Muḥammad, and finally in the person of Ḥamza (q.v.).

Arslān—One of the two ruling Druze families of Lebanon (the other is the Junbalāt family); they are of august Arab ancestry who originally ruled from Shuwayfāt near Beirut but now have their seat at ʿAlayh. The Arslāns are the traditional leaders of the Yazbakī political faction in Lebanon (heirs to the Yamanis, or South Arabs), while the Junbalāṭs are heirs to the Qaysi, or North Arab, grouping. The leading figure in this century was Prince Majīd Arslān (1904–1983), a veteran of many Lebanese cabinets since independence.

Arṣūn—One of the northernmost Druze settlements in Lebanon; formerly mixed in population with Maronites and Greek Orthodox but now largely Druze.

al-Asad, Ḥāfiẓ—Born 1928. One of the leaders of the Baʿth party coup in Syria, 1966; president since 1970. Member of the Alawite (ʿAlawī) sect, which like the Druze has Isma'ili Shia origins and keeps many of its tenets secret.

ʿāshūrā—Shia day of mourning and fasting that commemorates the anniversary of the martyrdom of Ḥusayn ibn-ʿAlī, grandson of the prophet Muḥammad, at Karbalāʾ in Iraq on the tenth day of the Muslim month of Muharram, A.H. 61.

Assassins—Name given to the Ismāʿīlīs of western Syria (near Latakia) and later Iran whose series of political assassinations terrorized both the Muslim and Christian Crusader leadership of Syria and Iraq in the twelfth and thirteenth centuries. Their name derives from the Arabic *ḥashīshīn* meaning "users of ḥashīsh," since the use of this drug was common among those carrying out their leaders' missions of political murder.

atʿābūha—Term used to describe the financial support given by a Druze man to the wife he has divorced. Although not legally required, it is a very common voluntary feature of marriage settlements in Druze society.

al-Aṭrash—Leading Druze family of the Jabal al-Durūz in Syria since the late eighteenth century. In this century the dominant figure was Sultān al-Aṭrash (1887–1982), leader of the Druze Rebellion of 1925 and the Syrian nationalist independence movements that followed.

ʿAtsha, Zaydān—Member of the Knesset for the Shinui party since July 1984. One of two Druze deputies in the current Israeli Parliament.

Awqāf—See *waqf*.

ʿawrāt—Literally, "genitals," sometimes translated as "nakedness" when referring to its use in describing the nature of women by the Druze holy man and sage, al-Amīr al-Sayyīd al-Tanūkhī.

ʿAyn Dāra—Site of the defeat in 1711 by the Qaysī (North Arab) faction of Lebanon's Druze over the Yamani (South Arab) faction, as a result of which large numbers of the defeated party and their families fled eastward beyond the Hawrān plain in present-day Syria, settling the then unpopulated region now known as the Jabal al-Druze.

ʿAyn Jālūṭ—Site of battle, near Nazareth, in 1260 that saw the defeat of the Mongols by the Mamlūks of Cairo, aided by their allies, including the Druze.

al-Azhar—Mosque and theological school, later university, established in the newly built Fatimid capital of Cairo in 972 as a center of Isma'ili worship and learning. After the conquest of Egypt by Saladin in 1174 it became and remained the leading educational establishment of Sunni orthodoxy in the Arab World. Along with the mosque of al-Hākim, founder of the Druze religion, it is one of principal architectural monuments of the Fatimid period.

Bʿabdā—Christian township in the foothills of Mount Lebanon directly to the southeast of Beirut, overlooking the city. Served as the administrative capital of Mount Lebanon during the *mutaṣarrifīya* of 1861–1914.

Bahāʾ al-Dīn—One of the principal disciples of Ḥamza and leading figure in the early spread and development of Druzism. An author of numerous epistles in the Druze

Canon, he is revered in the faith as the *muqtanā,* or imam's deputy, and the fifth of the dignitaries (*al-ḥudūd*), the Left Wing, or Follower.

Banū al-Maᶜrūf—Term by which the Druze are known and refer to themselves, literally the sons of Beneficence or Generosity, a reference to their universally acknowledged tradition of hospitality.

Banū al-Tanūkh—One of the Bedouin Arab tribes who form the known antecedents of the Druze community. They are thought to have emigrated in the third century A.D. from the area between the Tigris and Euphrates rivers (*al-Jazīra,* or "island") to the region of Mount Lebanon via the Arab client state of the Eastern Roman Empire, al-Ḥīra in Lower Mesopotamia.

Baᶜqlīn—Druze town in the central Shūf mountains, a center of the Druze faith since the earliest times of its penetration northward from the Wādī al-Taym.

Bārūk—Largely Druze town in the eastern Shūf at the foot of the mountain of the same name, noted for its large stand of ancient cedars, one of the few remaining in Lebanon.

Baᶜth—Political party (literally, "Renaissance") founded in 1940 by two Damascene ideologues, Michel ᶜAflaq and Salāḥ al-Dīn al-Bītār, the former Greek Orthodox and the latter Sunni Muslim. Based on western socialist thought, it strongly advocates secular government and rejects traditional catering to narrow confessional interests. It has been the ruling party in Syria since 1963, and its membership has been drawn disproportionately from various minority groups, especially the 'Alawis, Druze, and Christians.

bāṭin—Isma'ili Shia doctrine which teaches that Islām and the Qur'ān should be "interpreted allegorically and religious truth . . . ascertained by the discovering of an inner meaning (*bāṭin*) of which the outer form (*ẓāhir*) was but a veil intended to keep that truth from the eyes of the uninitiate" (Hitti, *History of the Arabs,* p. 443). Recognized by the Druze as a stage in theological development toward the ultimate goal, the *tawḥīd,* or perfect Unitarian Faith.

Bātir—Southernmost Druze village in the Shūf, the first Druze settlement on the road north from the Christian center of Jazzīn. From Bātir a road to the east leads to the Druze village of Nīḥā and the major shrine (*mazār*) of al-Nabī Ayyūb.

Bayt al-Dīn (Beiteddine)—Village in the central Shūf, formerly Maronite now Druze, and administrative center of the autonomous Druze canton of Lebanon; site of the arabesque palace of the amīr Bashīr II, Maronite Shihābī ruler of Mount Lebanon (1788–1840), built during the years 1812–1815 to rival the palace of his enemy the Druze amīr Bashīr Junbalāṭ of nearby al-Mukhtāra, whom he defeated and had murdered in 1825.

al-Biqāᶜ (Bekaa)—Valley in central Lebanon between the Lebanon and Anti-Lebanon mountain ranges. Its population is largely Shia Muslim, with large Sunni and Christian (Greek Orthodox and Greek Catholic) minorities. It is the source of two principal rivers of the region, the Orontes (*al-ᶜĀṣī*), which flows northward through Syria into the Mediterranean via Antioch in Turkey, and the Leontes (*al-Līṭānī*), which runs to the south into the Mediterranean near Tyre.

Biqᶜāta—Druze settlement in the central Shūf, which since the Lebanese civil war began in 1975 has grown into an important town and commercial center for the region.

Birrī, Nabīh—Lebanese Shia politician, leader of the *Amāl* party and paramilitary force, sometime ally of the Druze Militia and Lebanese Druze leader Walīd Junbalāṭ.

al-Buqayʿa—Druze village in northern Galilee, with large Greek Orthodox minority; among the more conservative Druze settlements in Israel.

Caliph—In Arabic, *Khalīfat Rasūl Allāh,* the successor to the Prophet of God, who, according to Sunni Muslim tradition, ruled the Islamic world as both its political and religious leader, beginning with the first of the orthodox (*al-rashidūn*) caliphs, Abū Bakr (632–634), and continuing in an unbroken succession until the institution of the caliphate was abolished by Kemal Atatürk in 1924, having been held by the Ottoman sultans since 1517.

caza—See *qaḍāʾ*.

Chamoun—See *Shamʿūn*.

ḍāḍ—Fifteenth letter of the Arabic alphabet, the velarized "d" sound of which is peculiar to the Arabic language, hence its description by the Arabs as *lughat al-ḍāḍ* (the language of the *ḍāḍ*); like a number of classical Arabic consonants, it has undergone changes in most modern colloquial dialects, but the Arabic spoken by the Druze has maintained its classical purity.

Dāliyat Karmil—One of two predominantly Druze villages on the eastern slope of Mount Carmel in Israel. With its population approaching ten thousand (all but 250 of whom are Druze), it is the largest predominantly Druze settlement in Israel and the third in size where large numbers of Druze are found (after Shafā ʿAmrū and Mughār). One of the two Druze deputies in the present Israeli Knesset, Amal Naṣr al-Dīn (LIKUD), is from this village.

al-Darazī, Muḥammad—Surnamed *al-nashtakīn* from the Turkish word *neştegin* meaning the son of a Turk by a non-Turkish woman; one of the early disciples of al-Ḥākim and Ḥamza, who quarreled with Ḥamza over both the leadership and theology of the Druze faith, resulting in his assassination in Cairo in 1019. He is traditionally credited with having carried the message of Druzism to southern Lebanon, where it took firm root, and with having given the new religion its popular name. Al-Darazī in Arabic means tailor.

darz—In Arabic, "seam, hem, suture," the plural of which is *durūz,* the same word as the plural of *durzī* (the singular for a member of the Druze community).

daʿwa—Literally, "call, appeal, bidding." In the Druze faith it is the Divine Call or summons to true Unitarian belief, proclaimed in 1017 and closed to further converts in 1043.

Dayr al-Qamar—Large Maronite town in the central Shūf district, natal village of Lebanese President Kamīl Shamʿūn (1952–1958); in Arabic, "Monastery of the Moon"; in the seventeenth century it was the seat of the Druze *amīr* Fakhr al-Dīn II.

Dirʿā—Administrative capital of the Ḥawrān district in southern Syria, a Sunni Muslim stronghold flanked by large Druze concentrations to the east (Jabal al-Durūz) and west (Wādī al-Taym and Golan).

dīwān—The reception area of a traditional Arab home where guests are received and offered hospitality. The English words *divan* and *davenport,* which describe comfortable pieces of furniture, derive from this Arabic source.

Druze—Anglicized form of *durūz,* the plural of *durzī,* or member of the Druze community.

Durūz—See *Druze*.

Durzī—See *Druze*.

Fakhr al-Dīn I—Lebanese *amīr* (died 1544) who was confirmed by the conquering Ottoman sultan Selim the Grim (having defeated the previously ruling Mamlūks of Cairo at the battle of Marj Dābiq in 1516 near Aleppo) as ruler of the Druze Mountain (Hitti, *History of the Arabs,* p. 729). Grandfather of Fakhr al-Dīn II.

Fakhr al-Dīn II—Leading scion of the princely Maʿn family of Mount Lebanon, whose enlightened reign (1590–1635) witnessed the opening of Lebanon to Western religious and cultural influence. Continually at odds with the Ottoman Porte in Constantinople, he was forced to flee his homeland in 1613 and spent the next five years as a guest of the Medici prince of Florence, Cosimo II. Upon his return home he introduced European technological innovations and ideas that were to make Lebanon a center for revolutionary change in the Islamic world. Outwardly a Sunni Muslim, inwardly a Druze, and possibly a Maronite Christian on his death, Fakhr al-Dīn II embodies all that is remarkable and, because of his tolerance, self-destructive in the Lebanon of today.

Fāṭima—Daughter of the prophet Muḥammad, his only child to survive into adulthood. Married to the prophet's kinsman ʾAli, she bore two sons, Ḥasan and Ḥusayn, both of whom are considered by the Shia sect of Islam to be the true inheritors of righteous succession to the caliphate.

Fāṭimid—Term that refers to the North African empire established by followers of the Ismāʿīlī (Sevener) sect of Shia Islam in Tunisia in A.D. 909. In 969 they overran Egypt, establishing their capital at Cairo, and for the next two centuries dominated much of the Islamic world, extending their boundaries into Palestine, Syria, and the Arabian peninsula. The sixth Fāṭimid imam-caliph, al-Ḥākim bi ʿamr-Allāh (ruled 996–1021), is the founder of the Druze faith.

Gemayel—Prominent Maronite family (al-Jumayyil) closely associated with the *Phalanges Libanaises* (*al-Kataʾib*), a militantly Christian party based on Fascist ideology that has adamantly refused to accept any but Maronite political rule in the modern Republic of Lebanon. The current president of Lebanon, Amīn al-Jumayyil, is the son of Pierre Gemayel (died 1984), founder of the Phalangist party.

ghayba—State of occultation into which the twelfth Shia *imām,* Muḥammad al-Muntaẓar, is said to have passed pending his return as the mahdi, or redeemer, and precursor of the end of time.

al-Ghūṭa—The rich farming district to the east and south of Damascus, an oasis formed by the waters of the Barada River. An early center of Druzism and still home to a small number of Druze in a handful of villages.

Golān—In Arabic, *al-Jūlān,* region directly east of the Sea of Galilee, assigned to the Syrian Mandate by the League of Nations and conquered by Israeli armed forces in 1967; annexed to the state of Israel in 1981 over universal international objection. Originally the home of more than a hundred thousand Syrian Arab and Circassian Muslims and Christians as well as a large Druze minority inhabiting four villages on the southern slope of Mount Hermon, it was forcibly depopulated by the Israeli occupying force. Only the Druze villages and one Alawi settlement were allowed to remain, and small numbers of Israeli settlers have established themselves in a handful of recently constructed Jewish townships.

al-Ḥadīth—Verbal pronouncements of the prophet Muḥammad, which along with the written testament of *al-Qurʾān* are considered by faithful Muslims to be all that is required for the foundation of their faith. These sayings were transmitted orally for generations before being at last verified and written down in an acceptable codification in the ninth century A.D., nearly two hundred years after Muḥammad's death.

al-Hāfiẓ, Amīn—Sunni Muslim Syrian army officer who came to power with the Baʿthi coup in 1963; overthrown by a second coup in 1966 led by ʾAlawi and Druze factions within the party.

ḥajj—The pilgrimage to the shrine of the *kaʿba* (Kaaba) in Mecca that takes place annually. It is included among the Five Pillars of Islām and is required of the Muslim faithful once in their lifetime, provided they are not financially or physically unable to perform it. Occasionally, pious Druze will perform the *ḥajj*, but there is nothing in their religion that requires or even recommends it.

al-Ḥākim—The sixth Fatimid imam-caliph, who ruled the Isma'ili Shia Fatimid empire from 996 until his disappearance and/or death in 1021. During the latter years of his reign the Druze call (*daʿwa*) was proclaimed (1017) and al-Ḥākim worshiped by devotees of the new religion as the fulfillment of Isma'ili theological expectation and embodiment of the godhead.

al-Ḥākimīya—Term by which the Druze were referred to early in their history by non-Druze Arabs, meaning "followers of al-Ḥākim."

Ḥalab—Arabic name for the city of Aleppo in northern Syria; literally it means the milking of an animal, and according to one tradition it marks the sport where Abraham "was very liberal in bestowing the milk" of his flock during his peregrination from Ur of the Chaldees (in Muslim tradition the city of Urfa, ancient Edessa, in Turkey) to the Promised Land (see Green, *Journey from Aleppo*, p. 2, *n.* [a]). In the early years of the *daʿwa* a principal Druze center.

Ḥalabī—Common Druze family name found throughout the Middle East but especially among the Druze of the northern Jabal al-Druze and Mount Carmel in Israel. Original meaning is someone from Aleppo.

ḥalāl—In Islam that which is permitted as opposed to that which is forbidden (*ḥarām*); with reference to food it describes which animals may be eaten and how they are to be slaughtered. The Druze traditionally follow Muslim custom in the preparation of meat.

Ḥamdān—One of the principal Druze families of Lebanon and Syria. Originally the Ḥamdān led the migration of Yemeni Druze from Mount Lebanon to the Jabal al-Druze in Syria following the defeat of their faction at the battle of ʿAyn Dārā. Once settled in Syria they were eclipsed in power and influence by the al-Aṭrash clan.

Ḥammādī, Marwān—Editor of Beirut's prestigious daily newspaper *al-Nahār* during the 1970s whose sister, although Druze, was married to the paper's owner and former Lebanese ambassador to the United Nations, Ghassān Tuwayni, a Greek-Orthodox Christian. After Walīd Junbalāt assumed the leadership of his family's faction of the Lebanese Druze community, Ḥammādi emerged as his primary spokesman and adviser.

Ḥammānā—Large Christian village in the eastern Matn region (Bʿabdā subdistrict) with an established Druze minority. Site of a large defection by Druze soldiers from the Lebanese Army in 1983.

Ḥamza ibn-ʿAlī ibn Aḥmad al-Zūzanī—Leading disciple of the *imām* al-Ḥākim and proponent of the Druze faith in the earliest years of the *daʿwa;* author of numerous epistles in the Druze Canon and highest-ranking of the five dignitaries (*ḥudūd*).

ḥarām—That which is proscribed by Muslim law and tradition and forbidden to the faithful. Certain of these proscriptions pertaining to food, especially meat and its preparation, are traditionally observed by the Druze.

Ḥasan—Elder son of ʾAli, son-in-law of Muḥammad, and Fāṭima, the prophet's daughter. He abdicated the imamate in favor of his younger brother Ḥusayn and lived out his life in retirement in Medina, according to Sunni historians; Shia sources assert that he was poisoned.

Ḥaṣbayyā—Predominantly Druze town in southeast Lebanon on the slope of Mount Hermon overlooking the Wādī al-Taym. Nearby is the *Khalawāt al-Bayyāḍa,* one of the main Druze shrines and site of the principal Druze theological school.

Ḥāṭūm, Salīm—High-ranking Druze army officer in the Syrian Baʿth party government, 1963–1966; led an unsuccessful coup against the Alawite establishment headed by Ḥāfiẓ al-Asad and Ṣalāḥ al-Jadīd in early September 1966, after which he fled to Jordan. Since then there have been no Druze officers within the inner circle of power in the Syrian military. He returned to Syria in 1967 and was executed.

al-Ḥawrān—Province (*muḥāfaẓa*) in southwest Syria between the Golan and Jabal al-Druze. Largely Muslim in population, with a small Christian minority. The term is sometimes applied to the whole southern region of Syria including the Jabal al-Druze, and the Druze of Lebanon often refer to their Syrian cousins as "Ḥawranis."

Hermon, Mount—See *Jabal al-Shaykh.*

al-Ḥijāz—Red Sea coastal region of present-day Saudi Arabia, site of the two holiest cities in the Islamic world, Mecca (al-Makka) and Medina (al-Madīna).

hijra—Often called "hegira" in English, the *hijra* is the flight of Muḥammad and his early disciples from Mecca to Medina in A.D. 622 to avoid persecution for their religious beliefs. The Islamic calendar begins with this event, and A.H. (after *hijra*) is to Muslim historical reckoning as A.D. is to Christian.

al-Ḥikmat al-Sharīfa—Literally, the Noble Knowledge that contains the sacred writings of the Druze, or Druze Canon, comprising 111 epistles in six volumes.

al-Ḥizb al-Ishtirākī al-Taqaddūmī—The Progressive Socialist party, founded in 1949 by Kamāl Junbalāṭ, whose membership remained largely confined to those Druze loyal to the Junbalat family.

al-Ḥizb al-Qawmī—The [Syrian] Nationalist party, founded by Anṭūn Saʿāda in 1932, which advocates the political union of Greater Syria (Syria, Lebanon, Jordan, and Palestine) under a secular government. Like the Baʿth party, it attracted large numbers of religious minority members, including Christians (chiefly Orthodox), Alawis, Druze, and Shias. Still very active and more commonly known by its French name, *Parti Populaire Syrien* (PPS).

Ḥizb al-Shaʿb—The People's party, an early Syrian Arab nationalist movement that joined forces with Sulṭān al-Aṭrash in the uprising of 1925.

al-ḥudūd—The five "dignitaries" of the Druze faith to whom cosmic rank were attributed by Ḥamza. Colors were later associated with each of the five and are mostly commonly represented in the so-called Druze Star.

Ḥusayn—Younger son of ʾAli and Fāṭima, who was martyred at Karbalāʾ in Iraq on the tenth day of the Muslim month of Muḥarram (A.H. 61, or October 10, 680) by forces of the second Umayyad caliph, al-Yazīd I. This event is celebrated annually throughout the Shia world.

Ḥusayn, Sharīf of Mecca—Ruler of the Hijāz and ally of the British against the Ottomans during World War I with the understanding that he would be made king of a Greater Arabia after a Turkish defeat. In fact, most of the territories promised him were given instead as mandates to the British and French, and Ḥusayn himself was overthrown by ʿAbd al-Azīz ibn-Saʿūd, founder of the Saudi Arabian state and dynasty, in 1924. His great-grandson, King Ḥusayn of Jordan, continues to rule a small portion of the greater inheritance that Ḥusayn of Mecca had claimed for the Hashemite (al-Hāshim) family—the line of the prophlet Muḥammad from which he claimed direct descent.

Iblīs—Satan, or the rival of Ḥamza, whom de Sacy in his "Exposé of the Druze Religion" equates with the calf image that the Druze were reputed to worship or revile in secret.

ʿīd al-aḍḥā—Major Islamic feast occurring at the end of the month of the annual pilgrimage to Mecca, the one Muslim religious celebration that is observed by the Druze.

ʿīd al-fiṭr—Major Islamic feast occurring at the end of the month of fasting (*Ramaḍān*); neither the fast nor the feast that breaks it is observed by Druze today, although in times past it was not uncommon for them to do so.

imām—In early Islām the leader of public prayer in the mosques, and so he remains in Sunni tradition. For the Shia the title *imām* was reserved for successors to the sons of ʿAli and their spiritual and political leaders.

īmān—In traditional Islām the term for religious belief. For the Isma'ili Shia it is the greater belief of which Islām (submission) is only a part, the first stage.

imāra—Territory ruled by an *amīr,* or prince. The *imāra* refers to the autonomous state governed by Fakhr al-Dīn II and his successors.

iqṭāʿ—A piece of land usually held under feudal terms; refers to the feudal domination under which most Maronite farmers were held by Druze landowners until the collapse of the system in the early nineteenth century.

ʿirḍ—A person's honor, or reputation, especially a woman's chastity before marriage and fidelity after.

ʿIsifīya—One of two Druze settlements on the eastern slope of Mount Carmel near Haifa in Israel. ʿIsifīya is the smaller of the two (population approaching seven thousand), of which more than 20 percent is Christian, largely Greek Catholic. One of the two Druze members of the Knesset, Zaydān ʿAtsha (Shinui party), is from ʿIsifīya.

Islām—Literally, "submission"; the religion inparted to the Arabs by the prophet Muḥammad and widely disseminated throughout the Middle East, North Africa, and central Asia after his death. The Druze faith is an outgrowth, nearly four centuries later, of sectarian theological movements well outside the mainstream religious development.

Ismāʿīl ibn Jaʿfar—Discredited elder son of the sixth Shia *imām,* whose followers refused to accept his having been passed over and acclaimed him and his successors as the true imams. They are known as Ismāʿīlis, or Seveners. Ismāʿīl died in 760, five years before his father, Jaʿfar al-Ṣādiq.

Ismāʿīl al-Tamīmī—The second in rank of the five Druze dignitaries (*ḥudūd*), called *al-Nafs,* or the "Universal Soul."

Ismaʿilis—Shia Muslims who revere the elder son of the sixth *imām,* Ismāʿīl ibn Jaʿfar, as the rightful successor to his father, rather than his younger brother Mūsā.

Isma'ilis are known as Seveners, since they consider Ismāʿīl to have been the seventh *imām* despite the fact that his father and the majority of other Shias refused to accept his claim to the title, on account of his dissolute ways. The larger group of Shias are known as Twelvers.

Jabal al-Aʿlā—Mountainous region in northwestern Syria near the Turkish border south of Antioch, which has been inhabited by small communities of Druze since the founding of the religion. The Druze population, contained in a dozen small villages, is estimated at anywhere from twenty thousand to forty thousand.

Jabal al-ʿArab—See Jabal al-Durūz.

Jabal al-Durūz—Hilly region to the east of the Ḥawrān plain in southern Syria inhabited by Druze since the early eighteenth century. It is closely coterminous with the province of al-Suwaydā and contains upward of 350,000 inhabitants, more than 90 percent of whom are Druze.

Jabal al-Shaykh—Arabic for Mount Hermon, the peak of Old Testament fame that sits astride the borders of Syria, Lebanon, and Israel.

al-Jadīd, Ṣalāḥ—One of the leading figures in the 1966 coup within the Baʿth party government that brought Ḥafiẓ al-Asad to power; like al-Asad, Jadīd was an ʾAlawi, but this did not prevent his being purged from the government in 1970.

jāhil—See *juhhāl.*

Jarbūʿ, Husayn—The senior of the three shuyūkh al-ʿAql of Syria. He is the Shaykh al-ʿAql of al-Suwaydāʾ, capital of the Jabal al-Durūz and largest Druze settlement in the Middle East.

al-Jazīra—Region in eastern Syria and western Iraq between the Tigris and Euphrates rivers; original home of the tribes of al-Tanūkh and al-Maʿn, two of the principal Arab Bedouin ancestors of the present-day Druze.

jihād—The so-called Sixth Pillar of Islām, literally "holy war," which Muslims are urged to wage against unbelievers.

jihāz—In Druze law and tradition regarding dowry, the "wife's requirements," i.e., clothing and jewelry, are considered over and above the strictly monetary settlement.

juhhāl (singular *jāhil*)—Literally, the ignorant, a term applied to Druze who are not among those initiated into the mysteries and secrets of their religion (the *ʿuqqāl*).

al-Jūlān—See Golan.

al-Jumayyil—See Gemayel.

al-Junbalāṭ—Leading political Druze family of Lebanon. Originally from Aleppo of alleged Kurdish stock, the descendants of ʿAli Janbulad (the autonomous ruler of the Aleppo region defeated and executed by the sultan in 1607) emigrated to Lebanon to seek protection from Ottoman wrath in the autonomous *imāra* of Fakhr al-Dīn II, an ally of their late chieftain. They settled in the Shūf mountains, where in time they came to be accepted as Druze and through judicious marriages gradually gained political strength, emerging after the watershed of ʿAyn Dāra as the leading family of the North Arab Druze faction. The Junbalats rivaled the newly Christian Maronite Shihābs for power in the mountain until the defeat of Bashīr Junbalāṭ by Bashīr II Shihāb at the battle of al-Simqānīya in 1825. Druze fortunes fell even further after the massacres and upheavals of 1860 and the ensuing intervention of the Maronites' French protectors; it was not until the independence of Lebanon after World War II that the Junbalāṭ family, under the leadership of the late

Kamāl (assassinated in 1977), began to reassert itself politically. Since the dissolution of the Lebanese state as an integrated territorial unit began in 1975, the current Junbalāṭ leader, Kamāl's son Walīd, has created (with the assistance of his locally powerful Druze Militia) an autonomous Druze canton encompassing nearly all the villages of Lebanon inhabited by adherents of the Druze faith.

Kafar—Small village in the Jabal al-Druze where a column of French infantry was annihilated on July 21, 1925, by Druze forces belonging to Sulṭān al-Aṭrash, thus beginning the Syrian Druze Rebellion of 1925 that spread to much of the French Mandate territories over the next two years. *Kafar* in Arabic means village or hamlet.

Kafar Sumayʿ—Small village, predominantly Druze (80 percent of some fifteen hundred inhabitants, the remainder of whom are Greek Orthodox), in north-central Galilee, a stronghold of conservative Druze practice and tradition.

Kafar Yāsīf—Large Arab village in western Galilee of more than six thousand inhabitants, 57 percent Christian (nearly all Greek Orthodox), 40 percent Muslim, and a mere 3 percent Druze. It is nonetheless the site of an important Druze shrine, the *maqām Sayyidinā al-Khiḍr.* In April 1981 a serious outbreak of violence between the Christians of Kafar Yāsif and the Druze inhabitants of neighboring Jūlis (home of the Shaykh al-ʿAql of Israel, Amīn Ṭarīf) resulted in several deaths and considerable destruction of property.

al-Kalima—Literally, the "Word"; term applied to the third-ranking dignitary (*ḥudūd*) of the Druze faith, Muḥammad ibn Wahb al-Qurashī.

al-Kataʾib—Arabic for *Les Phalanges Libanaises,* the right-wing Christian (chiefly Maronite) political party founded in the 1930s by Pierre Gemayel (father of the present Lebanese president, Amīn Gemayel) on the model of Fascist paramilitary political groups in Europe at that time. The Maronite Phalangists have been the most adamant force resisting political change in Lebanon, maintaining that the National Covenant (*al-mīthāq al-waṭanī*) that established Maronite political dominance in Lebanon is inviolable, regardless of any change in the confessional balance of population.

khalīfa—See *caliph.*

Khalawāt al-Bayyāḍa—One of the principal Druze shrines in Lebanon found in the hills above Ḥaṣbayyā and the Wādī al-Taym and the site of the leading Druze theological school. Founded after the 1860 massacres by Sitt Nayfa, daughter of Shaykh Bashīr Junbalāt (murdered in prison in Acre, Palestine, shortly after his defeat by the forces of Bashīr II al-Shihāb in 1825), and a prominent political and religious Druze figure in nineteenth-century Lebanon.

khalwa (plural *khalawāt*)—Place of Druze worship, also called *majlis,* or place of meeting, found in every village inhabited by the Druze in appreciable numbers. *Khalwa* is sometimes applied as well to shrines (*mazār* or *maqām*) where Druze holy men and women are buried and their memory revered. The average *khalwa* or *majlis* is a very simple, unobtrusive building where religious services are conducted every Thursday evening, village affairs discussed, and Druze religious beliefs rehearsed and studied.

al-Khāzin—Prominent Maronite family that, according to some sources, protected the young Fakhr al-Dīn II after the murder of his father by the Ottoman Turks. Some Druze historians deny this.

Kisrawān—Subdistrict and region of Lebanon northeast of Beirut, now wholly Maronite in population, but heavily Druze up to the time of ʿAyn Dārā (1711).

al-Khūri, Bishāra—First president of the Republic of Lebanon (1946–1952), a Maronite from the Shūf district, originally allied to the Junbalats but by 1949 estranged from his political connections with Kamāl.

kufiya—The cloth head covering (usually black- or red-and-white checkered) worn by many rural Lebanese and Syrian men, including the Druze *juhhāl*.

Lajnat al-Mubādarat al-Durzīya—The Druze Action Committee, a leftist organization of Israeli Druze opposed to the traditional cooperation of their community with the Israeli government since independence in 1948. They strongly oppose compulsory Druze military conscription and encourage Druze young men of military age to refuse service. Although a very small minority in the Israeli Druze community, they have enjoyed some success in this disruptive objective.

Levant—Term historically applied to the eastern Mediterranean from Smyrna (Izmir) in Turkey to Alexandria in Egypt, although some would argue that it begins at Alexandretta (Iskanderun).

al-Lijāʾ—Flat, volcanic wasteland known as "The Refuge" east of the fertile Hawrān plain of southern Syria to which the defeated Lebanese Yamani Druze fled following the battle of ʿAyn Dārā in 1711, later settling the more fertile foothills farther east now known as the Jabal al-Druze.

Madhabīḥ al-Sittīn—"The Massacres of Sixty," the term employed by Lebanese Christians for the events of 1860 in which many Christians were murdered by the Druze in central Lebanon and by Muslims in Damascus, following an incident of intercommunal rivalry near Dayr al-Qamar.

mahdi—In Shia Islām, the savior, or expected one, who will appear to usher in an era of Muslim righteousness.

mahr—Dowry, or bride price, paid by a young Druze man to his intended bride's family prior to his marriage.

Majd al-Shams—Literally, "the splendor of the sun"; in reality, a large Druze village of nearly seven thousand inhabitants in the northern Golan district of Israel who have strongly objected to and adamantly refused to accept Israel's 1981 incorporation of the territory seized from Syria in 1967. They and their fellow Druze in three neighboring villages have refused Israeli citizenship and military conscription, and they frequently invite IDF reprisals by flying the Syrian flag from their rooftops.

majlis—See *khalwa*.

Mamlūk (plural *Mamālīk*)—Literally, slave(s); in Islamic history they ruled Egypt during 1250–1517, descendants of slaves brought from the Caucasus to serve in the palace guard, who seized power from the Ayyubids and perpetuated their rule through their own military confraternity. It was during the early Mamlūk period that the last of the Crusader states were overrun and the Druze communities brought once again under rule from Cairo.

Maʿn—Ruling family of Lebanon during the first two centuries of Ottoman control; originally of Bedouin Arab ancestry from the northern Jazīra region of eastern Syria. Maʿnī power reached its peak during the reign of the *amīr* Fakhr al-Dīn II when the authority of the Druze *imāra* extended south into Palestine and east as far as Palmyra (Tadmur), 1590–1635. When the last ruling prince of the Maʿn family died in 1697 local authority in the Druze Mountain was transferred to the Shihābs.

mandīl—The white head covering worn by most Druze women, especially in the mountain villages; although often drawn across the mouth and nose, it is not a veil in the Muslim sense.

Manzikert—Battle fought near the village of Malazgirt north of Lake Van in southern Armenia in 1071, which saw the defeat of the Byzantine forces led by the emperor Romanus IV Diogenes at the hands of the Saljūq Turks under their leader Alp Arslān; in the ensuing two decades most of Asia Minor was overrun by the Turks who established themselves at Nicaea only a few miles from Constantinople; the emperor Alexius I Comnenus appealed to the West for aid, which manifested itself in the unexpected form of the Crusades.

maqām (plural *maqāmāt*)—Druze shrines and places of worship built around the tombs of holy men and women, usually on hill or mountain tops. In addition to providing a place of Druze worship they usually offer accommodation for whole families wishing to spend an extended period of time in religious retreat. Also called *mazār* (plural *mazārāt*) and sometimes referred to as *khalawāt* (see *khalwa*).

Maqām Sayyidīnā al-Khidr—Druze shrine in the largely non-Druze village of *Kafar Yāsīf* (q.v.) in western Galilee, one of eight such religious establishments in Israel.

mashā'ikh al-dīn—The Druze religious leadership, all *ʿuqqāl*.

mashā'ikh al-zamān—The Druze lay political leadership, drawn from the religiously uninitiated (*juhhāl*).

al-Matn—Subdistrict of the Mount Lebanon province (*muḥāfaẓa*), almost entirely Christian except for a small (2 percent) Druze minority; historically inclusive, however, of Bʿabdā subdistrict to the south with a large Druze population in such villages as Arṣūn, Qurnayyil, Ra'the-Matn, and Ṣalīma.

mawqaf—Literally, a place of stopping; an outdoor meeting place found in nearly all Druze villages, often in the form of a bank of steps or bleachers where public ceremonies such as funerals are held.

mazār—See *maqām*.

Mazraʿa—Literally, farm. Site, seven miles west of al-Suwaydā' on the border of the Jabal al-Druze and the Ḥawrān districts, where the French forces sent to engage Sulṭan al-Aṭrāsh and his followers were defeated on August 2, 1925, greatly embarrassing the French Mandate government and causing the localized Druze uprising to spread throughout much of Syria and parts of Lebanon.

Mazraʿat al-Shūf—Large Druze village in the central Shūf mountains directly across the Awalī River valley from al-Mukhtāra, the seat of the Junbalāṭ family. Until 1975 its population was one-third Christian, but once the news of Kamāl Junbalāṭ's assassination in March of 1977 became known, all those Christians in the village who had not fled were set upon by their Druze neighbors and massacred.

millet—Turkish for the Arabic *millah*, or nation. An Ottoman system of governing by which each religious community in the empire (termed a *millet*) was ruled by its own ecclesiastical law and leadership, the latter being ultimately responsible to the sultan for their respective communities.

al-mīthāq al-waṭanī—The National Covenant, Lebanon's unwritten power-sharing formula of 1943, by which the Maronite Christians and Sunni Muslims agreed to divide power in the new Lebanese republic between them.

mu'adhdhin (muezzin)—In both the Sunni and Shia branches of Islām the member of the local community who calls the faithful to prayer five times daily from the minaret of the mosque.

muḍāfa (plural *muḍāfāt*)—Guesthouses found in all Druze settlements, where visitors are lodged and given hospitality.

Mughār—Town of nearly twelve thousand inhabitants in eastern Galilee; majority Druze, but large Christian (25 percent) and Muslim (19 percent) minorities.

muḥāfaẓa (plural *muḥāfaẓāt*)—In Lebanon and Syria the term for province, each of which is subdivided into *aqḍiyā*ʾ (cazas), or subdistricts.

Muḥammad ibn Wahb al-Qurashī—See *al-Kalima.*

al-Muharram—See *ʿāshūrā.*

mujtahids—Shia theologians acting as intermediaries between God and the faithful in the absence of the *imām.*

al-Mukhtāra—Village in the central Shūf mountains, seat of the Junbalāṭ family and site of their early nineteenth-century palace.

al-muqaṣṣira—Literally, the state of being negligent or neglectful; used by Ḥamza to describe those Isma'ilis of Cairo who were "lagging behind" on their spiritual development toward the ultimate goal of *tawḥīd.*

al-Muqaṭṭam—Range of hills rising out of the Nile Valley to the east of Cairo, where the imam-caliph al-Ḥākim disappeared in A.D. 1021.

al-Muqtanā—See *Bahāʾ al-Dīn.*

murūʾa—The guiding principle of chivalry, knightly virtue, and sense of honor that governs Druze behavior.

mutʿa—The institution of temporary marriage practiced by most Shia groups (except the Zaydis of Yemen) but forbidden to the Druze, although it is known to occur in isolated instances (see Layish, *Marriage,* pp. 105–07).

muṭahhir—In Islām the performer of ritual circumcision on male infants and young boys.

al-mutaṣarrifiya—The autonomous governate of Mount Lebanon ruled by non-Maronite Christian governors under Ottoman suzerainty, 1861–1914.

muwaḥḥid (plural *muwaḥḥidūn*)—Believer(s) in the absolute unity of God; unitarians. The term by which the Druze commonly describe themselves.

nabī—Prophet.

al-Nabī Ayyūb—One of the principal *maqamāt* or shrines of the Lebanese Druze (literally, "the prophet Job") located in the southern Shūf district on a hilltop overlooking the village of Nīḥā.

al-Nabī Shuʿayb—Most important Druze shrine in Israel, located near Tiberias in eastern Galilee.

al-Nafs—Title (usually translated as "the universal soul") given to the second-ranking of the Druze dignitaries (*ḥudūd*), Ismāʿīl al-Tamīmī.

al-Nahār—Largest and most respected Beirut daily Arabic newspaper (literally, "The Day"). Owned by the Greek Orthodox Tuwayni family.

Naṣr al-Dīn, Amal—One of the two Druze deputies in the Israeli Knesset elected in 1984; member of the LIKUD bloc and resident at Dāliyat Karmil. See also *Zaydan ʿAtsha.*

Nayfa, Sitt—Daughter of Shaykh Bashīr Junbalāṭ (died 1825) and leading political figure among the Druze of Lebanon for many decades after her husband's death. Founded the *Khalawāt al-Bayyāḍa* (q.v.) near Ḥaṣbayyā after the upheavals of 1860

Nazīra, Sitt—Widow of Fuʾād Junbalāṭ (murdered in 1921), who ruled the Junbalatī Druze of Lebanon until her son Kamāl came of age and assumed his father's mantle of leadership in 1943.

Neştegin—See *al-Darazī*.

Phalanges Libanaises—See *al-Kataʾib*.

qaḍāʾ (plural *aqḍiyā*)—Administrative division (subdistrict) of the provinces (*muḥāfaẓāt*) of Syria and Lebanon; frequently written as *caza* in English and French.

qāḍī (plural *quḍah*)—Judges, originally of Islamic law, but also in contemporary society of secular law.

qāf—The twenty-first letter of the Arabic alphabet, a hard "k" sound pronounced at the back of the throat. In nearly all contemporary Arabic dialects it is dropped or altered to a hard "g" or "ch," sometimes "sh," sound. The Druze keep the original *qāf* sound of classical Arabic in their everyday speech (along with some Christians who live in predominantly Druze surroundings).

al-Qāhira—Arabic for Cairo, the capital of the Fatimid empire founded in 969 following their conquest of Egypt, near the site of Roman Babylon on the Nile and the early Muslim settlement of al-Fusṭāṭ.

qāʾim maqām—Title given to the two governors of Mount Lebanon (one Christian, north of the Beirut-Damascus road, and one Druze, south of it) during the period 1842–1861. After 1861 seven non-Maronite Christian *qāʾim maqams* governed the seven subdistricts of the governate (*al-mutasarrifiya*) of Mount Lebanon that lasted under European protection until 1914.

qāʾim al-zamān—The "Master of Time" or "Lord of the Ages," a title given to the anticipated Shia mahdi (q.v.).

Qalb Lawzah—Literally, "the heart of the almond"; Druze village in the Jabal al-Aʿlā of northern Syria built adjacent to a splendid sixth-century Byzantine church.

Qanawāt—Druze town a few miles to the northeast of al-Suwaydāʾ in the Jabal al-Druze built among extensive late Roman ruins. Seat of one of the three *shuyūkh al-ʿaql* of the Jabal al-Druze, and traditionally the Druze religious center of the region.

Qarmaṭian—Early sectarian movement within Isma'ili Shi'ism that posed a serious threat to Abbasid Sunni rule in Iraq and Arabia in the early tenth century.

Qays—North Arab tribe opposed to the ruling Umayyad caliphs (ruled in Damascus 661–750), whose battles with the South Arab, or Yamani, tribe that supported the caliphs were prolonged well into the eighteenth century by factions that took up either side of this rivalry, which had long ceased to have any real meaning. In Lebanon it divided the Druze to such an extent that it led to a major confrontation at ʿAyn Dārā in 1711, as the result of which much of Mount Lebanon previously dominated by the Druze was depopulated as the defeated party migrated in large numbers to the present Jabal al-Druze region of southern Syria. Maronites from the north filtered south into the vacuum created by the Yamani Druze exodus and the subsequent decline of Druze power in Lebanon.

al-Qurʾān—The literal Word of God as dictated to the prophet Muḥammad by the angel Gabriel and the major source of Islamic law and belief. Respected by the Druze but not revered by them.

al-Qurʾayyah (El-Kreié)—Village directly to the south of al-Suwaydāʾ, seat of the al-Aṭrash family.

Qurnayyil—Large Druze village in the eastern Matn (Bʿabdā *qaḍāʾ*).

al-raʾīs—In earlier times chief, or headman, of a tribe; today the title for president of a state.

al-Rāma—Large village in central Galilee, predominantly Greek Orthodox but with a substantial Druze and smaller Sunni minority. The Druze of al-Rāma are considered to be the least traditionally minded in Israel. Home of the contemporary Druze Palestinian poet, Samīḥ al-Qāsim.

Ramaḍān—The Muslim month of fasting (*ṣawm*), the observance of which is one of the Five Pillars of Islām. Not observed by Druze except in isolated cases, especially in the past when it was considered politically expedient.

Raʾs al-Matn—Large Druze village in the Matn (Bʿabdā *qaḍā*). Home of Druze professor and writer Sami Makarem.

Rāshayyā—Large Druze town in southeastern Lebanon, site of a Druze theological school; Greek Orthodox form a substantial minority (about 25 percent).

al-rāshidūn—Literally, "the rightly guided"; term applied to the first four caliphs of Islām, known in English as "the Orthodox caliphs": Abū Bakr (632–634), ʿUmar (632–644), ʿUthmān (644–656), and ʿAlī (656–661). All but the first died at the hands of assassins.

Saʿāda, Anṭūn—Brazilian-born Christian (Greek Orthodox) Arab of Lebanese extraction, who returned to Beirut via Germany as a German instructor at the American University; founded the *Ḥizb al-Qawmi* (Syrian Nationalist party, *Parti Populaire Syrien,* or PPS) in 1932, which calls for the union of Greater Syria under a secular, national, socialist-style government. He advocated revolutionary tactics, which caused the Lebanese government to ban his party and engineer his assassination in 1949; in retaliation his supporters assassinated Riyād al-Sulḥ, the Sunni prime minister and coauthor of the National Covenant (*al-mīthāq al-waṭanī*) in 1951. Still active today, the PPS continues to constitute a militantly divisive force in Middle East politics (most of the recent suicide car and donkey bombings against the Israeli Defense Force [IDF] and South-Lebanon Army [SLA] in southern Lebanon have been PPS inspired). Its membership cuts across confessional lines and has included small numbers of Druze.

Saḥmur—Shia village in southeast Lebanon, the site of a revenge killing of thirteen male villagers by Druze members of the South Lebanon Army (SLA) in retaliation for an ambush near the village, which killed three Druze soldiers, September 23, 1985.

Saladin—Westernized form of *Ṣalāḥ al-Dīn* (al-Ayyūbī), the fabled Muslim warrior of the twelfth century who overthrew the Fatimid dynasty in Egypt (1174) and recaptured Jerusalem from the Crusaders after routing them at the battle of the Horns of Ḥattīn in Galilee (1187). Founded the Ayyubid dynasty that ruled Syria, Egypt, and most of Palestine until 1250.

Salāma al-Sāmurrī—The fourth-ranking Druze dignitary (*ḥudūd*), who bears the title of "The Right Wing" or "Antecedent."

Ṣalīma—Predominantly Druze village in the Matn (Bʿabdā *qaḍāʾ*), site of a massacre by the Phalangist forces in 1976; retaken by the Syrian Army and now within the sphere of Junbalāṭ's Druze canton.

Salkhad—Druze town in the southeast corner of the Jabal al-Druze, Syria, site of an early encounter with French forces in the uprising of 1925.

Sārāh, Sitt—Niece of al-Muqtanā Bahā᾿ al-Dīn, who headed a peace mission to a group of Druze rent by division in the early years of the *daʿwa* and who is highly revered in the Druze faith.

Ṣawfar (Sofar)—Druze village on the Beirut-Damascus highway near the crest of the Lebanon Mountain; in happier times a popular summer resort dotted with Swiss-style chalets now serving as Syrian Army billets.

Seveners—See *Ismāʿīlis.*

Shahba—Small Druze town in the northern Jabal al-Druze built on the site of extensive Roman ruins.

Shamʿūn, Kamīl (Camille Chamoun, 1900–1987)—Second president of Lebanon (1952–1958), a native of Dayr al-Qamar in the Shūf and arch political rival of Kamāl Junbalāṭ.

sharīʿa—The code of Islamic law, of which there are four principal schools, one of which, the Ḥanafī, served to augment Druze law until very recently. As late as 1948 the Lebanese Druze Law provided that "the Muslim *sharīʿa* according to the Ḥanafī school . . . shall be applied to all matters within the jurisdiction of the court which are not expressly provided for by the Lebanese Druze Law" (Layish, *Marriage*, pp. 10–11).

al-Sharīf Ḥusayn of Mecca—See *Ḥusayn.*

shaykh (plural *shuyūkh*)—In pre-Islamic Arabic a tribal chieftain, and in parts of the Middle East including Lebanon a hereditary title; among the Druze the title accorded to their religious leaders, members of the initiated (*ʿuqqāl*).

Shaykh al-ʿAql—The highest-ranking religious leader within the Druze community, of which there can be more than one at a given time with defined geographical spheres of jurisdiction. At present there are one each in Lebanon and Israel and three in Syria.

Shīʿa—The major sectarian party within Islām, divided into two principal factions, the Ismāʿīlis (Seveners) and Twelvers (q.v.), of which the latter are by far the more numerous. The traditional center of Shia strength is Iran, although large communities are found in ʿIraq (where they are the majority of the Arab population) and Lebanon (where they form the majority of the Muslim population and are the largest single confessional group). The Seveners, from whom the Druze derive much of their religious philosophy, are today found in the Arab world only in Syria (fewer than a hundred thousand).

Shihāb—Leading Lebanese family, originally Druze, who succeeded the Maʿns in 1697 as the rulers of Mount Lebanon; in the mid-eighteenth century they became Maronite Christians (except for one branch, which embraced Sunni Islām) and governed until 1840, by which time Druze power in the mountain had been seriously weakened. In modern times a direct descendant of the Shihābi *amīrs,* Fu᾿ād, served as Lebanon's third president (1958–1964).

shirwāl—Loose-fitting trousers traditionally worn by Druze men but less and less frequently seen, except in the more remote and conservative mountain villages.

al-Shishakli, Adīb—President of Syria (1953–1954), who came to power by military coup and served as chief of state for less than a year before being toppled by a coalition of dissatisfied elements that included the Druze whom he had seriously antagonized. He was assassinated by a Druze in an act of revenge nearly a decade later in Brazil, where he had taken refuge.

al-Shūf—Subdistrict (*qaḍā᾿*) of the Mount Lebanon *muḥāfaẓa* in the mountains southeast of Beirut and inclusive of the coastal region of al-Kharrūb; by popular reckoning a region that includes much of the ʿAlayh subdistrict to the north. Heartland of the modern-day Druze canton and now almost exclusively Druze in population, except for the Maronite town of Dayr al-Qamar. The 1932 census showed the combined population of the ʿAlayh and al-Shūf *aqdiyaʾ* (90,872) to be 38 percent Druze, 32.5 percent Maronite, 14 percent Greek Orthodox and Greek Catholic, and 13 percent Sunni, the remaining 2.5 percent being comprised of Shia and miscellaneous Christian groups.

sijill—Proclamation, or decree, the most famous of which is the one issued by the caliph al-Ḥākim on the first day of A.H. 408 (1017) proclaiming himself to be the manifestation of the deity and encouraging his followers to worship him as such. Various *sijills* are included in the Druze Canon.

al-Simqānīya—Druze village in the central Shūf mountains midway between Dayr al-Qamar and al-Mukhtāra, site of the battle in 1825 at which Shaykh Bashīr Junbalāṭ and his Druze forces were defeated by the Maronite *amīr* Bashīr II al-Shihāb; marks the beginning of the decline of Druze power in central Lebanon.

al-Sūlḥ, Riyāḍ—First prime minister of Lebanon, 1946–1951; a leading member of the Sunni community, he coauthored the National Covenant with the first Lebanese president, Bishāra al-Khūri, in 1943 by which political power in the new republic was to be shared principally by the Sunnis and Maronites. Assassinated in 1951 allegedly by followers of Antūn Saʿāda (q.v.), founder of the PPS (Syrian Nationalist party), who had been ambushed and killed, allegedly by government forces, two years earlier.

Sunnī—Follower of the *sunna,* or "path," of the prophet Muḥammad, the so-called Orthodox or mainstream party of Islām that includes 90 percent of the faithful. In Lebanon the Sunnis are now considered to be outnumbered by the Shia.

al-Suwaydāʾ—Druze city in southern Syria, administrative capital of the province (*muḥāfaẓā*) of the same name, whose boundaries are nearly identical to those of the autonomous region of the Jabal al-Druze established during the French Mandate.

ṭalāq—Divorce; permitted under Druze law, but with more restrictions than under Islamic law. Unlike Muslims, divorced Druze may never remarry each other; Druze divorce is completely and absolutely final.

tanāsukh—The Druze belief in the transmigration of souls after death. When a Druze dies he is reincarnated in another Druze before birth.

ṭanṭūr—The decorative horn that was commonly worn by Druze and Maronite women until the middle of the nineteenth century; often between one and two feet in height and permanently attached to the hair, it was draped with the *mandīl* (either white or black).

Tanūkh—See *Banū al-Tanūkh.*

tanzīl—Revelation; in the system of Isma'ili theology it is conveyed by the First Intellect (*ʿAql al-Kullī*). According to Ḥamza it is the stage of belief after *bāṭin* (q.v.) on the path toward *tawḥīd.*

Taqī al-Dīn—Prominent Lebanese Druze family, a member of which, Shaykh Ḥalīm Taqī al-Dīn, a judge of the Druze court, was assassinated on December 1, 1983, on the first anniversary of the unsuccessful attempt on Walīd Junbalāṭ.

taqīya—Dissimulation; a Shia practice that permits members of this sect to adopt the outward forms of other religions in order to protect their lives while inwardly maintaining their real faith. A practice adopted by the Druze and commonly employed by members of the community and especially its political leadership in times past when it was deemed necessary to please the ruling Sunni establishment.

tarbūsh—The red fez commonly worn by Arab gentlemen until the middle part of this century.

Ṭarīf—Druze family of Jūlis in Galilee from whom the Shaykh al-ʿAql of the Palestine Druze community has traditionally been drawn.

tawḥīd—The Druze faith in the absolute oneness of God, achieved in various stages of Isma'ili theological development and revealed by al-Ḥākim through Ḥamza.

taʾwīl—The act of carrying the inner esoteric interpretation of *tanzīl* (revelation) to the extreme of denying the literal sense that is the outer law; in the Druze faith the final stage of religious development before achieving the ultimate goal of pure Unitarian religion, *tawḥīd.*

al-Tayāmina—Term by which the Druze were described in Arabic by non-Druze in the first centuries after their appearance; derived from the Wādī al-Taym, the principal Druze stronghold in southern Lebanon since the eleventh century.

thaʾr—Vengeance, blood revenge.

Twelvers—The principal group of Shia, followers of all the *imāms,* descendants of ʿAli and Faṭima, through the twelfth, al-Muntaẓar, who disappeared in A.H. 260 (A.D. 872/3) and is presumed by the faithful to have gone into a state of occultation from which he will emerge as the mahdi in the fullness of time. Known in Arabic as the *ithnaʾ ʿasharī* (Twelvers) as opposed to the Isma'ilis, who believe the imamate to have taken a divergent route via the elder son of the sixth *imām* (Ismāʿīl), passed over by his father (Jaʿfar al-Sādiq) in favor of the younger brother Mūsā, and thus known as Seveners.

ʿUbayh (Abey)—Large Druze village in ʿAlayh *qaḍāʾ;* site of early American Protestant missionary activity in the nineteenth century.

ʿulamāʾ (singular *ʿalīm*)—The religious leadership or elders of traditional Islamic society. Literally, the learned.

umarāʾ (singular *amīr*)—Princes.

Umayyad—First hereditary dynasty of caliphs in Islām, who ruled from Damascus during 661–750.

umma—Nation; the term used to describe the entire community of believers in Islām.

ʿunna—Male impotence; grounds for divorce initiated by a woman under Druze law.

ʿuqqāl—See *ʿāqil.*

Wādi al Naṣāra—The Valley of the Christians, a region in Syria's southern Latakia province, just north of the Lebanese border, which has remained a center of Greek Orthodox Christianity since the earliest days of the faith, despite the conversion of a small number of that ancient branch to the Catholic uniate church established in the eighteenth century, augmented by even smaller numbers of Maronite Catholics who emigrated from Lebanon to the south, and the more recent incursion of Alawis from the northern part of the Latakia district. Overlooking the entrance to the valley, in fact the upper reaches of the *nahr al-kabīr,* is the celebrated Crusader castle, "le Krak des Chevaliers" (*Qalaʿat al-Ḥuṣn*), whose antiquity is eclipsed by the Greek Orthodox monastery of Saint George (*Mār Jirjis*) a few miles to the northwest, which dates back to the time of the emperor Justinian in the sixth century.

Wādī al-Taym—Valley in southeast Lebanon on the western slope of Mount Hermon where the Druze faith took deep and early root during the years of the Divine Call (*al-daʿwa*), 1017–1043. Despite the pressures exerted at various times since then by the Sunni establishment and the surrounding villages and townships inhabited by Shia Muslims and Greek Orthodox Christians, the valley has remained a stronghold of Druzism to the present day. Above the principal town of the region, Ḥaṣbayyā, is the Khalawāt al-Bayyaḍa, one of the most important Druze shrines in Lebanon and the site of the leading Druze theological school.

Wahhābī—Name given to the followers of Muḥammad ibn ʿAbd al-Wahhāb (died 1792), a puritanical Muslim reformer from central Arabia who found the practice of Islām in his day to be deviant from the path intended by the prophet and "determined to purge it and restore it to its primitive strictness" (Hitti, *History of the Arabs*, p. 740). His message found fertile ground among the tribes of the Najd, principally the family of Muḥammad ibn-Suʿūd, whose descendants established the Kingdom of Saudi Arabia in 1924.

wāli—Governor, administrator; in the Ottoman Empire the term (*vali* in Turkish) given to the governors of provinces (*wilāya*, or *vilayet* in Turkish).

waqf (plural *awqāf*)—Literally, a "sufficient amount"; term applied to the establishment of religious foundations and charities in Islām perpetuated by gifts of property and/or money for their maintenance. *Waqf* properties exist among the Druze, primarily for the purpose of maintaining *khalawāt* and *maqāmāt* as well as providing for the needy in the community.

Yamanī—The South Arabian faction (literally, those from Yemen) opposed to the North Arabian *Qays* tribal machinations in the first century and a half following the death of Muḥammad. Long after the Umayyad dynasty (during which the North-South struggle began) fell in 750, internecine warfare between groups adopting one or either of these parties' political claims continued well into modern times; in the Druze community it culminated in the battle of ʿAyn Dāra in 1711, which led to a migration by the defeated Yamanī party into Syria and the consequent depopulation of whole Druze areas of Mount Lebanon to the ultimate detriment of the community and the benefit of the opportunistic Maronites.

yawm al-dīn—Literally, "The Day of Faith"; in Islām the Day of Judgment when the fate of all souls will be decided by Jesus of Nazareth (the prophet ʿIsā); for the Druze it is the culmination of a whole series of the soul's transmigrations toward the ultimate end of beatific vision.

Yazbakī—Following the defeat of the *Yamanī* Druze party at ʿAyn Dāra in 1711 by the North Arab *Qaysi* faction, a new rivalry developed along much the same lines between the Junbalāṭ clan and the *Yazbaki* clan (also known as the *ʿImāds*).

Yazīd I (ruled 680–683)—The son of the first Umayyad caliph, Muʿāwiya, and the first to rule by hereditary succession in Islām. It was during his reign that the son of ʿAli and grandson of the prophet Muḥammad, Ḥusayn, made his unsuccessful attempt to establish the hereditary rule of his family. He was defeated at Karbalāʾ in Iraq on the tenth day of the Muslim month of al-Muḥarram in A.H. 61 (A.D. 680) by armies loyal to Yazīd; his head was severed and sent to the caliph in Damascus, who, seeing the political implications of such a barbarity committed on the prophet's progeny, returned it for burial with the rest of Ḥusayn's body. Despite this gesture the supporters of Ḥusayn, who became known as the *Shīʿa,* or Sectarians, were unforgiving and to this day celebrate the anniversary of the Karbalāʾ incident with ten days of lamentation marked by a passion play reenacting Ḥusayn's struggle and suffering.

Yirkā—Large Druze village (population eight thousand) in western Galilee.

ẓāhir—In Isma'ili Shi'ism the outer form of faith contained in the *Qurʾan,* which was but a veil that only the initiated could pierce and thus achieve knowledge of the real religious truth.

al-Ẓāhir—Son of the imām-caliph al-Ḥākim, who succeeded him in 1021 and immediately rejected his father's pretensions to divinity that had given rise to Druzism. He persecuted followers of his father and Ḥamza, and successfully stamped out the new faith in major urban centers in Egypt; but he failed to stem its spread into more remote corners of his domains such as the Wādī al-Taym and Jabal al-Aʿlā. He died in 1035, eight years before the closure of the *daʿwa,* by which time Bahāʾ al-Dīn had firmly established the Druze faith in Lebanon and Syria.

zakāt—The act of giving alms, one of the Five Pillars of Islām. Although charity to those in need within their community is a feature of Druze society, the *zakāt* tax or tithe is not levied.

zifāf—Wedding ceremony.

Bibliography

Public Documents

Israel, *Census of Population and Housing 1961,* Bureau of Statistics, Jerusalem, 1963.
Israel, *Census of Population and Housing 1972,* Bureau of Statistics, Jerusalem, 1976.
Israel, *Census of Population and Housing 1983,* Bureau of Statistics, Jerusalem, 1985.
Jordan, *Awwal Taʿdād ʿAmm liʾl-Sukān waʾl-Musākin 1964,* General Bureau of Statistics, Amman, 1961–1965.
Palestine, *The General Census of 1931,* The British Mandate Administration, Jerusalem.
Syria, *The 1960 Census of Population and Housing,* Ministry of the Interior, Damascus, 1962.
Syria, *The Statistical Abstract of Syria, 1943–1956,* Ministry of the Interior, Damascus.

Books

Abou, Selim. *Le bilinguisme arabe-français au Liban.* Paris: Presses Universitaires de France, 1962.
Abū-Ismāʿīl, Salīm. *Al-Durūz: Wujūduhum wa Madhhabuhum wa Tawaṭṭanuhum.* Beirut: The Druze History Society, 1954.
Abu-Izzeddin, Nejla M. *The Druzes: A New Study of their History, Faith and Society.* Leiden: E. J. Brill, 1984.
Abū Ṣāliḥ, The Armenian. *The Churches and Monasteries of Egypt and Some Neighbouring Countries, Attributed to Abū-Ṣāliḥ, The Armenian.* Translated from the original Arabic by B. T. A. Evetts, with added notes by Alfred J. Butler. Oxford: Oxford University Press, 1895.

Alamuddin, Nura S., and Paul D. Starr. *Crucial Bonds: Marriage among the Lebanese Druze*. Delmar, N.Y.: Caravan Books, 1980.

Antonius, George. *The Arab Awakening: The History of the Arab Nationalist Movement*. London: Hamish Hamilton, 1939.

Arberry, A. J., ed. *Religion in the Middle East: Three Religions in Concord and Conflict*. 2 vols. Cambridge: Cambridge University Press, 1969. Especially vol. 2, chap. 18 (on the Druze) by J. W. Hirschberg.

Armstrong, Harold. *Turkey and Syria Reborn*. London: The Bodley Head Ltd., 1930.

Asher, A., ed. *The Itinerary of Rabbi Benjamin of Tudela*. 2 vols. Berlin: A. Asher, 1840.

Assaad, Sadik A. *The Reign of Al-Hakim Bi Amr Allah*. Beirut: The Arab Institute for Research and Publishing, 1974.

Baer, Gabriel. *Population and Society in the Arab East*. London: Routledge and Kegan Paul, 1964. Translated from the Hebrew by Hanna Szőke. First published 1960.

Bell, Gertrude. *The Desert and the Sown*. New York: Dutton, 1907.

Ben-Dor, Gabriel. *The Druzes in Israel: A Political Study*. Jerusalem: The Magnes Press, The Hebrew University, 1979.

Betts, Robert Brenton. *Christians in the Arab East: A Political Study*. Atlanta: The John Knox Press, London: SPCK, and Athens: Lycabettus Press, 1978.

Bouron, Narcisse. *Les Druzes: Histoire du Liban et de la Montagne Haouranaise*. Paris: Editions Berger-Levrault, 1930.

Buckingham, James Silk. *Travels Among the Arab Tribes Inhabiting The Countries East of Syria and Palestine*. London: 1825.

Carnarvon, Herbert Henry Howard Molyneaux, fourth earl of. *Recollections of the Druses of the Lebanon*. London: John Murray, 1860.

Castlereagh, Viscount. *Journey to Damascus*. 2 vols. London: Henry Colburn, 1847.

Chabry, Laurent and Annie. *Politique et minorités au Proche-Orient (les raisons d'une explision)*. Paris: Editions Maisonneuve et Larose, 1984. Especially chap. 6 ("Les visages multiples de la puissance Druze—Liban, Syrie, Israël").

Chamie, Joseph. *Religion and Fertility: Arab Christian-Muslim Differentials*. Cambridge: Cambridge University Press, 1981.

Chasseaud, George Washington. *The Druses of the Lebanon: Their Manners, Customs and History, with a Translation of their Religious Code*. London: Richard Bentley, 1855.

Churchill, Henry. *The Druzes and Maronites under Turkish Rule from 1840 to 1860*. London: Quaritch, 1862.

———. *Mount Lebanon: A Ten Years' Residence from 1842 to 1852, Describing the Manners, Customs and Religion of Its Inhabitants with a Full and Correct Account of the Druse Religion*. 3d ed., 3 vols. London: Saunders and Otley, 1853.

Cleveland, William L. *Islam Against the West: Shakib Arslan and the Campaign for Islamic Nationalism*. Austin: University of Texas Press, and London: Al Saqi Books, 1985.

Conder, C. R. *The Latin Kingdom of Jerusalem, 1099–1291*. London: Committee of the Palestine Exploration Fund, 1897.

Davis, Helen Miller. *Constitutions, Electoral Laws, Treaties of States in the Near and Middle East*. Durham: Duke University Press, 1947.

Durbin, John P. *Observations in the East*. 2 vols. New York: Harper and Brothers, 1845.

Frankland, Charles Colville. *Travels To and From Constantinople*. 2 vols. London: Henry Colburn, 1829.

Freshfield, Douglas W. *Travels in the Central Caucasus and Bashan*. London: Longmans, 1869.

Gordon, David C. *The Republic of Lebanon: Nation in Jeopardy*. Boulder, Colorado: Westview Press, 1983.

Green, John. *A Journey from Aleppo to Damascus: With a Description of Those Two Capital Cities and the Neighbouring Parts of Syria, To Which is Added, an Account of the Maronites Inhabiting Mount Libanus, &c.* London: W. Mears, 1736.

Guérin, M. V. *Description géographique, historique et archéologique de la Palestine: troisième partie—Galilée*. 2 vols. Paris: L'Imprimerie Nationale, 1880.

Guys, Henri. *La nation Druse, son histoire, sa religion et ses moeurs*. Paris: Chez France, 1863.

———. *Théogonie des Druses, ou abrégé de leur système religieux*. Paris: L'Imprimerie Impériale, 1863.

Haddad, George. *Fifty Years of Modern Syria and Lebanon*. Beirut: Dar al-Hayat, 1950.

Harik, Iliya F. *Politics and Change in a Traditional Society: Lebanon, 1711–1845*. Princeton: Princeton University Press, 1968.

Hill, Gray. *With the Beduins: A Narrative of Journeys and Adventures in Unfrequented Parts of Syria*. London: T. Fisher Unwin, 1891.

Hirschberg, J. W. See Arberry, A. J.

Hitti, Philip K. *The Origins of the Druze People and Religion*. New York: Columbia University Press, 1928.

———. *The History of the Arabs from the Earliest Times to the Present*. 9th ed. New York: Saint Martin's Press, 1967.

———. *Lebanon in History from the Earliest Times to the Present*. New York: St. Martin's Press, 1957.

———. *The Near East in History: A 5000-Year Story*. New York: D. Van Nostrand Company, 1961.

———. *History of Syria Including Lebanon and Palestine*. New York: Macmillan, 1951.

Hourani, Albert. *Minorities in the Arab World*. London: Oxford University Press, 1947.

———. *Syria and Lebanon: A Political Essay*. London: Oxford University Press, 1946.

Hudson, Michael C. *The Precarious Republic: Political Modernization in Lebanon*. New York: Random House, 1968.

Inchbold, A. C. *Under the Syrian Sun*. 2 vols. London: Hutchinson and Co., 1906.

Joumblatt (Junbalāṭ), Kamāl. *I Speak for Lebanon*. London: Zed Press, 1982. Translated from the French by Michael Pallis.

Khoury, Philip S. *Syria and the French Mandate: The Politics of Arab Nationalism, 1920–1945*. Princeton: Princeton University Press, 1987.

Knolles, Richard. *The Turkish History from the Original of that Nation, to the Growth of the Empire &c.* 6th ed., 2 vols. London, 1687.

Layish, Aharon. *Marriage, Divorce and Succession in the Druze Family*. Leiden: E. J. Brill, 1982.

Lewis, Bernard. *The Origins of Ismāʿīlism: A Study of the Historical Background of the Fāṭimid Caliphate*. Cambridge: W. Heffer and Sons Ltd., 1940.

Longrigg, Stephen Hemsley. *Syria and Lebanon under French Mandate*. London: Oxford University Press, 1958; reprinted Beirut: Librairie du Liban, 1968.

Madox, John. *Excursions in The Holy Land, Egypt, Nubia, Syria &c., Including a Visit to the Unfrequented District of the Hauran*. 2 vols. London: Richard Bentley, 1834.

Makarem, Sami Nasib. *The Doctrine of the Ismailis*. Beirut: The Arab Institute for Research and Publishing, 1972.
———. *The Druze Faith*. Delmar, New York: Caravan Books, 1974.
———. *The Political Doctrine of the Ismāʿīlis: The Imamate*. Delmar, New York: Caravan Books, 1977.
Meinardus, Otto F. A. *Christian Egypt Ancient and Modern*. Cairo: French Institute of Oriental Archaeology, 1965.
Momen, Moojan. *An Introduction to Shiʿi Islam*. New Haven and London: Yale University Press, 1985.
Najjar, Abdallah. *The Druze: Millennium Scrolls Revealed*. Translated by Fred I. Massey under the auspices of the American Druze Society, 1973, from the original Arabic, *Madhhab al-Durūz waʾl-Tawḥīd*. Cairo: Dar al-Maʿārif, 1965.
Nelson, Bryan. *Azraq, Desert Oasis*. Athens, Ohio: Ohio University Press, 1974.
Oliphant, Laurence. *Haifa, or Life in Modern Palestine*. New York: Harper and Brothers, 1887.
———. *The Land of Gilead, with Excursions in the Lebanon*. New York: D. Appleton and Co., 1881.
Osborne, Christine. *Jordan*. London: Longman, 1981.
Pococke, Richard. *A Description of the East &c*. 2 vols. London, 1745.
Puget de Saint-Pierre, M. *Histoire des Druses*. Paris: Cailleu, 1763.
Rabinovich, Itamar. *Syria under the Baʿth, 1963–66. The Army-Party Symbiosis*. Jerusalem: Israel Universities Press, 1972.
de Sacy, Silvestre. *Exposé de la religion des Druzes, tiré des livres religieux de cette secte*. Paris: L'Imprimerie Royale, 1838. Also portions appearing in English translation in a review of this book in *Foreign Affairs Quarterly Review*, London, 57 (April 1842): 168–203.
Salibi, Kamāl. *A Modern History of Lebanon*. London: Weidenfeld and Nicolson, 1965.
———. *Crossroads to Civil War: Lebanon, 1958–1976*. Delmar, New York: Caravan Books, 1976.
Sandys, George. *A Relation of a Journey Begun in A.D. 1610*. 6th ed. London, 1670.
Seabrook, William B. *Adventures in Arabia among the Bedouins, Druses, Whirling Dervishes, and Yezideee Devil-worshippers*. London: George C. Harrap and Co., Ltd., 1928.
Seale, Patrick. *The Struggle for Syria: A Study of Post-War Arab Politics, 1945–1958*. London: Oxford University Press, 1965.
Spagnolo, John P. *France and Ottoman Lebanon, 1861–1914*. (London: Ithaca Press, 1977.
Stanhope, Hester. *Memoirs of Lady Hester Stanhope, as Related by Herself in Conversations with Her Physician* [Dr. C. I. Meryon]. 3 vols. London: Henry Colburn, 1845.
Stark, Freya. *Letters from Syria*. London: John Murray, 1942. Her visit to the Jabal al-Druze was made in 1928.
Stewart, Desmond. *Great Cairo, Mother of the World*. London: Rupert Hart-Davis Ltd., 1969. Reprint. Cairo: American University Press, 1981.
Ṭabāṭabāʾī, ʾAllāmah Sayyid Muḥammad Ḥusayn. *Shiʿite Islam*. London: George Allen and Unwin, Ltd., 1975. Translated from the Persian and edited with an introduction and notes by Seyyed Hossein Nasr.
Thubron, Colin. *The Hills of Adonis*. London: William Heinemann, Ltd., 1968.
Tibawi, A. L. *American Interests in Syria, 1800–1901: A Study of Educational, Literary and Religious Work*. Oxford: Clarendon Press, 1966.

Torrey, Gordon H. *Syrian Politics and the Military, 1945–1958*. Columbus: Ohio State University Press, 1964.

Tuéni, Nadia. *Nadia Tuéni: la prose (oeuvres complètes)*. Beirut: Dar An-Nahar, 1986. Especially "Les Druzes: leur histoire et leurs 'textes sacrées'" (pp. 141–50) and "La poésie chez les Druzes," pp. 123–24.

van Dam, Nikolaos. *The Struggle for Power in Syria: Sectarianism, Regionalism, and Tribalism in Politics, 1961–1978*. London: Croom Helm, 1979.

Volney, Constantin-François Chasseboeuf, Comte de. *Voyage en Syrie et Egypte pendant les années 1783, 1784 et 1785*. 2 vols. Paris: Volland, 1787.

Winstone, H. F. V. *Leachman: "O.C. Desert."* London: Quartet, 1982.

Worrell, William H. *A Study of Races in the Ancient Near East*. New York: D. Appleton and Company, 1927.

Yaukey, David. *Fertility Differences in a Modernizing Country*. Princeton: Princeton University Press, 1961.

Yeats-Brown, Francis. *Golden Horn*. London: Victor Gollancz, 1932.

Zeltzer, Moshe. *Aspects of Near East Society*. New York: Bookman, 1962.

Al-Zuᶜbī, Muhammad ᶜAlī. *Al-Durūz: Ẓahiruhum wa Bāṭinuhum*. Beirut, 1972.

Periodicals

Aucapitaine, Henri. "Etude sur les Druzes." In *Nouvelles annales des voyages*, edited by Arthur Bertrand. Paris: Librairie de la Société de Géographie, 1862.

Bryer, David. "The Origins of the Druze Religion." *Der Islam* 52 (1975): 47–84; 53 (1976): 4–27.

Chamie, Joseph. "Religious Groups in Lebanon: Descriptive Investigation." *International Journal of Middle East Studies* 11 (Apr. 1980): 175–87.

Crow, Ralph E. "Religious Sectarianism in Lebanese Politics." *Journal of Politics* 24 (Aug. 1962): 489–520.

Deeb, Marius K. "Lebanon: Prospects for National Reconciliation in the mid-1980's." *Middle East Journal* 38, no. 2 (Spring 1984): 267–83.

Drysdale, Alasdair. "The Syrian Political Elite, 1966–1976: A Spatial and Social Analysis." *Middle Eastern Studies* 17, no. 1 (Jan. 1981): 3–30.

Graham-Browne, Sarah. "The Poetry of Survival." *Middle East* no. 122 (Dec. 1984): 43–44.

Hammer-Purgstall, Joseph von. "Sur les Druzes." *Journal Asiatique* (Nov. 1837).

Hodgson, Marshall G. S. "Al-Darazī and Ḥamza in the Origin of the Druze Religion." *Journal of the American Oriental Society* 82 (1st quarter 1962): 5–20.

———. "Durūz." Entry in the *Encyclopaedia of Islam*, vol. 2, pp. 631–37. Leiden: E. J. Brill, 1965.

Kheirallah, G. "The Druzes." *The Arab World* 1, no. 2 (1944): 17–21.

Mayer, Egon. "Becoming Modern in Bayt al-Shabāb." *The Middle East Journal* 29 (Summer 1975): 279–94.

de Nerval, Gérard. *Les Druses*. Scènes de la vie orientale. Vol. 19 (1847), pp. 577–626.

Oppenheimer, Jonathan W. S. "'We are Both in Each Others' Houses': Communal and Patrilineal Ideologies in Druze Village Religion and Social Structure." *American Ethnologist* 7 (Nov. 1980): 621–36.

Le Père * * *. "Documents sur la théologie des Druses." *Revue orientale et américaine* 4 (1860): 451–61.

"Réligion des Druses." *Revue de l'Orient* (1846): 225–46.

Saab, Ann Pottinger. "English and Irish Reaction to the Massacres in Lebanon and Syria, 1860." *The Muslim World* 74 (Jan. 1984): 12–25.

Salem, Elie A. "Lebanon's Political Maze: The Search for Peace in a Turbulent Land." *Middle East Journal* 33 (Autumn 1979): 444–63.

Schilcher, L. Schatkowski. "The Hauran Conflicts of the 1860's: A Chapter in the Rural History of Modern Syria." *International Journal of Middle East Studies* 13, no. 2 (May 1981): 159–79.

Toubi, Jamal. "Social Dynamics in War-Torn Lebanon." *Jerusalem Quarterly* 17 (Fall 1980): 83–109.

Weiss, Shimon. "A Traitor in Everybody's Eyes." *New Outlook* 23 (Aug. 1980): 38–39.

Unpublished Theses

al-Aṭrash, Jābir (Jaber al-Attrache). "Législation coutumière chez les Druzes du Hauran." Unpublished Doctorate of Law thesis, Université de Saint-Joseph, Beirut, Lebanon, 1946.

Ayoub, Victor F. "The Political Structure of a Middle East Community: A Druze Village in Mount Lebanon." Unpublished Ph.D. dissertation, Harvard University, 1955.

Betts, Robert Brenton. "The Indigenous Arabic-Speaking Communities of Greater Syria and Mesopotamia: A History of Their Rites, a Demographic Survey of Their Geographical Distribution, and an Analysis of Their Rôle in the Political, Social and Economic Life of Lebanon, Syria, Jordan, Israel, and Iraq since National Independence. Unpublished Ph.D. dissertation, The Johns Hopkins University School of Advanced International Studies, February, 1968.

Izzedin, Nejla Mustapha. "The Racial Origins of the Druzes." Unpublished Ph.D. dissertation, University of Chicago, 1934.

Newspapers and Magazines Consulted

Daily Telegraph (London), *Times* (London), *Sunday Telegraph* (London), *Sunday Times* (London), *Observer* (London), New York *Times,* Los Angeles *Times,* Washington *Post, International Herald Tribune* (Paris), *Wall Street Journal, L'Orient-Le Jour* (Beirut), *al-Nahār* (Beirut), *Economist, Middle East, Middle East International, Middle East Journal, Israel & Palestine* (Paris), *Report on Palestinians Under Israeli Rule* (Paris), *Jerusalem Post, Journal of Palestine Studies, Revue du Liban, Guardian Weekly, Christian Science Monitor* (International Edition), *Middle East Times* (Nicosia), *Tablet* (London), and *Spectator* (London).

Index

Persons and Subjects

Place Names

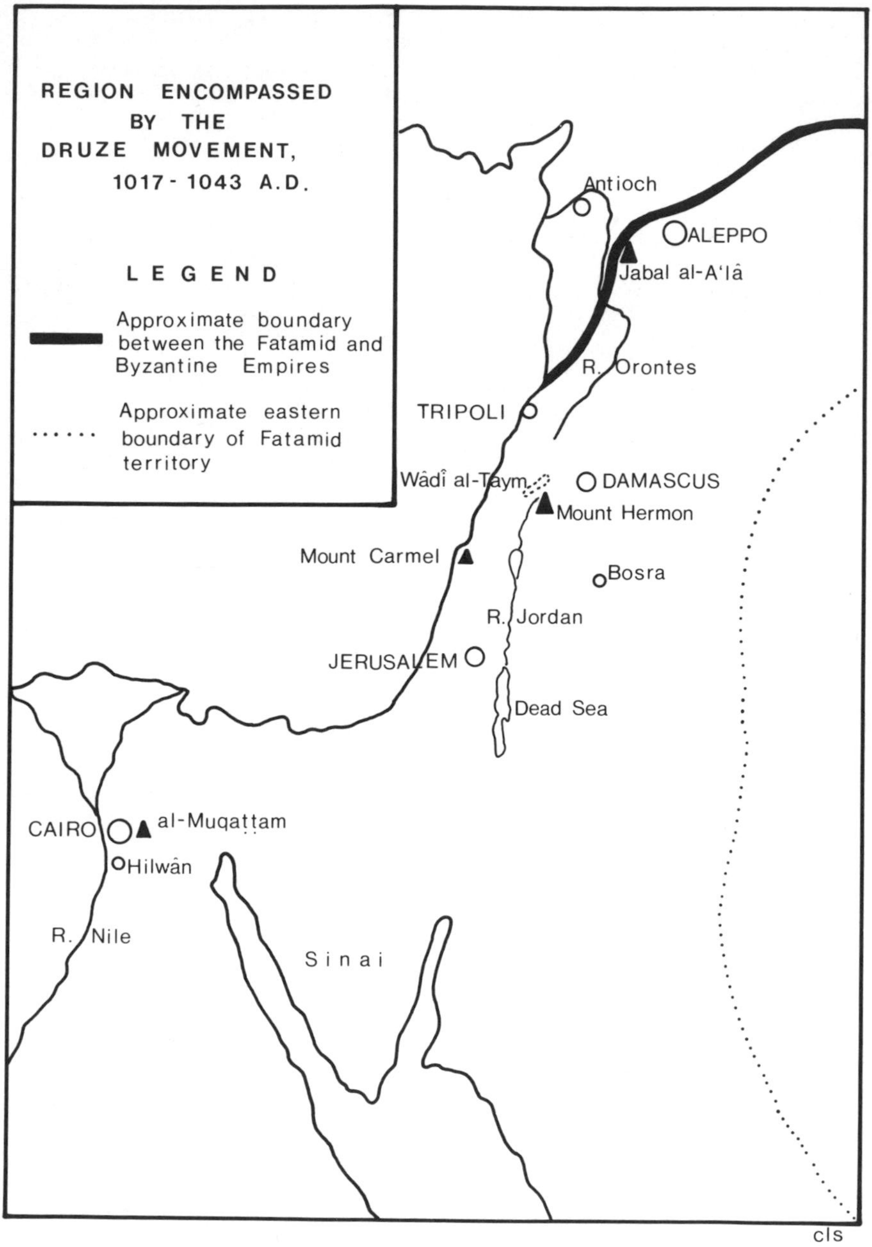
REGION ENCOMPASSED BY THE DRUZE MOVEMENT, 1017-1043 A.D.
LEGEND
Approximate boundary between the Fatamid and Byzantine Empires
Approximate eastern boundary of Fatamid territory
Antioch
ALEPPO
Jabal al-A'lâ
R. Orontes
TRIPOLI
Wâdî al-Taym
DAMASCUS
Mount Hermon
Mount Carmel
Bosra
R. Jordan
JERUSALEM
Dead Sea
CAIRO
al-Muqattam
Hilwân
R. Nile
Sinai
cls

MAP 1.

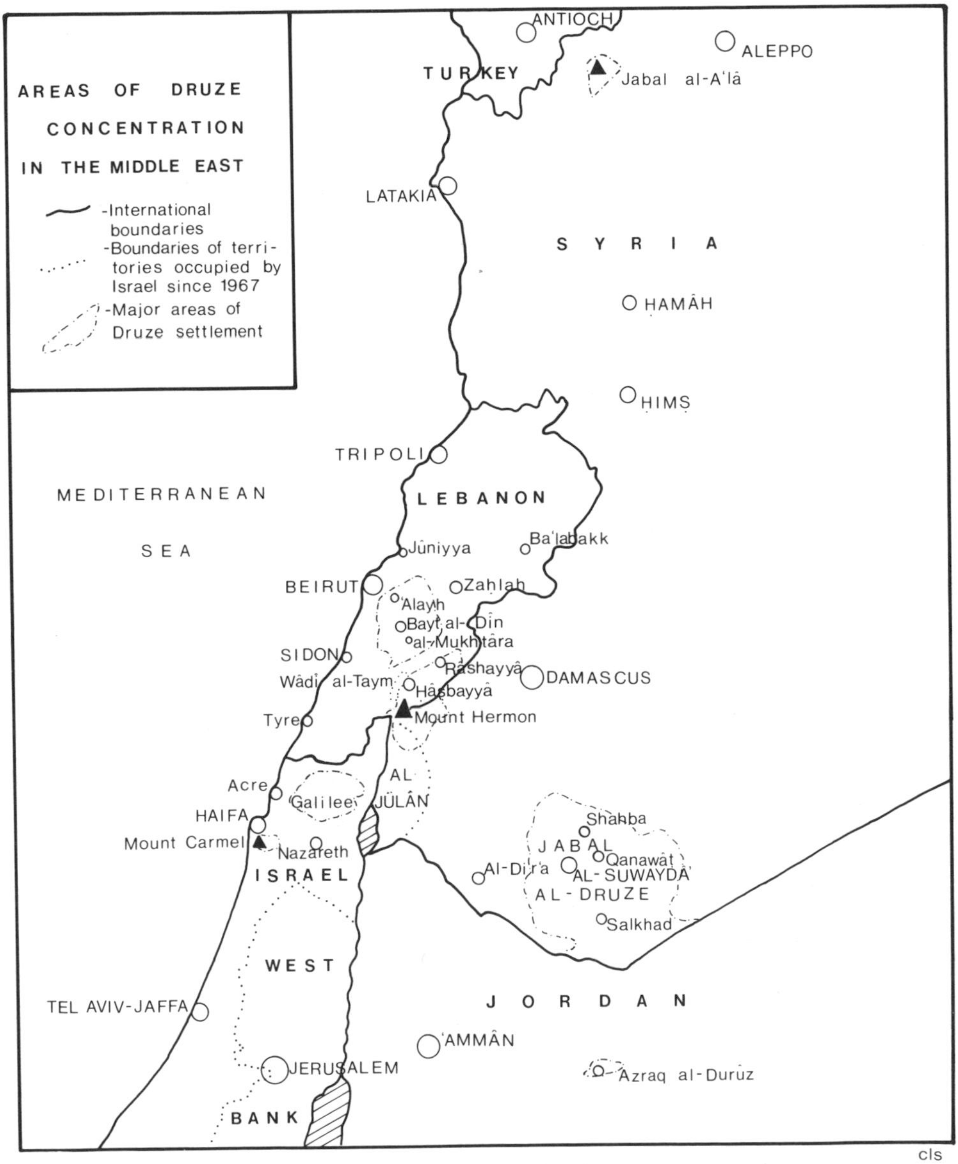
AREAS OF DRUZE CONCENTRATION IN THE MIDDLE EAST
-International boundaries
-Boundaries of territories occupied by Israel since 1967
-Major areas of Druze settlement
ANTIOCH
ALEPPO
TURKEY
Jabal al-A'lâ
LATAKIA
SYRIA
HAMÂH
HIMS
TRIPOLI
MEDITERRANEAN SEA
LEBANON
Jûniyya
Ba'labakk
BEIRUT
Zahlah
'Alayh
Bayt al-Dîn
al-Mukhtâra
SIDON
Râshayyâ
DAMASCUS
Wâdî al-Taym
Hâsbayyâ
Tyre
Mount Hermon
Acre
Galilee
AL JÛLÂN
HAIFA
Mount Carmel
Nazareth
Shahba
JABAL AL-DRUZE
Qanawât
Al-Di'ra
AL-SUWAYDÂ
Salkhad
ISRAEL
WEST BANK
TEL AVIV-JAFFA
JORDAN
'AMMÂN
JERUSALEM
Azraq al-Durûz
cls

MAP 2.

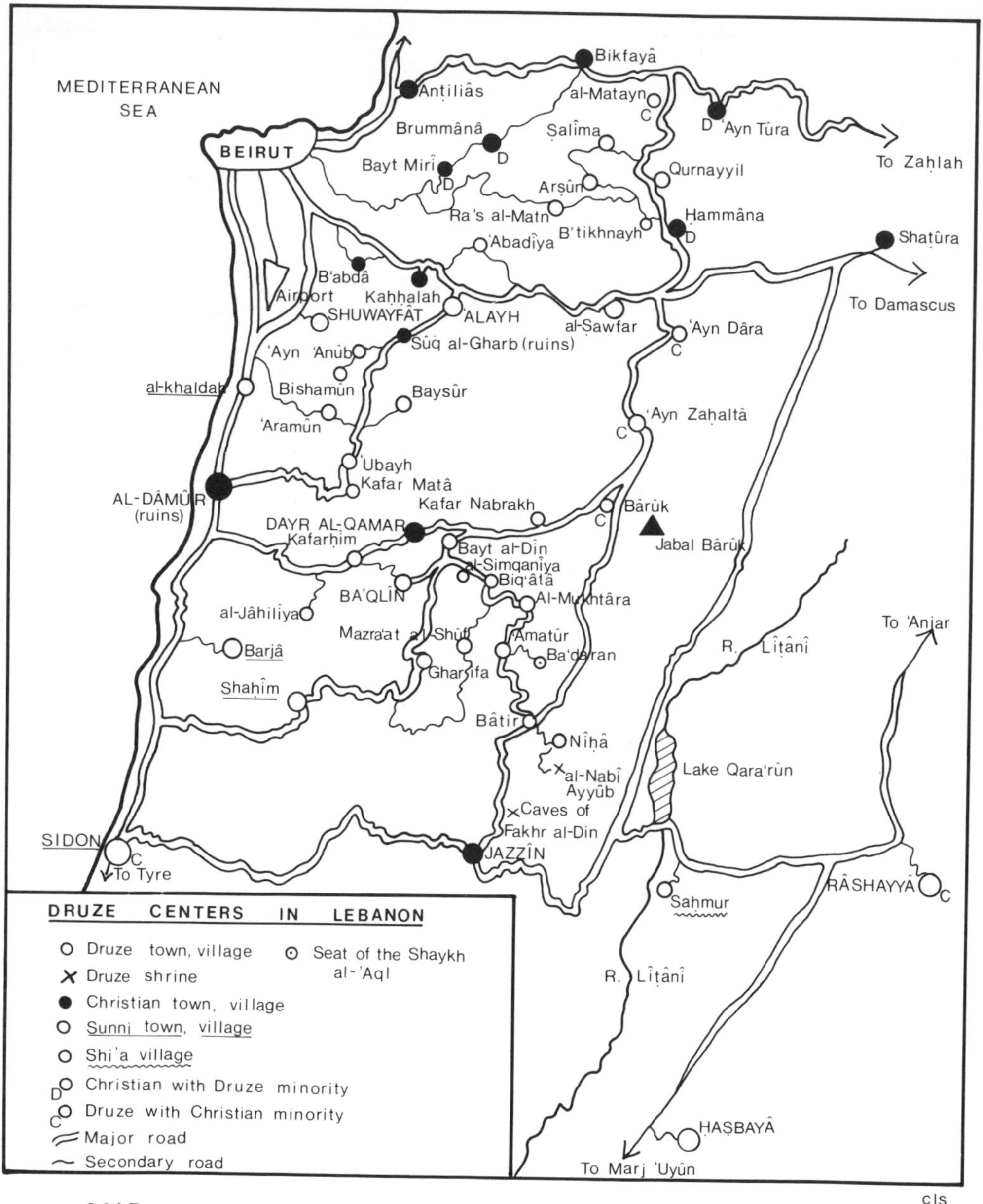
MEDITERRANEAN
SEA
BEIRUT
Airport
Anṭiliâs
Bikfayâ
al-Matayn
C
D
'Ayn Tûra
To Zaḥlah
Brummânâ
Salîma
Bayt Mirî
Qurnayyil
Arṣûn
Ra's al-Matn
Ḥammâna
B'tikhnayh
'Abadîya
Shaṭûra
To Damascus
B'abdâ
Kaḥḥalah
SHUWAYFÂT
'ALAYH
al-Ṣawfar
'Ayn Dâra
Sûq al-Gharb (ruins)
'Ayn 'Anûb
al-khaldah
Bishamûn
Baysûr
'Aramûn
'Ayn Zaḥaltâ
'Ubayh
Kafar Matâ
AL-DÂMÛR
(ruins)
Kafar Nabrakh
Bârûk
DAYR AL-QAMAR
Kafarḥim
Jabal Bârûk
Bayt al-Dîn
al-Simqanîya
Biq'âtâ
BA'QLÎN
Al-Mukhtâra
al-Jâhilîya
Mazra'at al-Shûf
'Amatûr
Ba'darân
To 'Anjar
R. Lîṭânî
Barjâ
Gharifa
Shaḥîm
Bâtir
Niḥâ
al-Nabî
Ayyûb
Lake Qara'ûn
Caves of
Fakhr al-Din
SIDON
JAZZÎN
To Tyre
RÂSHAYYÂ
Sahmur
HAṢBAYÂ
To Marj 'Uyûn
DRUZE CENTERS IN LEBANON
Druze town, village
Seat of the Shaykh al-'Aql
Druze shrine
Christian town, village
Sunni town, village
Shi'a village
Christian with Druze minority
Druze with Christian minority
Major road
Secondary road
cls

MAP 3.

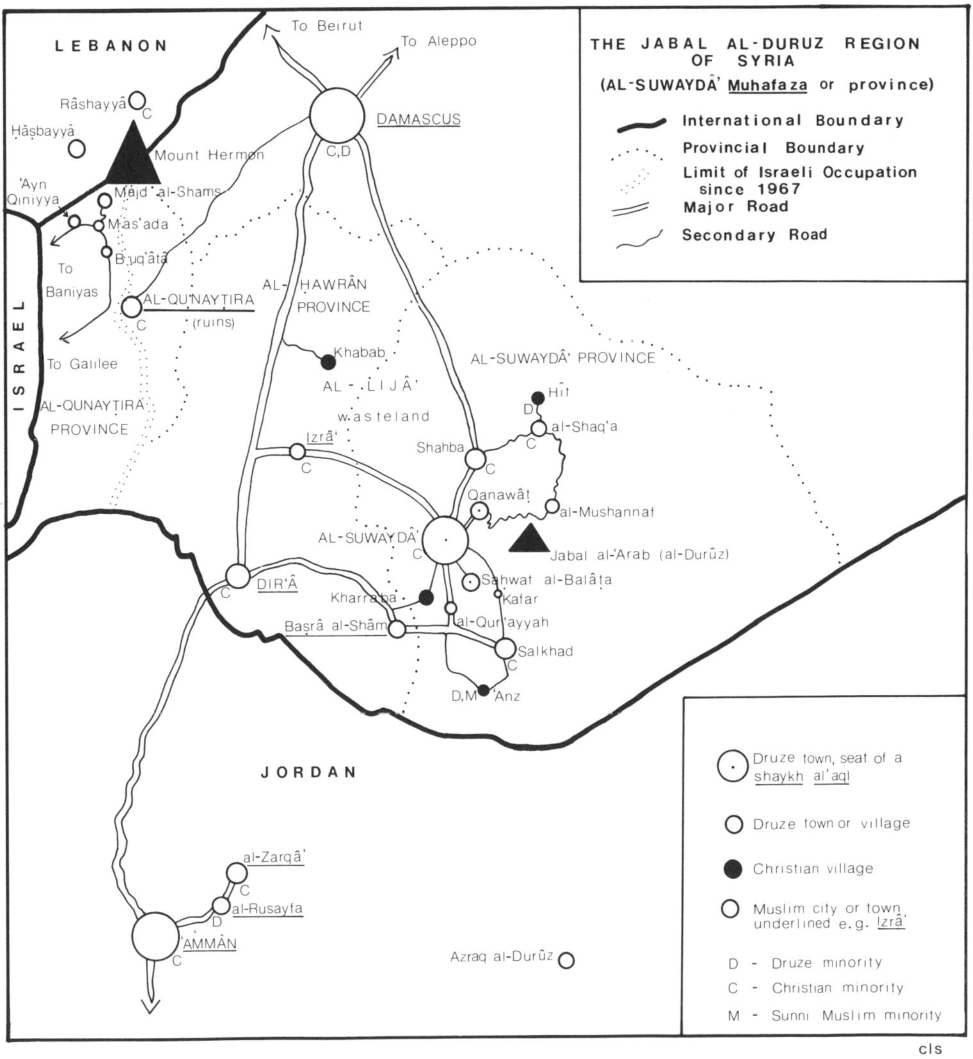
THE JABAL AL-DURUZ REGION OF SYRIA
(AL-SUWAYDÂ' Muhafaza or province)
International Boundary
Provincial Boundary
Limit of Israeli Occupation since 1967
Major Road
Secondary Road
LEBANON
To Beirut
To Aleppo
DAMASCUS
C,D
Râshayyâ
C
Ḥâṣbayyâ
Mount Hermon
'Ayn Qiniyya
Majd al-Shams
Mas'ada
Buq'âtâ
To Baniyas
AL-QUNAYTIRA
C
(ruins)
To Galilee
ISRAEL
AL-QUNAYTIRA PROVINCE
AL-HAWRÂN PROVINCE
Khabab
AL-LIJÂ'
wasteland
Izrâ'
C
Shahba
C
AL-SUWAYDÂ' PROVINCE
Hit
D
al-Shaq'a
C
Qanawât
al-Mushannaf
AL-SUWAYDÂ'
C
Jabal al-'Arab (al-Durûz)
DIR'Â
C
Kharraba
Ṣahwat al-Balâṭa
Kafar
Baṣrâ al-Shâm
al-Qur'ayyah
Salkhad
C
D,M
'Anz
JORDAN
al-Zarqâ'
C
al-Rusayfa
D
'AMMÂN
C
Azraq al-Durûz
Druze town, seat of a shaykh al'aql
Druze town or village
Christian village
Muslim city or town underlined e.g. Izrâ'
D - Druze minority
C - Christian minority
M - Sunni Muslim minority
cls

MAP 4.

MAP 5.

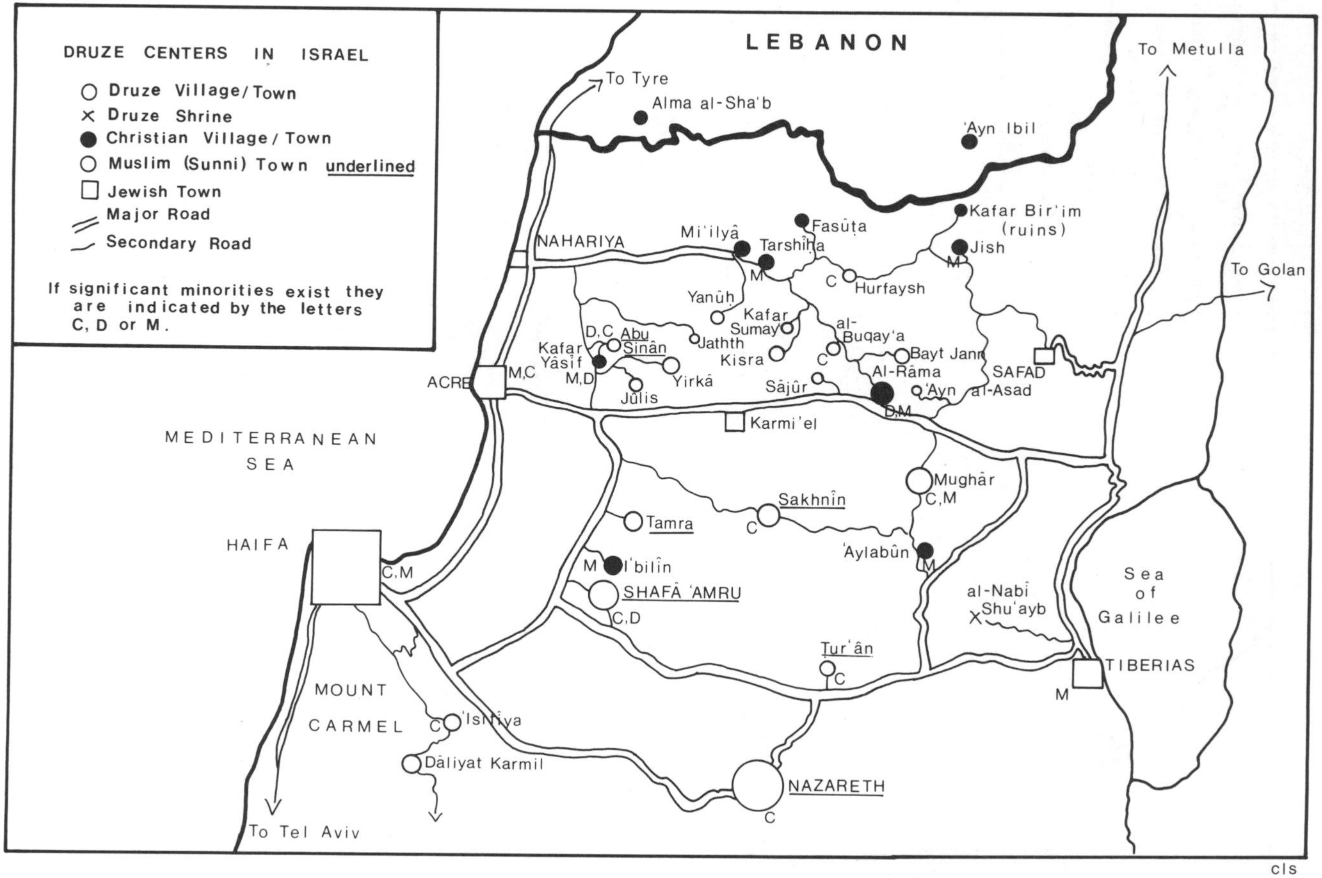
DRUZE CENTERS IN ISRAEL
Druze Village/Town
Druze Shrine
Christian Village/Town
Muslim (Sunni) Town underlined
Jewish Town
Major Road
Secondary Road
If significant minorities exist they are indicated by the letters C, D or M.
LEBANON
To Tyre
Alma al-Sha'b
'Ayn Ibil
To Metulla
To Golan
Kafar Bir'im (ruins)
Jish
Fasûta
Mi'ilyâ
Tarshîha
NAHARIYA
Hurfaysh
Yanûh
Kafar Sumay'
al-Buqay'a
Bayt Jann
SAFAD
D,C Abu Sinân
Kafar Yâsîf
M,D
Jathth
Kisra
Al-Râma
'Ayn al-Asad
Yirkâ
Jûlis
Sâjûr
ACRE
M,C
Karmi'el
MEDITERRANEAN SEA
Mughâr
C,M
Sakhnîn
Tamra
'Aylabûn
HAIFA
C,M
I'bilîn
SHAFÂ 'AMRU
C,D
al-Nabî Shu'ayb
Sea of Galilee
Tur'ân
TIBERIAS
MOUNT CARMEL
'Isfiya
Dâliyat Karmil
NAZARETH
To Tel Aviv
cls

PLATE 1.
The ruined mosque of al-Hakim bi^cAmr Allah, Cairo, in 1852.

PLATE 2.
The restored mosque of al-Hakim bi'Amr Allah, Cairo, in 1986.

PLATES 3 and 4.
Doors from the tenth-century al-Azhar mosque, now in the Islamic Museum in Cairo, carved at the top with inscriptions in honor of the caliph al-Hakim that read: "Our governor the prince of believers, the imam al-Hakim biʿAmr Allah, the prayers of God be upon him and upon his pious ancestors, and peace."

PLATE 5.
The village of Dayr al-Qamar in the Shuf district of Mount Lebanon. The women in the foreground are wearing the *tantur.* Taken from an engraving by William Bartlett in John Carne's *Syria and the Holy Land,* 1836.

PLATE 6.
Courtyard of the palace of Bayt al-Din, looking toward Dayr al-Qamar. Engraving by Bartlett in Carne's *Syria and the Holy Land,* 1836.

PLATE 7.
The Druze village of Baruk in the eastern Shuf Mountains of Lebanon. Engraving by Bartlett in Carne's *Syria and the Holy Land*, 1836.

PLATE 8.
Mount Hermon and the Wadi al-Taym in southern Lebanon. Engraving by Bartlett in Carne's *Syria and the Holy Land*, 1836.

PLATE 9.
The village of al-Mukhtara in the central Shuf Mountains, with the palace of the Junbalats at the very top, July 1975. The dense terraced cultivation of olives evident here is characteristic of Druze settlements.

PLATE 10.
The shrine of the Druze saint al-Nabi Ayyub in the southern Shuf Mountains near the village of Niha, July 1975.

PLATE 11.
Entrance to the shrine of al-Nabi Ayyub, July 1975. The wrought-iron gate includes the five-pointed Druze star.

PLATE 12.
The tomb of al-Nabi Ayyub (in plastic protective covering) in the interior of the eponymous shrine, July 1975.

PLATE 13.
Druze *shaykhs* on the steps of the *khalwa* of Qanawat in the Jabal al-Druze, Syria, July 1975.

PLATE 14.
Druze farmer threshing grain near Qanawat, July 1975.

PLATE 15.
The ruins of the Byzantine church at Qalb Lawzah in the center of the Druze region of the Jabal al-Aʿla in northwestern Syria, July 1985.

PLATE 16.
Entrance to the former palace of the Junbalat family (now a school) in Aleppo, Syria, July 1985.

PLATE 17.
Entrance to the new *majlis* of ʿAyn al-Zaman in Suwayda, Jabal al-Druze, July 1985.

PLATE 18.
ʿAnz, a mixed Druze, Christian, and Muslim village in the southern Jabal al-Druze, July 1985. Black basalt houses are typical of the entire region.

PLATE 19.
A new *mawqaf* at ʿAnz, July 1985.

PLATE 20.
A *mudafa* constructed from ancient Roman material in the remote village of Mushannaf in the eastern Jabal al-Druze, July 1985.

PLATE 21.
The Druze shrine of al-Nabi Shuʿayb, near Tiberias in Galilee, Israel, September 1985.

PLATE 22.
Entrance to the shrine of al-Nabi Shuʿayb, with a version of the Druze flag painted on the wall, September 1985.